ripping, cutting, stitching

Creative Interventions in Global Politics

Series Editors:
shine choi, Cristina Masters, Swati Parashar and Marysia Zalewski

The landscape of contemporary global politics is complex and oftentimes violent. Yet the urgency to provide solutions or immediate practical actions to this violence oftentimes leads to inadequate knowledge. This is despite the abundance of theoretical, conceptual and methodological tools available – much of this produced through conventional academic disciplines, notably International Relations, Political Theory and Philosophy. But the constraints imposed on these traditional disciplines profoundly limit their ability to incorporate and make effective use of more creative and innovative methodologies found in other disciplines and genres.

This series provides a unique opportunity to offer creative intellectual space to work with an eclectic and rich range of disciplines and approaches including performative methodologies, storytelling, narrative and auto-ethnography, embodied research methodologies, participant research, visual and film methodologies and arts-based methodologies.

Titles in the Series

ripping, cutting, stitching

feminist knowledge destruction and creation in global politics

shine choi, saara särmä, cristina masters,
marysia zalewski, michelle lee brown,
and swati parashar

(an ugly feminist writing collective)

ROWMAN & LITTLEFIELD
Lanham • Boulder • New York • London

Published by Rowman & Littlefield
An imprint of The Rowman & Littlefield Publishing Group, Inc.
4501 Forbes Boulevard, Suite 200, Lanham, Maryland 20706
www.rowman.com

86-90 Paul Street, London EC2A 4NE

British Library Cataloguing in Publication Information Available

Library of Congress Cataloging-in-Publication Data

Names: Choi, Shine, author.
Title: Ripping, cutting, stitching : feminist knowledge destruction and creation in global politics / shine choi, Saara Särmä, Cristina Masters, Marysia Zalewski, Michelle Lee Brown, and Swati Parashar.
Description: Lanham : Rowman & Littlefield, [2024] | Series: Creative interventions in global politics | Includes bibliographical references and index.
Identifiers: LCCN 2023034913 (print) | LCCN 2023034914 (ebook) | ISBN 9781538171370 (cloth) | ISBN 9781538171387 (paperback) | ISBN 9781538171394 (epub)
Subjects: LCSH: Feminism--Political aspects.
Classification: LCC HQ1236 .C4835 2024 (print) | LCC HQ1236 (ebook) | DDC 320.56/22--dc23/eng/20230814
LC record available at https://lccn.loc.gov/2023034913
LC ebook record available at https://lccn.loc.gov/2023034914

'Touch me here'.

Touch me here.

I wanted to open by writing that our book cover and this page is for Sharain. To be honest, this is also for us: those who loved her (touch), those who are difficult or prickly (me), those who feel isolated or alone (here).

Dr. Sharain Sasheir Naylor was born in Pennsylvania and faced many obstacles as a child in the US foster system and as an adult. She found ways through them: graduating from Penn State University, the Defense Language Institute, then earning a PhD in political science from the University of Hawai'i at Mānoa. A trained Chinese linguist and intelligence analyst in the US Navy, Dr. Naylor (Sharain to those who knew her) became a fierce critic of war and militarism. She was a queer activist and 'life-long' member of the LGBTQIA community.

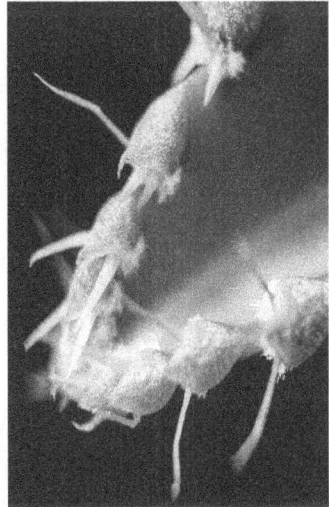

Dragon fruit plant (Sharain Sasheir Naylor, 2015, Honolulu, Hawai'i)

In addition, Sharain was a talented photographer, ceramicist, and figure artist. Art was something she enjoyed throughout her education. After earning her PhD, these art forms became important processes for how she understood herself and the world around her.

We may read or hear 'Don't speak ill of the dead'. After Sharain's unexpected death in October 2021, I learned that can also mean 'Don't publicly show their flaws while hiding your own'. I was taught it is healthier to be honest both internally and externally. So when we write, share, and talk abut how a woman or nonbinary colleague, friend, or family member was diffi-cult, or intense, or challenging—let us not omit our own actions, inactions, and flaws in those relationships. Let us use those moments to assess our own internalized biases and expectations, adjust, then act.

But that is easier to type out than do when we *feel* in many ways, often simultaneously.

Sharain was intense and passionate. So are all of the authors here. She also had a huge heart and never gave up on caring—even when she was hurt so deeply it brought her to angry tears years after the events. Her capacity for hope, anger, care, and action was extraordinary.

When I speak and write about kinship in this book—know that it is active. We do not just find or lose kin. Each day we make decisions about what, who, and where we give our attention. Some of the decisions (or absences/ lack of support) with Sharain may hurt us to acknowledge them. Kinship is active; we make daily choices. Sometimes our inaction or withdrawal is necessary for our own boundaries or well-being. Sometimes, our inaction and withdrawals are to avoid other harder aspects of care: reciprocity and repair.

Sharain helped me pack and clean our last apartment in Honolulu. In that wonderful intense-caring way of hers, we laughed because she was stressing me more with how visibly stressed she was. Leaving is hard to do gracefully. She cried, I cried, and she shared how she was both happy for me and incredibly sad as she would feel more alone. Feeling alone was something she struggled with for a long time. I understand that more now as I am here in a new place, feeling the absence of deeper connections, deeper kinships here. I have been thinking about our conversations, her future plans, how we connected people around the world with Sharain dur-ing her last 48 hours in the ICU, and the nursing staff noting how many people cared for her.

Sharain loved and admired many of us involved with International Rela-tions (IR), Feminist Studies, and Global Politics. When she felt unsure in her own work and voice—not seeing her brilliance after years in the doctoral degree process—it was attending the International Studies Association con-ferences that renewed her. Scholars she admired responded to and supported her and her work. When I would become frustrated with the disciplining in the field—sure that I should leave and go elsewhere—Sharain reminded me of all the 'pretty awesome' people within it doing important and transforma-tive work. She was right. Her insight is why I am a part of this book you are reading.

We will keep Dr. Sharain Sasheir Naylor with us, our memories of her and our love for her motivating us to be better kin with each other now. Not just in the future: right here, right now. I am grateful to this collective for deciding on her artwork for the cover, bearing with me as I write this, and keeping her with us as we rip and cut and stitch, determinedly yet generously.

Michelle Lee Brown
January 13, 2023

A monstrously queer table of contents

Acknowledgments

We warmly thank all those who have supported and cared for us while we have been working on this book. And to those who didn't help us, who hurt us—well, here's the book anyway!

A special shout-out to our co-travellers, V. Spike Peterson and Laura McLeod, and our very generous and supportive reviewers.

A contributing cast of characters

Chaos: I am trying to get unstuck. This is creating all sorts of problems.

Surprised writer: I can only do quirky made-up versions of feminism. Getting weirder every day.

Interventionist: What can I say, I'm a chronic interventionist. I find academia suffocating.

Nuance queen: I am your nuance queen, who sees time, death and destruction as essential ingredients for creation. Everything is complex. I don't mind being a fence sitter and watching from a distance. No one has the keys to the queendom!

Nokia: I know a lot of people in academia and love bringing people together. I'm curious, I resist boundaries and want to smash them. I am all about disrupting IR malestream and their 'serious' academic performances.

Tattooed laydee: Even while stuck in this assigned analytic, two things remain true: 1. No, you can't touch them; 2. Yes, they have meaning. Now about my paper. . . .

Eelusive: I'm not quite IR, but keep coming back for amazing people working along the fringes and edges.

Black cat: Not impressed at all by all the things we're supposed to be impressed by.

chine: a typo, a translation . . . of what? Does it matter? chine is a mistake.

Malestorm: A typo?

Marge: Margins, marginalia, marginal.

Kali: She is not your usual Indian goddess. Part of the Hindu pantheon of goddesses, her origins can be traced to indigenous traditions as well. She is chaotic, she is dark, angry, bloodthirsty and destructive. But she is also the nurturing mother. She cannot be appropriated for bourgeois interests, she is the goddess of the poor and the marginalised, the ugly and the invisibilised.

She breaks caste and class barriers and her worship and rituals are available to all without discrimination.

Zzzzzzz: We're just so tired, also depressed, but hanging in there somehow.

Professor feminist: Battling oxy/morons . . .

Professor Man/Cosmo Man: The bad guy, the regular guy, the everywhere IR guy. A terrifying character who sometimes disguises himself as a cat. Beware. He is everywhere.

white feminism/s: Have read Kimberlé Crenshaw, Maya Angelou, and bell hooks, yet assist in the reproduction of whiteness and patriarchal coloniality.

Professor Woman: She is always trying so hard to keep up with and be one of the boys. She'll step all over you if need be. Or just because she can.

Real Researcher: A ghost that haunts (some of) us.

Gromit: Tirelessly placing down (railway) tracks, building bridges, carving out trails.

A very short list of abbreviations

BISA—British International Studies Association
EISA—European International Studies Association
FTGS—Feminist Theory and Gender Studies Section (of ISA)
IFJP—International Feminist Journal of Politics
IR—International Relations
ISA—International Studies Association

PART I

Chapter 1

how to read this book
that is not a book

First, leave all expectations behind.
Or bring them with you and (super)impose them on the text.
Documenting the brokenness.
Putting the pieces back together, differently, sometimes badly.
Not pieces of a whole.
Multiplicity of 'I's.
Imagine yourself as one, some *or* one of the many 'I's animating the text.

Collage by Ugly Feminist Collective

This book is something of a thought-writing-feeling-educative experiment, in part channelling Le Guin (1976, 3): 'This book is not extrapolative. If you like you can read it . . . as a thought-experiment.' We challenge—through creation, collaboration—the expectation that the work of critical scholars could/should achieve reliable and sustained changes to hegemonic orders and thinking structures. Drawing some inspiration from *Frankenstein*, our work in part involves (un)stitching stories—and ourselves—about global politics together, though perhaps in unfamiliar and unpalatable forms. It has also involved stitching our 'selves' to one another in the hopes of laying bare the mythical power of our distinctiveness—to disrupt the knowing subject, and reimagine 'it', whatever the 'it' may be. So, it is also about de/compos(t)ing ourselves as authorial individuals. It is an experiment.

So, how to read this book? With an open heart, mind and imagination. It might not be the most comfortable, satisfying or pleasant of journeys, but we do want to tell you some stories through these pages. And we really want to puzzle you. And comfort you. And be visible to you. We feel a little bit compelled to provide something like a set of tools to 'read the book' (methodology?). But we also don't really want to do that. Or not yet anyway.

So, let's start with this. . . .

Chapter 2

frankenstinian encounters: feeling the ways

Setting: The last day of the four-day conference, Interpersonal Sociopathic Association (ISA). The conference brings together 'international scholars', together with ambition, vulnerabilities, competitiveness, jealousies, malicious gossip, plenty of suited&booted men feeling important and manly, and just maybe some friendship.

The last panel is about to start; Surprised writer is on the panel and presents their paper on Frankenstein.

Last paper: Surprised writer

Hi everyone—and thanks for turning up for the last panel in the last time slot!

Ok, so, my presentation is something of an introduction to the 'idea' of 'the frankenstinian subject'—and to talk about why the project we're working on has this as something of a muse—an epistemological and affective 'muse' if you like. Inevitably, talking about anything described as 'frankenstinian' conjures something 'stitched up' or 'stitched together'—disparate parts. In one sense, we are the disparate parts that have come together in this project to stitch up our various views/research/experiences. . . . Perhaps I should briefly say a little more about the source of this muse or inspiration—though I would be very surprised if there's anyone in this audience who doesn't know what I'm referring to when I say 'Frankenstein'. I am, of course, referring to Mary Shelley's book *Frankenstein* first published just over 200 years ago in 1818 (so 2018 was the book's 200th anniversary). *Frankenstein; or, The Modern Prometheus* 'tells the story of Victor Frankenstein—a young scientist who creates a hideous, sapient creature in an unorthodox scientific experiment' (or at least this is how Wikipedia describes the work). The book remains in print and has been reproduced in many films and plays. The image of Boris Karloff as 'the monster' with bolts sticking out of his neck has become something of an iconic image of 'the monster'—though confusingly the 'monster' is commonly mistakenly referred to as 'Frankenstein'.

But why turn to Frankenstein to begin imagining this project? It's not so much about the story per se, or the many arguments about 'who was the "real" monster' in the book (though this remains an intriguing argument which we don't necessarily turn our back on). Rather, Mary Shelley's story—and all the trails that twist around and in(to) it—is such an intriguing merging of 'messiness, emotion and ugliness'. The life-frame of the book itself—Mary Shelley, her life, her mother, her writerly imagination—it's a wonderful messy combination of the personal, the intellectual, the scientific, politics, nature, the political, category destruction and creativity. I'm so intrigued and moved by the whole mess of it—the stitched-up subject at its heart (or one of its broken hearts), and all the disasters and the pain that come from it all. What a muse to help us think through and write through our struggles! So much to do with humanity and identity and what a human is, isn't and can become. The human dripping, searing messiness of all of that—

But what is to be done with all this messiness? And am I presenting messiness as positive? If I were, this would be unusual in conventional disciplinary methodological and political idiom. Our training as academics (if we really want to describe our 'learning' as training) urges a tidying of mess—a clear 'sifting and sorting' en route to producing clean, straight knowledge. Though any of us working with more creatively and radically inspired foundational questioning methodologies might be happy enough to start with mess—but this isn't quite my starting point here. In a way I'm starting at the 'other end', this 'important' international conference, the world of global politics, in other words the conventional, hegemonic, mainstream world 'out there/in here'. And I pose a simple question about this—why does this world(s) relentlessly get stitched back together in such familiar ways? Patriarchies, heteronormativity, hypermasculine Eurocentric whiteness—they could all fall apart easily, but they don't. How does it all get stitched back together in these very familiar forms? Tell me somewhere or somehow that it doesn't—at least more than fleetingly, temporarily or superficially. It's this question—and its many offshoots—which leads me/us to want to work with the muse of the Frankenstinian subject, at least initially and as a kind of hovering, oozing ghost—as a thinking muse to keep us off the disciplinary beaten, beating track.

But I also cannot get away from the mess of the subject brought forth by Frankenstein—'the man/the monster'. He/she/it—they are a complete wretched victim, and this stitched up plaything of scientific white man

Stitched heart by mz

inevitably (?) ends up being/doing violence. How can he/she/it not? This creation—made of everything and nothing, the flotsam and jetsam of refuse and the dead(ly)—has no way to think or to know, but becomes—becomes a confused brain, a destroyed-destructive life. Such a sad thing.

Messiness. Arbitrary piecing together. Still looks so much the same. So, the frankenstinian subject as a hovering, insistent and broken deathly muse to try and hold on to and work with some of that confusion and complication. And the pain.

In 1852, thirty years after Percy Shelley died and a year after Mary Shelley's death, Percy's heart was found in Mary's desk along with sheaves of his poetry. A story of love?

Discussant

The discussant delivers his comments, a little puzzled, a little destroyed and a little destructive in the process, critical without a mission, erasing and cancelling with a vengeance. Were they expecting a paper like this? There is very little time for discussion, but the Chair opens it up for a few final questions/comments from the audience. Glancing at the audience looking for comments, the Chair sees something unusual. A black cat sitting in the corner looking very much unimpressed. 'Could it really be, or is my jet-lagged brain playing tricks on me? Maybe it's just someone's sweater on the floor'.

Interventionist hesitates but since the discussant mostly omits Surprised writer's intervention, which for Interventionist, seemed most provocative, her hand shoots up before she can stop herself. She hears herself saying:

I hear your voice in my head repeating, 'but Frankenstein is not the monster. . . .' And you're right of course, Frankenstein is/was not the monster, not exactly anyway. This slippage and/or confusion between creator and created, subject and object, student and monster, author and subject, however, is an interesting vantage point to feel our way through the fleshy politics of global politics. There's something fecund about this slippery triad of Mary Shelley, Frankenstein, and her-his monster for our thinking here. Especially when we consider she was writing a little over two hundred years ago, as a teenage mother no less, about what it meant to be human, to live and be alive, and, arguably, in challenge to the utter masculine arrogance in thinking they had it better figured out, better placed to 'know' and make sensible the 'human', 'life', 'living', to create the perfect One. Sounds terribly familiar in our venerated discipline, no? Anyway, feeling her way in the dark, Mary Shelley was working at the limits of what was known. . . .

The chair cuts her off just as Interventionist gets to her question. Interventionist wanted to ask Surprised writer what she thought about how we might harness the aesthetic affect of the patchwork corpse/monster to do more creative, more radical work here. But no, the Chair thanks the presenters and the discussant for their interesting thoughts on how we might 'innovate' our thinking. The audience applauds. Surprised writer makes her way over to Interventionist, who is chatting with Nuance queen. The three lament how awful it is when one is trying to present work that's shaking things up a bit and one is often met with awkward silence or a belligerent omission or deliberate erasure. Pushing at the limits of thinking and writing, pushing at the limits of being in spaces which were designed for hegemons—sharing this so openly, perhaps brazenly—what gets left in that space, how is it felt/experienced?

Broken heart by mz

Surprised writer puts on a brave smile. She's used to it; it's been happening for years! Yes, for years, but it always crushes, it always shatters . . . always re-stitching to do . . . again and again and. . . .

Interventionist and Surprised writer continue their conversation animatedly. Interventionist continues,

What I was trying to say before being cut off by the Chair is that feeling her way in the dark, Mary Shelley was working at the limits of what was known, at the (bloody) edges of the 'real', 'science' and 'fantasy', playing with (im)possibilities; in an attempt to write a better ghost story than the boys (for real). Her patchwork corpse a challenge to smug perfection, singularity, surety, to asshole men. I want to embody her, be her! But it would be far too easy to align with Mary in repudiation of Frankenstein. We'd also be wrong though to think the choice is between these two, option a or b, either/ or. Thinking so, a measure of how caught up we are in binary and hierarchical frames. I say, 'fuck that shit'. There is another option (there's always another option, often breathing down our necks setting off ripples of goose pimples across our flesh), of course, a monstrous one swirling with desire, fear, hope(lessness), horror, ugliness, beauty, (in)justice, and swimming in blood-spattered imagination, creativity, invention and failure. The monster is who we hope to become and write, saturated with the stuff that haunts us, moving us in this fucked-up world we live in. Why is it so difficult to write monstrous stories that challenge and trouble the subjects of IR—the academic as rational subject, the bloodless and bodyless objects of knowledge, our arte-facts/outputs as bounded and innocent corpuses and corpses of knowledge?

Nuance queen listens, half interested, half impatient. She does not get it, she wants to get it, but really, what *is* this Frankenstein business? She does not want to be disparaging, she is also used to it, not getting the seemingly immediate relevance or newness among feminists, as if because we are femi-nists, we should get it. And this constant pressure to say something 'new', something 'original', something striking and extraordinary. How can that happen, panel after panel, book after book, one journal article after another. She must meet Chaos at the lobby anyway, so they can discuss some ideas together. She wanted to talk to Professor feminist about serving as possible external examiner to her doctoral student who was going to defend her thesis soon, but no, this is not the right time. She is running late anyway. . . .

Nuance queen walks into the lobby. It looks like a bazaar or a village fair where you can ply your wares in different ways, a perfect site for the unfold-ing of a new *Raag Darbari*, that famous Indian novel by Shrilal Shukla. So many weird characters and such fine nuances. Suited&booted men in grey and black hover around with pasted smiles and anxious looks, trying to spot familiar faces in the crowd. Oh, why do they wear ties and coats like corpo-rate employees all trying to look the same? Some think that they don't need introductions; that they exist is already well known and appreciated, and that their presence in the hotel is to make lesser mortals aware of their profound intellect for the duration of the convention. They are looking for admiring eyes of mostly junior scholars, and those actively seeking them out for polite conversation. There are women too, who come in all shades, from confident, high-heeled power dressers to nervous young women trying to fit in, anxious to be seen with the right kind of 'rich and famous' in this crowd. And then you notice (or don't), those awkward women of colour (men of colour are faring better as there exists a big-buddy culture), trying to invisibilise them-selves by either looking for familiar faces and corners and pillars behind which they can fold their minds and bodies and hide. 'How many panels are you on? Oh, did you get promoted last year? Did Professor Man invite you for dinner? Were you nominated for any awards this time? Have you finally got tenure/promotion? How is your new book doing in the market? Did you

Conference collage by ss

get any research funding? Which publishers are you approaching this time? Which receptions will you attend? What is your conference fashion statement this year?' These phrases are liberally sprinkled in polite conversations, introductions and friendly banter. Seems like an urban jungle of human stick figures, all alike outwardly but you have to look closely to see how different they are. One thing is evident. They are all looking for external validation, they are all anxious even as they perform confident white masculinity in charge. The hotel check-in staff, concierge, taxi guys, coffee shop workers are in charge, not the pretentious stick figures whose greatest fear is to be called out, exposed for their difference, for the emptiness of their lives, for their racist and sexist worldviews. In this jungle, why can't I spot Chaos? Oh, might that stick figure be her?

Snatched Chats in the Lobby

Nuance queen: Chaos, why are you dressed like that? Like all the other ridiculous people. I would have never spotted you.

Chaos: Shhh, I am trying to blend in, you know, be taken seriously so I can get somewhere, you know. . . . But more seriously though, don't I look great? I clean up nicely. It's like magic.

Nuance queen: So how many 'postcolonial', global south invitations do you have? Are you ready to decolonize just about everything *they* want us to? And you are trying to decolonize by blending in the crowd? Terrible business, this blending. Like the smoothie where that chia seed is still recognizable, settles in neatly at the bottom once the blending process is over.

Chaos: Haha, it is a heavy load to carry. And that is precisely why we studied for our higher degrees?

Nuance queen: No, of course not. But that's what we have been made into. I am called for all things 'postcolonial' and global south, as if that is my intellectual home and identity. PhD sounds a bit like 'Please Help Decolonise!' So, what skills and smart mantras do you bring to the table?

Nuance queen and Chaos laugh and have a conversation about how despite:

how differently they look and speak,
how different their respective 'Asia' is,
how their interest in global politics does not quite ever meet though both of them are interested in 'postcolonialism', 'feminism' and 'Asia',
how both are simply and unidentifiably grouped as 'women of colour', 'academics of colour', 'persons of colour'.
As if the rest of course have no colour.

Nuance queen does not like these titles, she tells Chaos.

Regardless of their differences, both are taken as basically doing and being the same thing when they are 'in dialogue' with their white counterparts, in their 'Western' contexts. But is it really a dialogue when only certain people get to determine the terms of conversation, its tone, and whose sensibilities we should be careful not to hurt?

Ranting (a break to rant/a rant that breaks)

We are tired of ranting. We are not even generally angry; anger is not our general disposition, but it is that we get no opportunity to compost the moments that anger us, that enrage us when we are just trying to do our jobs, to do work. To get to the work bit, we have become the caricatures they have made us into: the quintessential angry brown woman, or the tiger ice queen, who must do the labour to decolonize and educate those who have nothing to learn. While many of my white colleagues pursue their intellectual interests and projects, our primary job is to decolonize. We are invited on panels, very often as the token person of colour, or to offer a postcolonial/decolonial perspective. It can be genuine but when you are a token presence, you just know. . . . What is the right thing to do? Decline such requests? Accept and 'do a good job'? What is a 'good job'? If we don't speak up, will it be another lost opportunity? If people don't get it, and all they hear and see is rage, is this bad?

We/I rage and rage about what we study, how, who is included and who is excluded. By the way, men of colour don't often share this burden. Let me repeat: *Men of colour don't often share this burden* (especially if they are straight). They are (often) completely mainstreamed, working in elite institutions, speaking in and occasionally speaking from their own closed circle, about all things post and de/colonial in their eloquent, deep knowledge about colonialism, about colonial realities, about the intricate histories. They don't see gender, class or other privileges and sometimes are worse kinds of sexists and racists than white men. They do not know (and refuse to see) the colonialism, domination here, now, in the very room that they repeat, in the very way they speak that they speak only to certain people who have proven themselves, and are free, free, free. But free from what? The taint of femininity? The taint of woman? Of depravity? Of history? Of the injustices that we supposedly are trying to correct? Are we 'in it' together? How does this freedom come about? What is this freedom for? They are part of small cliques where they intellectualise the discipline by reading and citing themselves, each other and only the 'best' of them—only the texts they think will last. They very rarely include women, and when they do, you have to perform a certain kind of femininity within an alternative mainstream masculine space to belong. This is possible for younger/ than women of colour, but even then only until the veil of mystery, only the possibility that you might be that exceptional feminine complementary version—if a better version, even better comes along, watch out—you will be replaced, because they like only the 'best', only the ones who will last. They only read and cite the 'best' women, those who have shown them as mere mortals by her unambiguous success as a public intellectual of global scale. They only embrace women who they are forced by the white world to celebrate. Tell us that whiteness is not structuring postcolonial intellectual networks that reproduce elitism, hierarchies of universities and programmes, myths of prestige and legacies? Tell us. . . .

And the esoteric language that they continue to use! Why must we develop these complex textual constructions that prevent meaningful engagement with ideas? If it is ideas that matter, then why build so many barriers to them shaped by a particular aesthetic that is 'sophisticated' and 'clarifying' only for some?

And there are economic dimensions to all of this elitism and closed networks. A very famous postcolonial globalization Professor Man wants a pot of money (to compensate him for his time away from family) to deliver a keynote talk. Rather than read another page of a book, we put aside time to see if this can be arranged but alas, we cannot afford it, and expectedly he decided to skip the event that he affirmed was so important, potentially historic! Turns out, Professor Man was an alleged sexual predator and was named in #metoo by several women of colour. Another famous Postcolonial Professor Woman is known to only fly business class and up so you cannot even invite her to events. And some are so high and mighty that lesser mortals must be careful even in their requests or what to expect from them. The invites they receive must be worth their stature. Or else, no response is guaranteed. Some Dr Up and Coming never organises anything but just expects to be flown in for workshops By Invitation Only and public events as the token junior person of Clear Brilliance. They never simply share their ideas either, but always speak to be heard and seen by those that Add Value to Knowledge, which often means being ruthless to those who appear weak minded.

We find ourselves raging all the time against all of this and more. They say I 'speak my mind', which is basically a euphemism for not blending in enough. How do I economise on my rage? is what bothers me.

But when did we start raging? I used to barely speak; I enjoyed myself the most when I could just take things in, but then I had to stop being a student, stop being just me, and had to get a job in academia. Yes, I think that is when I started talking because I quickly learned that unless you know how to talk, you count for shit in academia, which is still very puzzling to me . . . why does thinking and being reflective about the world require us to be coherent, amazing public speakers? Shouldn't we be bad at speaking because we spend a lot of time thinking, reading, observing? I dunno; anyway, when I start talking, of course I don't get to talk about things I want to but what is required of me, or required from me, so I can actually get to the bits of the conversation I wanted to be part of in the first place. People I was talking to made me into a ranter. How terrible.

Yes, I am also not a script performer. I rage, I digress, I tell stories, I become silent. My anger has turned me into a monster I sometimes don't recognize. Am I the monster though, a monster with nuances, angry and benign, passionate and indifferent? Was Frankenstein's monster all of these too? After fighting monsters all my life, have I become one too? I have inhabited so many different contexts and worlds and the Kali in me is never fully at rest. She has only small phases of quiet calmness. Then she dances around to let off her incorrigible anger. She dances in sync with herself and the universe. She becomes Kannagi, the Goddess who burnt down an entire city. Her anger is frightening but necessary. Kali, the monster mother, has her own red bloodthirsty tongue. As Chhinnamasta, she decapitates her own head in anger, and drinks her own blood. Kali, the Goddess within me, is raging all the time. But must she always be the bloodthirsty monster mother? When do monsters 'become' monsters—how do they acquire monstrosity, or is it thrust upon them? Or are they born that way? Why does monstrosity look so necessary, so banal in these times?

Monsters

Eelusive is sitting and waiting for some big-name Professor Man to show up for a meeting with her. She's thinking International Relations (IR) as a field doesn't make sense to her: inter-nation-al relations includes lands, waters, and the nonhuman and human communities connected to them that we gather on each year. But year after year that doesn't register at/with these fancy international conferences. Maybe that's asking too much, when many well-known IR scholars she's observed can't even be civil to the hotel staff. . . .

interlude one: tidal turns

When my mother would beat us, her eyes would turn black. Not as a metaphor (her eyes were already quite dark) but as a real, observable phenomenon. After shielding ourselves, clinging to sturdy furniture legs, learning how to coax her to use the strap not the buckle end—I became old enough to fight back.

One day, after being pinned down for a 'tickle session' I did not want—I fought back. So intensely that she stopped. I calmed down. My mother stepped away from me and said 'Your eyes went black—it's like I didn't know who you were anymore. i couldn't reach you. You scared me. You were . . . crazy'.
I remember thinking 'Good. Now you know what it feels like'.

I became afraid in a whole new way.

The tides had turned; I was beaten much less after that. But something else stirred. Nana had told me stories of us—of our lineage being birthed from a fearsome goddess and a giant serpent: Mari of the dark eyes and flames. Sugaar of the lightening and teeth.

Maybe all of these had coalesced into something far more scary. Myself.

A few weeks later, I was at a pool party. Boys were chasing girls around a four-foot pool, splashing them and trying to pick them up. As someone who chopped and carried wood (and lots of library books)—I was stocky but strong. I thought it would be great fun to turn it around—I scooped up the nearest boy and dunked him three times quickly, deeply—laughing and splashing. Making lots of waves. Until I realized no one else was laughing.

They were all staring. Whispering to each other.
I stopped and put him down as quietly as I could. I suddenly felt too large, too 'husky', too . . . something.

*A girl next to me said 'you can't **do** that to him. Don't act all . . . crazy'.*

The boy (whose name I still remember, Tommy) brushed it off, saying it was fine. And it was—as long as I stayed out of the pool and away from everyone. My mom came to pick me up early.

What does it mean to be made from monsters?

'Sorry for intruding, I couldn't help but overhear, are you talking about monsters [excitedly]?'

The others smile and nod, so Eelusive dares to go on despite feeling like an impostor. I'm working with some monsters myself, trying to develop this idea of postmonstrous. I'm interested in how to elude the ever-present 'real' monster of colonization? Could we mutate it into the postmonstrous, embracing the potential to become the monstrous, but channelling those energies, grounding them in renewed practices, stories, and relations?

I'm looking at *Lilith's Brood* by Octavia Butler alongside *The Monstrous-Feminine* by Barbara Creed and placing the monstrous in female hands. Have you read them? You should! They're amazing. I think they are such a fertile place for what I like to call 'monstrous feminist thought' in its many-tentacled forms: whether we are the monsters giving birth to humans exemplifying more of the qualities we aspire to, or whether we give birth to wonderful and terrifying hybrids who exemplify these same qualities, moving *beyond human-bounded ideas* of how they might be manifested. I have transplanted these monstrous roots to stretch them; allowing the concept to push out different embodiments of the monstrous while dropping the hyphen to signify its mutation into something speculative and beyond: the posthuman.

The Professor Man was around after all but was hanging around looking for more important people before settling on showing up late to meet Eelusive. He whisks her away before she has time to change her mind about this meeting, which no longer feels all that important. Chaos and Nuance queen also decide to get on with their lives with promises of reconvening to brainstorm 'real ideas'; anxieties, frustrations and rants are not real ideas in academic spaces. Chaos heads to the bathroom.

Glitter

Chaos enters the bathroom, and sees someone covered in . . . is that glitter? And what a fun pink fluffy dress! For a moment Chaos unashamedly takes in this vision of a woman covered in glitter who also has pink hair and cat-eye shaped glasses, and finally asks: 'Are you my fairy godmother?'

The pink & glittery woman is a bit startled, not sure how to take the question because she's suspicious of Chaos. She looks like the sea of corporate types she ran away from in the hotel lobby. She coldly replies, 'I'm Nokia'.

Chaos is used to cold responses in first encounters in life and in work. She kills it with overenthusiasm: 'Nice to meet you, Nokia! So, why are you covered in glitter? How fun'!

Nokia starts explaining carefully, while thinking 'what is up with this cheeriness?':

Conference glitter by ss

'I just came from this innovative panel where we made some collages together and I accidentally burst open a bag of glitter. I was meaning to glue some of it on the collages, but now most of it is on me and on the floor of the room. I was trying to clean some of it off there, but had no luck, now I feel bad that someone has to go and clean it. . . . '

Chaos interrupts, all excited: 'An innovative panel with glitter as props! Please tell me more, what was it about? Collaging, where did that idea come from'?

Nokia: 'You know ISA runs a series of innovative panels each year; I'd been to a few before. There was one on martial arts mixed with art presentation, and one year there was a bunch of fabrics all around the room. Don't really remember what that was all about, but we wanted to experiment this year by getting the audience to make something during the panel, that's why glitter and collaging. I've done some collages in my own work and wanted to see what would happen if they were done collectively, multiple people working on the same collage'.

Chaos, even more excited: 'How did it go? I was talking with Nuance queen—you might know her?—in the lobby about being taken seriously and dressing the part, but isn't this glitter business a bit risky in that sense'?

Nokia sighs: 'Nuance queen, oh yeah, I should catch up with her. . . . Yeah, this is definitely risky stuff. I'm actually a bit—or a lot—upset and pissed off how this panel turned out. Most of it was really inspiring and fun and people were really involved, but as we were talking about the risks of doing this kind of creative work in this discipline, I was told by a Professor Woman that it's not risky if you do it well. I think she implied that since I see it as risky, I'm not doing a good job. I so used to look up to her, she's always been one of my feminist idols and now . . . I'm so disappointed; I was hoping she would have loved the session, that's why we asked her to be the discussant. The collaging part though, it worked, but I have to give it some more thought what it all means to do this collectively compared to doing it by myself'.

Chaos, scribbling on a piece of paper torn from the 400-page program book: 'This sounds fabulous and so interesting, but I have a flight to catch, please please email me soon, I would love to hear more, and maybe Nuance queen and us can do something together for next year'.

Nokia is left mumbling to herself still, trying to clean all the glitter: 'Next year, maybe something about inappropriate disciplinary performances, hmm, wonder if Professor feminist, Interventionist and Eelusive would also be interested, must email them all soon. . . . '

The Tattooed Laydee shimmers in the conference bathroom for a moment. She shudders.

I am still not used to that shift from a categorical analytic.
She inhales deeply and stretches her arms. *For a few minutes here, I am a person in a particular place in time.*
She waves and laughs. There are tattoos on her arm, and—is that one on her ankle? Maybe they are some somewhere else. . . .
Seriously? I am speaking for only a minute here. As myself, through this analytic. What I may or may not have elsewhere is not important here—but I get it. The whole Tattooed Lady imaginary ingrained in Western cultural references. Whew, were some of them problematic.
She shrugs. *I get placed into the Tattooed laydee category whether I like it or not. These*—she looks at herself—*are not for show. But they help me show up.*
She shudders once again and sighs.
I can only break out of this analytic for so long in these academic spaces. I will return later.
The Tattooed Laydee vanishes.

Chapter 3

on writing

> She had been warned of the risks she incurs by
> letting her words run off the rails. . . .
>
> (Trinh T. Minh-ha 1987, 5)

We are fighting 'writing'—'the category that is not a category, the category to hold what cannot be held' (Hustvedt 2014, 5). Or better perhaps fighting the ways we are pushed to put our words and thoughts together. The idea of the frankenstinian writer is sometimes about disjointing ways of shaping knowledge for conventional disciplinary usage. It is about the struggle of writing. Writing as a way to unlearn so much and learn differently; to write in ways that don't break us or leave us as empty and shrivelled husks of ourselves. Here we try to link the thinking in our minds with Mary Shelley's *Frankenstein* and perhaps to the madness of that/our work. Madness is drenched with gender and race and 'strangeness' not welcome in disciplines.

In Charlotte Perkins Gilman's story *The Yellow Wallpaper,* the female narrator tells us she is 'sick'. Her husband, 'a physician of high standing', has diagnosed her as having a 'temporary nervous depression—a slight hysterical tendency'. We try to be sensible; we try to be measured. To not tell of disciplinary and worldly sickness. Though why have we tried so hard when so much of the living in global politics which we are immersed in, or touched by, or are resistant to, or covered over by—when this bears such a heavy violent weight of gender, pain, white entitlement, coloniality and and and . . . and various entanglements that surpass these very terms we have for now. Perhaps we are here to give up that trying—and to show some of the layers of all those 'giving ups'. Perhaps 'for now' we are here where the language we have is, and to find ways to work with it *and* without.

21

Words put together in comfortable, pretty ways always mask violation. Poetry as a kind of frankenstinian word-form helps us to think about this, especially disordered and disjointed poetry. And especially poems which so well expose the brutalities of white/patriarchy—though white/patriarchy is already beginning to seem too small a phrase, even when we mark its disjointedness through the slash (*'but it was always too small, never a center'*, *whisper shouts Marge*).

Acting as frankenstinian writers works as a kind of permission to let the writing (un)do itself—fall apart. To follow what the writing wants to say and take a rest from being
                    the stitcher
                        the maker
                            the authoritative controller of words
Perhaps only in those kinds of moments is white patriarchy passed over, laid aside, ignored.

This book experiments with thinking and writing. It 'runs off the rails' and touches the edges of 'what makes something unthinkable'. It is a book which takes risks and some 'steps into the dark'. Its purpose is multilayered; though it is primarily offered as an ethical, epistemological, experimental and affective journey collated to help make critical thinking field(s) shiver—sometimes those in International Relations (IR). Our aim is not to make readers think or 'feel' anything in particular, but our queered method of 'latticework' and disruptive methodologies and texts will, we think, foreground affective and therefore intimate aspects of thinking and reading practices, displacing, even if momentarily, the cognitive and causal. One of the reasons for piecing this work together in these ways is to act overtly, even brazenly, as critical thinkers and creative makers and readers to push at the decolonization of knowledge in the study of global politics. As Maya Angelou (2017) says, 'I've learned that people will forget what you said, people will forget what you did, but people will never forget how you made them feel.'

The writings in this collection work to show what lies in/between, in the gaps of the various kinds of work and writing/speaking that we do as IR scholars, which ranges from inhabiting (without cynicism) the position of an expert in diplomacy, to judging a student's work (without cynicism), to dabbling in a range of IR theoretical frameworks, to writing (without cynicism) on a wide range of topics we know something about or know very little about in the beginning and sometimes in the ending, to colouring in (without cynicism) pages in our notebook the unicorn or cat we drew for fun at work. Cynicism is easy within IR—it hides behind the critique and relies on 'The Canon' to provide shields and ammunition. We are genuinely—perhaps even naively? (a word laced with gender and race)—playful about our rage and laughter as we try to catalogue the various kinds of work involved in performing 'seamlessly' the role of an academic and treat this work not too easily as intermediary steps towards making the performative process the output.

This is our frankenstinian project: working at and with the stitches—ripping, cutting, stitching—keeping them alive and lively, refusing to paper over them with dead words and deeds, or filing away at the rough edges with a sharp instrument until it is/we are the sanitized and edgeless right shape, size and fit. Refusing to ignore festering wounds, or to lick them privately in a dark corner far away from the sites of their infliction, pretending the hurts/joys/pleasures/indifferences of the multitude of ties that bind us aren't there. We refuse to trim off the hanging threads; we want to dangle from them, swing from one to an/other, maybe even let go to see what happens, to feel what we might feel, to think what we think, to see what we can(not) do. Who knows where we might (not) end up!

Dear reader, will you write another paragraph here? For others. For us?

Chapter 4

collective writing/writing collectively

Part of the work of this project is to *shred the illusion of the monograph.* A *thing* that contains hours and hours of labour by friends, colleagues and family members rendered (nearly) invisible. Only sometimes becoming fleetingly visible in the acknowledgment section. This project tears away the monograph to reveal how much more rich and complex collaborative work can be. Inventive kinnections rather than connections—ideas and concepts do not exist in singularity but are connected to larger networks of human and nonhuman relations. These tangle and snarl, and demand to be woven into our rage and play. This does not mean our work will be perfect—in fact, *we are offering imperfection(s)*—however, in the *here* of this writing and your reading—there will be multiple worlds moving inbetween us, ravelling and unravelling. This may seem dangerous, unacceptable, yet we are committed to this sensuous, emotive, rough-edged and patient pedagogy, and we insist on gathering discarded, abused and disabused stories, moments that are feminized and racialized, and colonial stories and patriarchal nightmares together in a strange patchwork, to help teach us all differently about the worlds of politics and our many kinnected everydays.

As much as it sometimes feels like we each are using our respective individual research to contribute to a larger pool, the collaborative project, for some of us, also feels at times like a jar from which our individual projects are drawing for how it interrupts the questions we are asking in our respective projects. Let us start here with an admission that the mode of research many of our respective individual research projects requires is a particular version of our personality or sense of authority. The differences that result from the decisions we make or don't make as researchers whose difference is so minuscule and intimate that only the researchers feel it and yet, these small imperceptible differences seem so important to work through. So, a

compelling reason for the work of this book is to experiment with collabora-
tive writing and meaning making, to delve more recklessly and more atten-
tively into our senses and sensibilities as we navigate and negotiate
what collaborative knowledge formation

looks and feels like
how it falters
continues and stagnates at the same time
travels
how it gains and gives layers
sheds light on things
tends to tears shed
shares
and keeps us caring and cared for.

What if we thought of collective writing, doing, working on whatever
—as just listening to one another?
That all that we need to do is be a better listener, and here it might be
worth emphasising from the very beginning that this includes also a prac-
tice of listening that is 'a not',
for example, a not forcing ourselves to listen to tunes, tones, voices that
we do not want to (but learned to listen to that just numbed our aural
sensibilities).
Of course, that we need to state this, and to state it as 'a not', is indicative
of who-what has been arbitrating conversations about listening as well as
speaking, who-what has been structuring conversations, who-what has been
choosing the tunes.
So yes, what about this question, what if?
What if we thought of collective writing first as listening, not an act of
speaking?
Could we think of speaking or writing as what we do in between silences,
listening for those moments of silences?

Academe is a tough place for us to be in—so we find each other, we slide and
slither, smash, rip and tear our way into spaces and places. Here's to laying
eggs and planting hybrid offspring throughout it, in the walls, the offices,
in the minds of colleagues and those we teach, and in the words and art we
publish. If we do that enough, we'll take it over from the inside out; turning,
twisting, collectively birthing something that is more than what academe
was—old-yet-new technologies of thinking, being and doing.

Academe being a place and an amalgam of technologies perhaps, at one level, explains why the book starts from and works with anxieties around writing, writing collectively, and the production of knowledge about global politics. As a place, it privileges writing (*if you can't write, then . . .*), and the technologies of academe—reading, writing, crafting, object-making— rely on subjects that survey and surveil, master (over) or become mastered (over), accumulates, dispenses and disperses. The multivocality that matters here in the collective writing subject is not only about the 'us' as individuals coming to this project with different backgrounds, experiences, desires. Multivocality here also engages with a wide range of disciplinary voices, positionalities, dispositions, and affective and aesthetics categories that are brought into and are also shaped by academe as a place and a set of technologies of subject and object creation(s). We are in/from various geographical locations and work in different locales with particular academic cultures. We're at various career stages and not all of us have permanent jobs. We are all involved in one way or another in the study and the writing of global politics, many of us are working within or at the margins of the academic discipline of IR. But how we speak with, to and for IR is complicated and contested amongst us; we're unsure how much we want to give voice to it, how much or little to turn down the volume on its talk, where it belongs in our effort to do otherwise. Surprised writer, Chaos, Nuance queen, Interventionist, Nokia, Eelusive, Professor feminist and various other characters in the book are stitched together into a frankenstinian subject—a monster, maybe even more than one—as we work through and around our differences in writing this project. At times, it took us collaging (and drinking wine!) as a method of seeing where we were at a given moment and moving on again. And again. And again.

The pressure to do this kind of work only seems to become more important when 'we live in disturbing, mixed-up times, troubling and turbid times' (Haraway 2016, 1). Or for Lauren Berlant (2012), 'living within crisis and the destruction of collective genres of what a "life" is; and about the dramas of adjustment to the pressures that wear people out in the everyday and the *longue durée*'. Currently, both the discipline of IR and the landscape of global politics seem enclosed in contradiction, confusion and intermittent crises. In the former (IR), this, in part, involves the difficulties critical scholars face in producing ethical and productively responsible knowledge in the context of the neo-liberal university in which the masculinized 'gaming' of research most succeeds. In the latter (global politics), this involves all the dramas of 'cruel optimism' (Berlant 2012) given the realisation that the world cannot sustain 'organizing fantasies of the good life'. Both of these arenas—the landscape of global politics and the discipline of IR—bubble and boil with seething vats of violence, though so much violence remains unnoticed though perhaps worse, uncared for.

Who do you care for? What do you care about? How do you care? Who cares for you?

Chapter 5

playground relations

Something throws itself together in a moment as an event. . . .

(Kathleen Stewart 2007: 1)

Never does one open the discussion by
coming right to the heart of the matter.
For the heart of the matter is always
somewhere else than where it is supposed to be. . . .
There is no catching, no pushing, no directing, no breaking through, no need for a linear
progression which gives the comforting illusion that one knows where one goes. . . .
The story never stops beginning or ending.
It appears headless and bottomless for it is built on differences.

(Trinh T. Minh-ha 1989, 1–2)

Moved by Berlant (2012), 'this is not a time for assurance but for experi-ment', we write this 'statement of performance', or affective playground—it might be called a methodology section in a regular book—to help readers to navigate their way through the text. Though it isn't meant to be a 'map' (to map is laden with colonial desires), or if it is, it is an idiosyncratic, resisting map, one meant to inspire engagement with the experiment that is this book. Less so to offer a sure guide—indeed there is little 'sureness' to be found in the following pages—but instead to offer some gifts of creative slowness, dissonance and disjuncture. Or as Kathleen Stewart puts it, 'to slow the quick jump to representational thinking and evaluative critique long enough to find ways of approaching the complex and uncertain objects that fascinate us . . . not to finally know them' (2007, 4).

Collage by Ugly Feminist Collective

The 'to' here ('to slow the quick jump') is also not just about what lies between and beyond representation and evaluative critique, and what kind of doing or being is possible in this space or mode. It is also about questions of destination; where are we headed? Where do we find that we have landed? Where are we trying to get to when working with the gifts of slowness and disjuncture? Who are we bringing along in our journey to get there, and who are we leaving behind for now, since after all, we cannot speak to everyone, do and be everything? And does destination ever really matter, and for whom, how, when? In what sense does it that we are thinking and asking questions such that what we create is the visual of a *spectrum* of questions? How does this spectrum that we travel through, as if travelling can happen only in the motion of *through*, of moving from point a to point b to point c, misrepresent and distort by ordering how thinking supposedly happens? Even this very linear arrangement of questions—*as a series*—exhibits the destination-orientated way many of us think we think in the first place. So, yes, there is much to return to in the ellipses (and other markers of dissonance) (*what happens in the brackets is almost more interesting*, Interventionist utters).

For some of us, being 'here'—in whatever point we are along our journey—also means being with, breathing with various simultaneous timescales and realms—multiple worlds that Winona LaDuke notes 'all sit in the present time' (Pechawis 2014, 38).

Um, hi. When I first started this journey, I was still figuring out graduate school. One of the things that helped me get through was ISA and these people I met there. I polished up a seminar paper. I presented it with this collective, even Spike read it! And liked it! I got surprisingly positive feed-back from amazing people. That transformed what I thought I was able to do and not do. It changed me, so I changed—again. Interestingly, that paper didn't fit as the book evolved. Parts of it are still here. Some of it could be something else, or it can just roam monstrously within the margins—a liminal state. Like people often see eels as. I wanted to note that for me this book started here. And me writing and pre-senting that? That was transformative. But I didn't know it then—I just said yes to what felt right. Which is what we are taught eels do. Did I mention eels are cool? So cool. And given my name here and where I come from, transformation is what I'm all about. Transformation to suit a purpose, to go deeper, to go farther. To come up to shallow surfaces or roll as collective wriggling balls across muddy, muddy terrain. Yes, we can roll and move on land and through fresh and salt water if we want to. But those transitions take time and energy. We have to be in a specific form and sometimes in a group to roll across unexpected terrain. Perhaps next ISA or another conference, you might see some of us rolling together, consuming, growing, learning. That's what we do in that state—as young eels and as emerging scholars. But we consume not just to take and take, we consume to transform. Being attentive to what we consume, and the reciprocity involved. Some consump-tion times are intense—ingesting a great deal so that we can undergo a massive transformation again—going deep and far into the ocean. Moving into other disciplines and returning with things to share. Seeding new ideas that will hatch and transform. Becoming their own lines of thought, lineages within subfields that are connected through time and space through care. Eelusive pauses, realizing they've undergone another transformation. *Aw crap. Just when they got used to grad student form and functions.* They look up, flexing this new form, then retreating slightly. *Well, in any case what I wrote. Then, and what you will read,* was something I felt so good about at the time. *As it changed so did I, that's OK too. It doesn't make what it was any less.*

What I can give to you throughout this book is something more than just me
writing to express my thoughts. It's thinking and moving with others—so I'll
move in and out.
As we do.

What disjunctures are there between these overlaps? Between the wor(l)ds
each of us bring to this collection? How might we pause to sense them? How
do we make them meaningful, visible, and 'here' with words on a page?

Slowness and disjuncture are not the usual methodological tools of aca-
demic books—and we do think of this as an academic text, or at least one we
hope is read by academics and students in our field(s). Though we also hope
this book will be read and shared across a much wider spectrum of readers
than those in academia. We will gesture as we go along why we were drawn
(or not) to these two affective and destabilising senses and their methodologi-
cal largesse—*slowness* and *disjuncture*—as well as how we work with them
across other affective registers. But first we move to describe some of the
reasons that brought us together to collate this book; though before that, a
few digressions. And be warned that in the coming pages, there will always
be digressions. We like to digress. We are aggressively digressive.

Disjuncture # 1: Slowness

When slow food, slow scholarship, the 'celebration of slowness' is men-
tioned, often we nod . . . as if we already know what it means for others,
or even for ourselves. Slowness is a conscious decision to work differ-
ently, thus it often becomes something (else) to be applauded, strived for,
achieved.

Slowness in an academic sense, however, requires particular temporalities,
themselves requiring certain resources, and support. Or lack of support
and resources. 'Slow scholarship' can itself be fetishised in ways
that are unattainable to those in more precarious positions within academe
or who are neurodivergent. Not all can do it the same way; even among
our collective, slowness—the ability to dive into these thoughts and
threads—is not the same across position, place, or points on our academic
career timelines. Slowness in this sense isn't singular or experienced the
same for all of us. What looks 'slow' might in fact feel breathless, hectic,
demanding. For others, slowness, a putting aside of other practical respon-
sibilities and personal proclivities, is an indulgence in decadent lifestyle
because writing is a decadent practice.
Writing is luxury.

And writing is hard, who doesn't recognise this?: 'I'm afraid to write. It's so dangerous. Anyone who's tried, knows. The danger of stirring up hidden things—and the world is not on the surface, it's hidden in its roots submerged in the depths of these' (Lispector 2012, 5).

Anguish. In one production of *Frankenstein*, Mary Shelley is part of the play, the action itself; she moves around the set with her table, her notebook and her pen. We witness her tussling with her ideas and struggling with her 'inability' to write and to keep hold of what she is thinking. But as she gets further into the narrative of her 'monster', in some anguish she cries out, 'oh for a bridge of words! For this nightmare is woven through my imagination like my own blood!'.

And her words arrive.

Disjuncture # 2: More on Slowness

Getting more embodied, if this slowness is experiential, it is not always about emptying out to do the work. For some, it can signify an unleashed *intensity*: hyperfocus *as* slowing down through permission and a safe space to let the mind and body dive deep into this tentacularity, submerging in the work-play and losing track of particular quotidian temporalities. This might mean you forget to eat, drink water, or care for others (as female/female presenting academics and students are often expected to do); it may mean forgetting yourself by showing your nakedness, being vulnerable, putting words and thoughts out there to become entangled in unexpected ways. Sometimes this slowness cannot happen—due to financial, workload, family, health issues, natural disasters, the messiness that is life. Anger or rage might ensue: which, after it has unfurled, might edge into a different kind of emptiness/stillness. Thus, troubling slow scholarship is not to demean it or render it as a useless or a highly privileged concept . . . though it can be, as some do not have tenure or a permanent job, funding, or family support to savour the work as much as they would like. And sometimes lacking all these is precisely why you can take in and do this thing called scholarship very, very slowly. Rather we take up these tensions to frame what we do have: each other.

Each other.

Collaboration works as a way to add speed (in terms of output/productivity) and slowness (who has what resources to give, who can focus on parts of the text for a length of time). The result isn't speed or slowness per se—but stacked temporalities that this work can move through.

This multitemporal slowness affects the way we write [IR]—the way we write/live theory. It loosens the tightness of theory-writing, allowing edges to (un)ravel or fray, sharp edges to bump and run against each other. By making temporal space, disjunctures become more apparent and can be held up, rather than glossed over or squashed.

a big disjuncture with no number: pandemic times/spaces of pandemic
For Nokia the Covid-19 pandemic has meant a forced slowing down as she is someone who thrives in hectic social environments such as conferences and seminars. Trying to do what she loves doing, connecting people, feels almost impossible and so forces in the disembodied spaces of emails and Zooms. Not being able to be in the same spaces with other people did a number on her creative mind.
For the Black Cat the pandemic was a gift, having been stuck hiding in the corners she for once was allowed to feel her whole being fully, she came out of hiding, stretched out, and lay on the couch purring, demanding attention and affection.
Zzzzzzz thinks that depression may not feel like a gift at the time, but when it makes you stop completely and listen to yourself more fully, maybe you learn not to ignore it for so long the next time. Or not. Zzzzzzz could afford to stop and take all the time she needed, because of institutional affordances. Strong unions and the welfare state ensured long sick leaves that are compensated for well; funding institutions flexibly grant extensions.
Chaos just sat in the whirl of chaos that was always there in her home. When chaos tried to get unstuck in place, without physically moving because the borders were closed, things around her imploded and led to some interesting un-sticking, unexpected experiences of being unstuck.
chine split into a separate character during the pandemic, a mistake. Marge came by to say hello when Eelusive swam through muddy water, marge thought as she muddied the water.
Surprised writer stopped. Just stopped. Giant black cats. Small black screens. Surprising comfort.
Turning into . . .
the dark . . . too much unwanted dark
Breaking, broken . . .
Eelusive, shedding grad student skin.
Intervention had nothing to intervene in but herself. It got ugly.

Our happenstance collective was partly drawn together and to each other because we were (and very much remain) angry. Amorphous clusters of angriness and rage which emanate from varying avenues of the everyday and academia every day. Casual insistent racism. Exhausting levels of sexism.

Pandering sticky stealthy ageism. Insidious body shaming and ableism. Sinuous trails of misogyny. Quietly screaming violent acts of silencing. Relentless and unyielding returns of the bodies and needs of the abled, white and masculinized to the centres of visibility, 'truth' and power. This, and more, we witness, we feel, we experience, we see, we notice, we sense, we hear and feel across the varied ranges of our different lives—personal, political, intellectual, psychic, emotional and professional. In the varied places 'where we are'—academia, universities, home, city streets, global politics, conference hotels, public transport, dance floors, IR, lecture halls, seminar rooms, cafes, local shops, libraries, different countries/cities/villages—these felt harms materialize periodically, intermittently, insistently though oftentimes very quietly. Piling up like dirty laundry in a corner, ignored only for so long, the dirt never easily scrubbed and washed away. Stains, smells and residues remain, sticking to us, marking our skin in intimately ugly tapestries of accretive violence.

interlude two: controlled burn

My daughter is about ten. We're discussing self-defence and channelled energy. She asks how do I become like . . . that.
'You know that rage feeling, that heat, in your gut'?
I will never forget her reply.
'I can feel it, it really scares me'.
We talk about control, healthy outlets. I take up running again, she joins me now and then, in addition to Aikido and kickboxing classes.
Six years later . . .
My daughter and I complete our first half-marathon together, running almost side by side (though she still bemoans that I finished 63 seconds before her).
I was reminded of the last lines of the book Monster Mama *as we crossed the finish line:*
'Your Mother is something else' the boys told him admiringly.
'It runs in the family' replied Patrick Edward.

Yet paradoxically what also brought us together is fun, laughter, the lightness of performing *together* in one physical space a loosely scripted collective paper, which was how this project started—a conference panel at the International Studies Association annual convention. Some of us wore Benedict Cumberbatch masks (aka Bodysnatch Cummerbund, Buffalo Custardbath, Bumbelsnuff Crimpysnitch). Some of us took off our shoes. Some of us giggled. Some of us stayed wilfully silent. Some of us cried. Some of us got angry. Imagine having a bit of fun and getting a bit of 'feels' in an academic conference space that is so disciplined by seriousness, professionalism, and showing off one's best-and-yet-unfinished-work ('cutting edge'). It is a space that really requires those who want to be part of it to be good at what we do, as if what we do and for whom we do this good work are shared (shared in academia seems to be a euphemism for ordered, that there is a clear singular order of how everything fits), and thus sensible in such a way across the different locations of our work that we can compare excellence, rigour and originality across these sites.

So, what motivates some of us to be here, to do this, and take this risk is the fun factor of wearing a Benedict Cumberbatch/Bumbelsnuff Crimpysnitch mask, goofing around, and doing whatever comes to mind during a conference session without second-guessing ourselves. After our first performative panel at the ISA, we continued to carve spaces within the official conference program over several years for doing whatever we wanted in panels—singing, rapping, working with puppets (Jack!)—and much more! All of this continues to animate the writing-down of stuff in this project. When the goofing around happens in official sessions and spaces, it becomes a controversial thing, but also an event that builds the groundwork for legitimising it as a particular mode of intellectual work, of working through emotionally heavy—enraging, devastating, traumatic, unwieldy—topics that are the stuff

Masks and notes by mz

of life and of global politics. These performances create(d) collective support—presenters and audience/members and participants—that strengthen the space and hold it for one another to laugh, cry, get angry, confess, swear, fail, discover, soar, crash: to unleash.

This sense of 'one can let go' (of) questions of appropriateness once a year for the length of the panel session, one hour forty-five minutes, liberating when for the majority of our working hours as academics, we find ourselves going about our (feminist) business constantly being interrupted and challenged and as a result second-guessing if we have gone too far (what is too far and who gets to decide this? And how is 'too far' raced and sexed?), revealed too much of our personal thoughts and baggage, was too angry, was too aggressive, was too long-winded or was too light-weight in how we present(ed) our ideas (ourselves/oneself) in the eyes of serious, professionalised critical scholars. Academia so often requires us to keep other parts of ourselves 'othered', closeted, whether this other is the artist, performer, activist, maker in us in so many ways: these are to be kept separate and as far from IR as possible. Not to mention being parents, daughters, siblings, nervous, bold, wilful—an unwieldy unfinished list making up a person, to professional recoil. Embracing rough and messy fun within these conference settings and publishing formats is necessary to help stitch/quilt/suture ourselves back together through monstrously disobedient performances pregnant with radical possibilities.

Fun is also necessary to perform and let loose not just as what happens after the official sessions or outside official spaces between close colleagues and friends, but as a valid mode of doing our intellectual work. Firstly, because serious IR work is also driven by a fun factor as it has been viewed by a small, entangled lineage of traditions, people, ideas and practice/craft*man*-ship. Secondly, because lightness and experimentation are not incompatible, but are imperative in work that takes risks. Risks take jumping, which often involves what Nokia terms 'do first, think later'—jump not with certainty but with a hope that one lands in ways that are not too crushing, that the cracks of the landing are workable, that the edge that one lands on is not the edge that finally pushes you off the realm of resonance, shared concerns, intelligibility. Fundamental to this collective endeavour then is the unexpected. The stuff we can't and don't anticipate, the stuff we can't and don't know in advance, the stuff that sneaks up and surprises us, lays beyond or slips out of our control, our scripts, our desires. We hope to do 'something' with the unexpected, the unplanned for, the surprises that have brought us here—although an uncertainty lingers with what to do with what happens in three-dimensional space and how we bring it to the flatness of the page.

To work in a collective, however loose, also means that these landings can be cushioned by the support of others; the cracks and gaps not just made workable but (lovingly) held and held up as beautiful, striking, breathtaking, essential, meaningful. So, in a sense all risky work, serious or not, is 'light' but in privileging the fun factor, we are trying to make sensible how risky work can have different inflections, taste levels and sensualities that are important to firstly recognise and secondly to diversify. Doing this collective work is therefore an attempt to make *a home* or *to be at home*—a sense of belonging, worthiness, necessity, comfort—for that which is too often (un)seen, (mis)understood, taken to have 'no business' in the 'serious business' of academic scholarship and how one should conduct scholarly research.

This is not, however, about making comfortable and safe what we do and are doing. Indeed, the very opposite. One of Donna Haraway's recent urgings is to 'stay with the trouble', which we might take as emblematic for this book and the work we are engaged in. . . .

> . . . *the 'might' flags the problematic ways Haraway has erased Indigenous political theory and praxis from her citation practice. So, we want to stay with the trouble and also make trouble for those who pull Professor Woman moves!*

For Haraway, the task is to become more capable, to 'make inventive connections as a practice of learning to live and die well with each other in a thick present' (2016, 1). To paraphrase her, the words we use *to world* worlds matter as we stay with these troubles. As such, our collective matters even more—to make sure that many facets are covered, that our approaches note the routes and roots of what we play and rage with, of how we might dream (IR) otherwise. This lateral strength means we don't just touch on things or skim over them, our tentacularity can entwine deeply across a vast area.

> Yet when it comes to knowledge about global politics—
> more capable of doing what?
> The responses to this question matter a great deal.

[crack]
shit, is this going to further marginalise the already marginal place I have in International Relations, International Studies, the Social Sciences? Not if you do it well, as that Professor Woman said in response to a similar question from the floor in a panel session on art as method. But what if my method is not driven by 'doing it well'? Worse, what if my effort is evaluated as being pretty bad despite my best, honest, genuine effort? Is there no place for

bad-quality risk-taking? Can efforts to know and their failures always need to sound . . . so goddam eloquent, polished, conceptualised? I do like my highly polished conceptual way of writing, and sometimes when I read them, in print, I marvel—wow did I write that? That I like eloquent, well-crafted theoretical sentences is not the point. Liking what is high-quality is not the point. We all like nice stuff (beautiful stuff, sublime stuff, clever stuff). I am just wondering why this predilection, this taste, is not questioned, its edges felt out a bit more, destroyed in greater frequency, not because what we have and how we do things is bad necessarily but just to see what has been structuring writing, research, theory all along, just to see what happens. Am I self-sabotaging by being curious about this? Where is the boundary line? Other people seem to intuitively know and I am not privy to this script. Please share your knowledge script so I jump with my eyes open!
[crack, CRrrrACK]
I have no idea what I'm doing here. It's terrifying, yet exhilarating. Not knowing somehow okay when I'm not alone. . . .
[splat]
. . .

Disjuncture # 3: Care

Slowness, hmmmm . . .
Some of us are unsure that this is the *right* methodological (?) sense we (want to) work with (what does it mean to be right here?). In one sense slowness feels right, capturing the mood and tempo of a project underway for several years, waxing and waning with the annual tempo of the ISA's Annual Convention, marked by short bursts of excitement and months and months of distracted postponements by the constant tug of the neoliberal university streeeeetching us, exhauuuusting us, squeeeeeezing every bit of life, creativity, generosity out of us. Too often leaving us with little left to give; spent, wrung out.
So, slowness sounds just about right. Yes, please. More, please.
The project first took flight with a performance in protest—a performative protest—to the infamous Sapphire Series and its all-white panels at the ISA in New Orleans 2015. Armed with our Benedict Cumberbatch/Buffalo Custardbath masks we powerfully, if unexpectedly, disrupted the discipline and deeply unsettled those in attendance (Shepherd 2015) and, interestingly, ourselves. Urgency and a rage-fuelled sense of care tinged with good doses of cynical exhaustion (the sheer repetition of disciplinary practices of silencing and marginalising enough to exhaust anyone) animated us.

Slowness had little to do with the moment, instead a pressing sense that we had to respond and do so quickly, because we cared deeply and angrily about the persistent and blatant exclusion of feminist, postcolonial, and queer scholars from a series meant to 'highlight key issues, current events, and new challenges' in the discipline. We cared (and dared) enough to throw caution to the wind. Do the unexpected. Go out on a limb. We made ourselves vulnerable, implicated, our own skin crawling with the sheer discomfort of a performance—and while to a degree calculated—that took on a life of its own. Viscerally confronting us with the violence of exclusionary practices so palpable in our discipline and the politics engendered therein. It was shocking, unexpected and surprising in its effect.

On the panel we performed a similar racialised and gendered exclusion to the Sapphire Series. There were five of us on the panel, four white women and one woman of colour. We agreed to actively marginalise and exclude Nuance queen. We made space for the Professor feminist to speak. We made space for the up and coming (white) feminists to speak. We carried on as though Nuance queen didn't exist. We pontificated and pontificated some more. When we exhausted ourselves and invited engagement from our audience, they refused to engage until Nuance queen spoke. But she refused to speak, despite the performative exclusion having ended. Getting up and walking away to the back of the room with her back to all of us. This wasn't in the script. We pleaded and urged her to speak. She wilfully remained silent. Some got up and held space with her at the back of the room. Some cried. One person got up and left. All of us were undone.

We enacted the structural racism and sexism of the ISA, IR, the university and were forced to sit with it for the duration of the panel. A smidgen of time that felt like an excruciating forever. It's still within us.

Why then, you might ask, have we settled on slowness rather than care, love, anger, rage or some other affective entanglement as our aesthetic and methodological sensibility? Have we settled at all? We/I don't ask this question because it is an either/or scenario. Surely it isn't. But it's curious that we've alighted on a far more majestic and luxurious aesthetic of slowness than the far more mundane and less glamorous one of care. And while slowness evokes care, evident in common and everyday refrains to 'go slowly', 'slow down'—in other words, to 'take (greater) care', 'be careful'—they are not readily interchangeable. Care might sometimes signal slowness, or the very opposite: immediacy, gut reactions, NO TIME, time is of the essence, a demand of 'now' not later.

Maybe we should slow down, more carefully consider the senses we are working with in this collaborative effort to ask what type of aesthetic

subject, what kinds of relationalities, ethics, and politics, and with what
capacities for feeling, knowing, and acting might be activated by and
through each of these senses (Ngai 2005).
As a sense, care is interesting because it functions both as a verb and noun.
As a verb it signifies to feel concern, to take interest in, attach importance
to, or to have 'feelings', often strong, about something or someone. And to
care is to invoke concern, sometimes worry. One is often troubled or goes
to trouble for someone or something, is bothered and bothers, one looks
after, takes care of, attends to, notices and tends to the needs of others and
oneself, takes charge of, fosters, protects, guards, watches over. This project
is rife with care: what we care about (or not)? Where we think care does
or doesn't happen or needs to happen? Who cares, who doesn't? Why do
we sometimes care about those who don't care about us (academia—we're
looking at you)? Why should we/you care? And surely prompted by strong
feelings about many things! Though how we care often looks sharper,
angrier, and also interestingly playful, loving, giving, open. And we can
also be 'carefree': throw off the disciplinary and institutional shackles that
confine us, hold us forcefully down and back.
As a noun, it also conjures the provision of health, welfare, sustenance,
and protection of something or someone. In this sense it is more obviously
bound up in relations of power than slowness: the one who cares, the other
who is cared for, although these positions need not be mutually exclusive,
binary, hierarchical. It also gestures to careful attention and consideration
of the possible effects of one's actions in an attempt to avoid damage; it
involves caution, carefulness, wariness, attentiveness, vigilance, circum-
spection, observance, and even guardedness.
Care gestures to geographies of home, domesticity and servility that make
us as feminists understandably nervous/wary, maybe wanting to walk a
wide circle around care, a pressing need to move away—far away—from
it. And while care might be more slippery, precarious, and ambivalent in
its widely and wildly divergent modes of expression—which also raises a
more uncertain and complicated status between labour and play so vital to
our performances of the frankenstinian subject/s—we would be remiss if we
didn't pay close attention to who care is typically addressed to as a demand:
women and, more particularly, women of colour who are far more likely to
feel the weight of the 'address' to care productive of marginalised subject
positions. Woman as a 'caring subject'. Thus, care's gendered, raced, and
classed baggage might be why we shy away from it. Ironically, it might
very well be the reason to embrace it, to face head-on the uncomfortable yet
unavoidable power relations signified in it; to reclaim, reformulate, perform
otherwise. Care's various intensities, temporalities, and geographies might

be an interesting monstrous methodology for thinking creatively about
global politics:
'Care is anger improved.
Care is the aftermath of anger.' (Vuong 2022)

We write because we care.

Too much, too little. Badly.

interlude three: song for a monster

*In March of 2017, I was formally diagnosed with 'moderate-to-severe'
ADHD. This was after weeks of testing and meetings, including IQ tests I did
not want (I have taken many of them, and test well. I have learned that this
then shapes expectations and perceived failings on my part to meet expected
benchmarks and performance markers. I agreed to take these tests to sup-
port my diagnosis—if I was not told the scores. On my last meeting, the psy-
chiatrist told me scores excitedly, as one was the highest she had ever had
in her office.) . . . but were necessary to support an adult diagnosis and the
prescription I received. I've struggled to find meaning in this—the fact that
I am the first in my family to not only to go to college but get a PhD. I have
two master's degrees as well—obtained as part of the meandering path to my
PhD. I tore myself apart to make it through. Sometimes others tried to tear me
apart. Only when I was confronted with the massive structure and planning
of the proposal and comps did I stall out and seek help.*

*I told my primary care doctor (an amazing woman who we're lucky to have
practicing in a low-cost clinic) 'Something is wrong with me. I'm . . . broken'.
She promised me we'd come too far together, she'd followed my academic
journey too long, to let me fail now. I carried the bottle of generic Ritalin
with me that she'd prescribed for a full day or two—afraid to take it. Afraid
of what I might be—more zombie than monster. Ultimately it was concern for
my daughter, sister, and my adopted kin and mentors—how hard it can be to
live with monsters—that prompted me to take it.*

It works. I am careful with it.

*I still see Dr Chelsea, to refill the prescription and check in. She laughs
sometimes and says 'If I took that medication—I'd be so productive! I'd . . .
like . . . get everything done'!*

*How do I explain that I take it so I don't rage out? So I can get out the
tentacles of ideas and sounds and images and fully composed paragraphs in*

my head into forms that are more understandable? So I don't exhaust those I love by navigating being more easy/more manageable/more 'sensible'?

Sometimes no matter how far I run, how much I train, or whether I take the medication as prescribed—the beast comes out. So I sing to her.

Academe is a tough place for us to be in—so we find each other, we slide and slither, smash and tear our way into spaces and places. Here's to laying eggs and planting hybrid offspring throughout it, in the walls, the offices, the minds of colleagues and those we teach, the words and art we publish. If we do that enough, we'll take it over from the inside out, collectively birthing something that is more than academe was—old-yet-new technologies of thinking, being, and doing.

Chapter 6

calling out (via) disjunctures

The slow, fragmented, playful conversation-as-a-method approach to writing this book is directly related to what we can say, and what we can do in the world. The premise of this approach is from the consensus in the group—though for different reasons, extent and effect, and our character-driven writing voice is an effort to feel out and make the differences perceivable and make space for dissonance to rework points of (non)consensus—that academic writing does not serve; it is not fit for purpose for changing the orders, relations, in the world. The pervasive and normalised disjuncture between theory and practice in academia, which again takes various forms, is symptomatic of how academic writing as a mode of doing good research, as an ideas-driven practice for developing better politics, as an activity that brings together people. Here we are talking about:

- Disjuncture between what people write and claim to believe, but in practice as colleagues, mentors, teachers, fellow humans, we consistently see a character that directly works against their ideas.
- Disjuncture between what people say and how they say them, to what effect.
- Disjuncture between who people are in public and who they are in private, intimate exchanges where what comes to pass, what happened is ambiguous and often feels circumstantial.
- Disjuncture between who people are as researchers and who they are as teachers, who people are as intellectuals and who they are as guest speakers, who people are as anonymous readers and who they are as readers with names, institutional positions and reputations, and vice versa. What do we do about the brilliant colleague who is shitty and racist to their PhD student?

- Disjuncture between thinking and bodies where we ask certain bodies to continually erase their specificity in the name of high theory, the good smart stuff.

Categorising and separating out spaces, relations and ways of thinking is necessary and inevitable, for instance differentiating how one is 'at the job', and how one is 'off-duty' makes for better practices, relationships and human beings. Boundaries established to balance demands, intensification in labour practices and human intimacies especially in cases of power asymmetry makes for a more reflective environment where negotiations and pushbacks are possible. At the same time, the possibility that the world and aspects of one's life can be categorised into distinct spaces, relations and modes has also been abused in academia to do less to the detriment to others in more vulnerable positions, and to establish boundaries that prop up the ego-driven performances of selfhood when perhaps letting go of the 'I' could have opened up new possibilities of not-I, perhaps even a 'we'.

But to claim that exposing disjunctures and bad practices in academic knowledge production and in university spaces would then somehow produce a different, more progressive, open, functioning and even benevolent institution requires some critical reflection. A question here might be: If we shift how we produce knowledge, would the Professor Man who governs and disciplines the boundaries of academic knowing subjects disappear? Could there be more plural knowing subjects that radically break from the Professor Man? Can we even desire this position given how fundamentally the academic space and practices are shaped by them? Would this effort create other hierarchies and relations that are as toxic, deliberating, disciplinary and variously fraught (but perhaps involving a different constellation of bodies that get abused, made invisible, torn apart)? Would the supposed new grounds of knowing and learning have different politics (of violence)?

What about writing just for the sake of writing,
not in the way we understand the job of the public intellectual.
What about writing what we feel we need to write
so we can continue in our respective salaried jobs,
but not to tick off boxes in promotion or fortifying a CV for rewards,
recognition.
There is no prestige here.
It might become scandalous.
Wanting to be able to do meaningful work *in* the academy.

We want to create more meaningful work. Partly we understand public anger against academics and the university as an intellectual enterprise. An aspect of populism is a revolt against the privilege and colonisation of knowledge. What if then we started with the premise that the world does not need changing, and rather than problem-solving or critical orientations toward the world, we first start with something smaller, trying to change the academic spaces we are part of, including perceptions on the outside of academia. In other words, what if we turn on its head the commonsense notion that the problem is 'out there' not 'in here'?

Taking feminist care and collaboration which means genuinely taking unpopular positions to build a community, rather than co-opt mainstream practices of violence and exclusion. Part of this is self-silencing and censorship that makes violence possible. Yes, friendships are at stake . . . when you discover your friends and close colleagues are racists and sexist, abusive, negligent, exploitative, unkind, elitist, delusional? How do you challenge them, show them the mirror? How do we do this without hiding our own reflections in it? Especially when we are complicit too. How do you call out/ in without calling out? Can you name and shame without attending to the masculinist politics of name and shame? How do you construct empathetic critique and empathetic REFUSAL?

Starting from the shitty 'here and now' to demonstrate the unequal worlds of invisibilised, erased and deliberately silenced peoples against the hypervisible, ever-present, always speaking and space-occupying people in IR, where the journey is not valued and productivity is the destination. We want to make present the journey and refuse the pristine destination of productivity.

What do you do when . . . ?

1. You're invited to an all-white women panel on diversity and publishing and instead of asking who is on the panel before agreeing, you say yes and then deflect blame and refuse responsibility.
2. High-flying Professor Woman treats a black doctoral student dreadfully (belittling them in public; leaving them to sit outside their office while they speak on the phone despite a scheduled meeting; an hour goes by and they still wait).
3. A prominent white Professor Man is well-known for being a sexual predator and/or sexist.
4. A prominent brown Professor Man is well-known for being a sexual predator and/or sexist.
5. You find out feminist x has plagiarised feminist xx.

6. You hear feminist y has published a journal article using feminist yy's ideas which the latter shared tentatively in a workshop; the published ideas feel too true to feminist yy's sense of the world. The published journal article does not mention feminist yy or offer alternative lineage of the ideas; surely ideas have lineages especially in the current conferencing and workshopping culture.

7. You can, in theory, write that shiny important article that might set you apart from others but you are unable to.

8. You can charge all your expenses to institutions by passing on to the workshop organiser the receipts of bottled water and snacks at the airport.

9. You sit through (maybe not great) paper presentations by the most junior scholars in the room and the most senior scholar shames them for taking away the opportunity from more 'deserving' academics.

10. You work with stubborn and defensive 'well-meaning' colleagues who consistently discipline scholars different from them through the framework of 'mentoring', 'global south', 'empowerment'.

11. You are part of a hiring committee and you find yourself part of conversations that make the candidates with non-Western, non-traditional research focus over-prove themselves.

12. When it is—again—an all-white male shortlist for a senior job.

13. You are part of meetings where established and not-so-established mediocre men take up so much space that the newcomer women in the room have to do so much labour to shape the conversation in ways that bring the group together, push the agenda of changing up curricula on course, and let their male colleagues take the credit for coming around to and sometimes coming up with the ideas.

14. When your male straight theory colleagues trash your feminist work.

15. The people who see you do not see others that are 'too different' often dressed up as, 'oh I don't understand feminism', or 'oh that is a bit weird, isn't it?'

16. When students get told your course is 'the feminist one'—with a perceptible nudge and a wink.

17. You hear that the very competitive funding you finally managed to get was because 'the review panel must've been really weird this year'.

18. When you ask for help from your 'boss', explain why you need it (pressured into saying and making yourself vulnerable) and he replies 'fuck off'. Ok, not so explicitly—but says no and can't be bothered to even acknowledge the 'why'. (I re-write a lot of those emails in my head—the way they should be written if the people in charge were better—maybe even a bit feminist/queer/kind.)

19. You sit through an entire work-related dinner where the topics of conversation are mainly driven by the loudest, fastest-talking conversationalists.

20. You walk into a cutting-edge critical IR panel session to hear someone you admire immensely, and you are the only person of colour in the room, both up front and in the audience.

21. You walk into a cutting-edge postcolonial and critical IR panel session and you quickly realise it is a session of a closed network of intellectual masturbation orchestrated for or by the Big Shot holding court.

22. Many, many send you direct messages in solidarity on X, formerly known as Twitter, in a thread about xx but do not post publicly in your support.

23. People privately offer sympathy for the bullying you've put up with, but stay quiet in public.

24. When you publicly support an X, formerly known as Twitter, thread about xxx but find out later that there was more to the story that put it in a new light and revealed hidden violences.

25. Men try to be helpful and make you write in clearer ways that you are not interested in, but these men are your friends and supporters. And you are no longer a PhD student.

26. Colleagues are just too nice to point out blatantly wrong premises for decisions in meetings so you stand (up) alone, because being 'too nice' is not an option for you.

27. When IR men will only hire non-IR political theory people who can also teach 'soft' critical IR.

28. When political science/theory men will only hire non-feminist women researchers who can also teach the one gender and politics course in the department.

29. When in a hiring committee someone says we are already doing feminism so why do we need 'another' feminist, as though feminists are interchangeable. And when one or two feminists is always more than enough. We can have five Marxists/critical theorists/Kantians, etc., but TWO WHOLE FEMINISTS?!?!?!? Unthinkable.

30. When you can't just be 'you' in the here and now—but get shackled to some mythical past. With all its sanctions.

31. When your feminist colleagues side with the mainstream men. Careers are more important than feminism.

32. When you hear 'well-meaning advice' from Professor Men that maybe you should look for jobs outside of academia because 'it's even hard to find permanent academic positions for those talented ones'.

33. Please add your own—

Do we step aside, say something, intervene? Take a deep breath and do the work (which work)? Take a deeper breath and try to shift the pain elsewhere for a while? At what cost? At whose cost?

Chapter 7

what is at stake?

Our approach to writing this book reflects what we agree is at stake in this experimental collaboration. This involves challenging and feeling out differently the reproduction of a range of violent orders including (but not only) whiteness, masculinity, heteronormativity, ableism, elitism and sexism in the university as a workspace and site of knowledge production. In feminist, postcolonial and critical scholarship that takes shelter in the margins. In public spaces where only certain bodies become visible and invisible, heard and ignored, valued and devalued, included and excluded. And in homes and intimate spaces that are always part of the usually more visible global, shared realities.

But 'challenging' and even 'feeling out differently' both fail to capture what is really at stake or what we are really trying to get at, because what we are really trying to expose is the <u>small</u> stuff, the stuff we often brush off, or more often are asked to brush off—FOR NOW—because the situation is so bad NOW (no time to experiment), because more important issues of humanity require our intellectual attention (no time to experiment), because <u>NOW</u> demands more efficient use of one's time and body (no time to experiment), because this career—or trying to make it one—demands you to be serious (no time to experiment). But NOW goes on and on and on. It lasts for what feels like forever.

How does one take writing and thinking risks for things seemingly so small, so petty, so light?

What is at stake is that I want my life to matter and be meaningful full-stop. Not something that is continually reduced to, captured or compartmentalised into 'work-life' balance, how many journal articles I publish, how many grants I get, how many mini-mes I produce—my 'status' in the discipline.

51

What is at stake is my own well-being at a point in my life, rightly or wrongly, I feel so privileged, with some padding, some breathing space, and I am not doing anything meaningful with it, nor do I see others doing anything meaningful in their comparable or even extraordinarily more padded positions. How does academic work matter? Does it matter and to whom?

What is at stake is kindness.

What is at stake is joy, pleasure, fun, laughter.

What is as stake is humanness.

What is at stake is being able to say you are sorry when you fuck up.

What is at stake is also forgiveness and the capacity to move on. We all fuck up once in a while . . . ok, maybe more than once . . . just human . . . and so tired. . . .

What is at stake is the need to acknowledge/see harm and do something about it.

What is at stake is exposing the sexist, racist and ageist centres at the margins.

What is at stake is refusing authoritative forms of knowledge embodied in absurd claims to originality and contributions evidenced in how we must write to get published in top-ranked journals. (What's the new publishing niche?)

What is at stake is a possibility of producing knowledge that is less certain, less surefooted, less arrogant, less authoritative.

What is at stake is producing and validating knowledge that is more open: open to interpretation, participation, scepticism, irreverence, and thus, doesn't simply reproduce dominant, racialised masculinist modes of knowledge and knowing subjects.

What is at stake is rethinking and reinventing strategies to address rampant racism, sexism and ableism in academic spaces which spill over to other aspects of life.

What is at stake is sharing the burden of those who are fighting these battles on their own, those whom the system turns into activists, whose time goes into everyday activism that prevents intellectual explorations.

What is at stake is shifting the big and small impacts and continuities of racialised colonial encounter. This should not be the burden of certain bodies simply because one is from India, Rwanda, the various non-Wests while working in a Western context. Educating white feminists, white men and also brown and black men is NOT one person's labour alone. This work is an attempt to do this work collectively from our many locations.

What is at stake is valuing failed and/or less than articulate attempts to think through complex, lived realities and the shitty, violent politics of global politics, the discipline and the academy.

What is at stake are real, living people and treating them as though they matter and are not simply 'data' for our research, badges of our superior intellect, baggage that needs to be shaken off quickly.

What is at stake is refusing the many, many ways we reproduce sexism, ageism, ableism and racism in our daily academic lives.

What is at stake here is writing. Why does it matter that we publish one more article, one more book, stage one more conversation if feminist knowledges continue to be marginalised and dismissed?

What is at stake is art. Who gets to do artistic stuff? Does art in IR have to be done 'well'? Does it have to be made by a 'real artist'? Or can anyone do art in IR? Who gets to decide what counts as art and what doesn't? IR may not get art, but art gets IR, all right. Do you have to have a degree in art or art history, or somehow otherwise prove that you've read enough of art history? What is enough? Who decides?

What is at stake is giving some figurations of academic ways of being/living/working that resists lot of the pressures to perform like a 'serious' academic & to become an asshole.

What is at stake are categories, compartments, identities, 'protected characteristics' (what a [bad] joke . . . and yet we all have to obey and 'pretend'—for so many bad reasons). Maybe we've been fighting categories all our lives—not thin enough, not clever enough, not bold enough, too shy, too self-conscious, too girly, too hetero, not queer enough, too young, too fucking old—starts about twenty-nine I think . . . what kind of fucked up thing is that? It's all so bewildering—all the time—why did she wipe the hand marks off the handle that person had touched? Why can't I go there? Why doesn't it feel ok? Why do I have to go in that sex/age/marital status box? Why are the options so limited? (Airlines—twenty-first century—really? Mr is your default category? Mrs is your 'main' female category?). Banal—first worldy perhaps. But it all counts. Let's focus on banalities—there the world spins. . . .

What is at stake is ridiculous shards of light sometimes—oh the joy and pain of thinking, writing! But what is this weird thing—this weird feeling we get when we're surprised people behave like shit. People who 'should' know better. How naïve. There's something at stake about how we 'logic' our ways of thinking, writing, speaking—we keep explaining and rationalizing. But sometimes—too often maybe—the answer is people don't care . . . current white hetero-patriarchal global (and local . . .) leadership is deep red testament to not giving a shit.

What is at stake is fighting categories. Then it gets worse. When the expectations are too high—position—apparent position is not all it seems—certainly for some. When people you think won't—do. When people you think will—won't. And find the power of the category and its rewards too appealing. And why not—why wouldn't they? Is that 'self-care'?

What is at stake is the obsession with the 'grand narratives' of feminism. Why do we selectively recognise struggles and voices? What is important to speak for and about and what is not? What differences are too different to recognise and negotiate? Why does diversity invite only tokenism? And what is authenticity? Is it not disingenuous to look for 'authentic voices' to tell stories that are so complex anyway? And how does lack of 'authenticity' or concerns about 'who can speak for whom and from where', insecure women?

What is at stake is that I/we don't know how to write an academic article. I/we are not even interested in reading most of them. I/we want to be able to write differently, in a fragmented and less structured way, not always spending time justifying why it matters to do feminist IR or pop culture in IR or arts-based stuff in IR. I/we just want to do it. I/we don't want to try to convince those who are not going to be convinced anyway. Been there, done that. But maybe open up some space for some others who are struggling with these same issues. Academic arguments are judged in a very particular way, the standards are set and 'everyone' knows how to tell if the argument is well made or not. We're trained to make these judgments; when faced with something that's not structured in the usual way it's easy to just dismiss it as not IR enough, not academic enough, or simply not good. I/we are worried what this formulaic way of working does to thinking, to ideas, to creativity. If everyone has to produce similar kind of work, doesn't that also mean something about what kind of (cookie cutter) people we have to become to 'make it' in academia? If so, I/we are not sure I/we want to stay. So maybe in this project what is at stake is my/our future(s) and my/our whole relationship(s) to academia; if this manages to change something, maybe there'll be room for someone like me/us in academia.

What is at stake becomes palpable in the minutiae, in minor moments of decision making that often feel like low-stakes stuff. We are interested in the low-stakes stuff because these are moments when relationality and positionality become visible, when relations come into tension, when reality becomes so hard to discern.

'Caring is risky because it is ethical' (Wołodźko 2020, 216). Hmmm, care—yes care. Care is very much at stake.

Pause: I was distracted . . .

I was distracted . . . by the rats at the back door
I was distracted . . . by my crying mother who worries she will never see us again
I was distracted . . . by not seeing my partner for months
I was distracted . . . by my inability to keep focus
I was distracted . . . by the global pandemic
I was distracted . . . by wanting to lie on the floor and die for most of September
I was distracted . . . by people trying to stop me caring for my own health
I was distracted . . . by emails which start 'I hope this finds you well'
I was distracted . . . by having to do everything myself
I was distracted . . . by crippling isolation in lockdown
I was distracted . . . by refusals and rejections
I was distracted . . . by caring for my family at a distance for so long
I was distracted . . . by exhaustion
I was distracted . . . by 'business as usual'
I was distracted . . . by relentless sexism
I was distracted . . . by the costs of 'working from home'
I was distracted . . . by the global pandemic
I was distracted . . . by *MasterChef Australia*
I was distracted . . . by a new baby in the family and my love for them
I was distracted . . . by exhaustion and depression
I was distracted . . . by my desire to find some passion in things I do and how I live
I was distracted . . . by the nausea from my SSRI meds
I was distracted . . . by doctor's appointments
I was distracted . . . by *RuPaul's Drag Race*
I was distracted . . . by therapy
I was distracted . . . by the global pandemic
I was distracted . . . by the hours spent caring for my sick dog
I was distracted . . . by 'my' government's entitled, greedy, obscene behaviour
I was distracted . . . by 'my' government's stupidity
I was distracted . . . by the absurdities of masculinity
I was distracted . . . by my bad back
I was distracted . . . by the chaos that is my house
I was distracted . . . by the smell of cat poo in my living room
I was distracted . . . by the global pandemic
I was distracted . . . by *24*

I was distracted . . . by my painful feet
I was distracted . . . by Twitter
I was distracted . . . by technological failures
I was distracted . . . by the global pandemic
I was distracted . . . by thousands of words proving in-person teaching is 'safe'
I was distracted . . . by thousands of words proving in-person teaching cannot be safe
I was distracted . . . by knowing 'evidence' is gendered, raced and authority 'owned'
I was distracted . . . by worrying about money
I was distracted . . . by *Dexter*
I was distracted . . . by the global pandemic
I was distracted . . . by the broken heart of academia
I was distracted . . . by sycophants
I was distracted . . . by wanting to write
I was distracted . . . by feeling so sorry for students
I was distracted . . . by my cat
I was distracted . . . by my unruly hormones
I was distracted . . . by wondering if I will see my mother again
I was distracted . . . by the harsh disregard for my health and well-being
I was distracted . . . by Duckspeak
I was distracted . . . by the blood on the hands of 'leaders'
I was distracted . . . by my questionable viewing choices
I was distracted . . . by the smoke and mirrors of university finances
I was distracted . . . by black holes where emotional intelligence should be
I was distracted . . . by encroaching agoraphobia
I was distracted . . . by my sister's bizarre views
I was distracted . . . by a multiplicity of 'Zooms'
I was distracted . . . by hardly moving sometimes
I was distracted . . . by the frozen soul of bureaucracy
I was distracted . . . by cheese
I was distracted . . . by virtual conferencing and how meaningless it felt
I was distracted . . . by hatemail
I was distracted . . . by a thing on social media
I was distracted . . . by a journalist asking for my expert view on a thing
I was distracted . . . by guilt (should not complain because others have it so much worse)
I was distracted . . . by my mother bringing around some food
I was distracted . . . by a crisis in the family
I was distracted . . . by having to cook lunch

I was distracted . . . by PMS and my cramping uterus
I was distracted . . . by tv shows that I don't remember watching
I was distracted . . . by the darkness of the winter
I was distracted . . . by worrying about daughters wanting to give up their jobs
I was distracted . . . by friends suffering relentless racism
I was distracted . . . by a pain in my backneckshoulderslegsfeet & a headache
I was distracted . . . by sunny weather
I was distracted . . . by students crashing and I am doing all I can to catch some of them
I was distracted . . . by deaths by suicide and memorial services on campus
I was distracted . . .

PART II

Chapter 8

black cats, the seduction of usefulness and cracks

Dear chine,

I was so excited about this idea of exchanging letters with you that I thought I'd get right on it. Yet here we are four days later, and I haven't written a word. Exhaustion kicked in before I even got started, or exhaustion was stronger than my excitement.

The past few weeks have been difficult as the public discussion about research funding (mainly on Twitter but also on some mainstream media) has been ridiculous. All kinds of important projects in humanities and social sciences have been labelled stupid, unnecessary, and undeserving of funding. My funded project hasn't been mentioned this time, that I know of, but it's made it onto those lists before.

I know I should just do my work and try to find joy in it. But it is so hard to ignore that noise. For four years I worked on that funding application every fall, spending who knows how many hours on it. Many other people helped me by reading and commenting; without them I'd never have succeeded. And now some journalists, politicians, and random people on social media think they are qualified to judge, based on the title and short public description, whether the research proposal has merits and deserves funding.

I think this is activating some old wounds of not getting the support for my work that I might have needed and why I find it so hard to ignore. Also, it just generally worries me, where we are going as a society, for how long will there be any room for critical intellectual work?

Yesterday, I was in therapy complaining about this dilemma of being excited about doing the work on this book and writing this letter and somehow spending the whole week avoiding actually starting to do it (am afraid to even count how many *Law & Order: SVU* episodes I watched instead). As I'm into visual work, my therapist asked me to pick out some cards describing how I feel. Won't get into those here, but at the end she also asked me to pick out an inspiring card that would perhaps work as a reminder that I am indeed excited about this work and maybe it would nudge me to get to the work instead of avoiding it.

Here's the card:

In therapy by ss

What do you see in it?

I see excitement, curiosity—feminist curiosity even. Hmm, isn't the saying 'curiosity killed a cat'? I hope curiosity is what keeps us going when academia is surely trying to kill us with overwork and never-ending demands. I see a hopeful future. Isn't that a crystal ball rather than a fishbowl?

Also, the cat is no longer black. Black cats are beautiful, but when I think of the figure of the black cat that I've connected to the discussions we've been having about exhaustion, I do hope it slowly changes colours and does not forever remain black. I think exhaustion and depression are definitely much more like cats. Cats do what they want in their own time. Exhaustion and depression surely take their time, and don't proceed as you would expect them to. I think the blackness of the cat (or dog), can be problematic in equating black with something bad or undesired (there's a long history of that equation, isn't there?) I've read some descriptions of severe depression (Hardwick 1999, Styron 1990) and the darkness they describe is truly black, thus I was thinking of the black cat. But my exhaustion and (not severe) depression have rather been quite grey: the past looks grey, the future looks grey, the now looks and feels grey. So maybe the black cat is not the best metaphor. Maybe there are multiple cats. The black one is always there as well, but not demanding all the attention all the time.

I can't believe it's been a year and a half since we last got to hang out in person right before the pandemic. I'm regretting going to bed early and not going dancing and drinking together in Nashville. Little did we know how fast things would change from then on. Now that I think back, there were so many signs of depression and exhaustion at the time, and I kept ignoring them. I've always enjoyed conferences a lot, getting to hang out with some of my favourite academics and listening to inspiring and interesting presentations. At the IFJP conference in Nashville I hardly found any enjoyment in any of that, nothing really sparked my interest. I don't even know how long that had been going on at that point. And I'm afraid that if it hadn't been for the pandemic, I would've kept going. There was going to be ISA Hawai'i the same month and BISA Newcastle in July. And I was planning some research visits, to various places.

I think I would've kept going. And going. I would have been underachieving and miserable, and I don't know for how long I would have just kept on going until the next thing, and the next, and the next. Maybe the whole three years of my project.

So, in a way, I'm glad the pandemic forced me to stop and take time off to recover. I still feel like I don't have much to say about anything, but at least I can write about exhaustion and cats. I think our letters (and more/other things) exchange will bring me some joy in the upcoming dark season. I'm trying to find a way to *work with* the darkness instead of struggling against it, taking inspiration of Kaisa Kortekallio in *Monster Talks* (2020).

It's sunny today here, so I think I'll go outside to get some of that natural bright light.

Have a restful weekend! I'm looking forward to where this exchange will take us.

Zzzzzzz

dear Zzzzzzz,

In excitement, I am writing back right away, though who knows how long it will take me to actually finish writing it? the picture of the cat card just had me burst into a laugh and tears. I don't know where the tears came from, specifically I mean. just like you, I've come to a stop these days with the help of the pandemic-related restrictions, and with this stop find myself not only surrounded by cats but surrounding myself with sad music, sad stories, and just generally attracted to dark, melancholic things that make me tear up. in the beginning of the pandemic, I even bought a book on tears, Heather Christie's *The Crying Book*. it turned out not quite to be the book I wanted, not the kind of thinking about tears i needed so I read a few pages and stopped. it felt too intellectualized; i did not want to read things that have been intellectualized then but maybe I will return to the book now, now that I am tearing up differently.

I remember you talking about your plans, the world tour you were on last year. I was also following an exhausting work schedule that required a lot of international travel and meeting people that hearing of your plans, they felt normal and fun insofar as work can be fun. I've been wondering what that phase of my work life was about and why I created it. I think in part it was because I had so many things I finally get to do that in the past, when I was just fresh out of PhD, I felt like I was closed to people like me. somehow (miraculously!) I found my people, got grants, had a stable job, that I was actually able to put into motion things I imagined/thought up, and I got to meet people and share my ideas-in-formation that in the past I just had to figure out all on my own (often while being talked at, erased from literature). So I think I understand what you mean about how you feel about the local assholery over funding projects, why it bothers you so much every year, even if your own project is not under attack—is it related at all, do you think, to just finally getting to do what you need and wanted to do because you have worked so hard to not fall through the cracks, and then you realise, oh wait, there is this other big aggression against your work, and like, of course there is.

I was in a reading group conversation on feminist nuclear politics, you know the one that Y and I got going for ISA Hawai'i. Two phrases struck me from that, 'seductions of usefulness' which were my words just observing what people were saying about their problems with the critical approaches that are not feminist (or maybe it is better to say, critical approaches from *nowhere* because that is how men in the field theorise, seems like the only way they know how to talk about the international). but the other phrase from that reading group that keeps ringing in my ears is how someone was telling us about how she had encountered this text we were discussing and in telling her story, she described it as 'falling through the cracks', how moving between critical IR from the United States and United Kingdom, she fell through the cracks, and what remained unsaid by her but what I also heard her say, is how existing feminist networks too often only contribute to this falling, rather than do anything to reshape 'the field' so people like her can also be part of feminist conversations more easily, that at the moment people like her have nowhere to go but . . . be alone with the men. I think there are so many ways to respond to that, but I really felt that—that feeling of falling through the cracks, like no one cares if I do but me, and that at the macro theoretical debate level or at the global political level, it does not matter if certain people in the existing academic landscape fall through the cracks and disappear except the people who don't make it, you know? but how can anyone tell another human being—however 'privileged' or whatever—they do not matter? who gets to say that? how can people think they get to say that? who made you god?

Trying to answer these questions just gives me a headache, literally, I give myself migraines with these kinds of questions. But I wonder if we are talking about the same related phenomena—you, me, this conversation, that conversation I had in the reading group. Let me see if I can articulate this idea: . . . hmm. I cannot. All I can think of it, it is the whole fucking thing that is the problem, that is impossible! Things feel impossible!!!! That clarifies nothing; I will come back to this.

I am really into just stopping these days, I used to just keep going, finding a way to keep going (though even then I was maddeningly messy and late handing in everything, and just an unapologetic procrastinator). when the border closed after I hurriedly returned from the Nashville IFJP conference where I saw you last, not only did my calendar get cleared out but also all the things that were structuring my day, you know? like I no longer had to set my alarm (that I would not get up to), check emails (to then not respond in a timely manner anyway), go to a café and create a change of scene (so I can work and stay 'active', though my default mode is to be just home and do nothing), smile and be expressive (when I'd rather be that person sitting in the back row and just watch), and so on. I just had the things that structured my not not-going-to-disappear, and as part of this, I also stopped reading things

I felt I had to because they were good for me, or whatever. I just stopped and waited and interestingly, when I just stopped reading the 'thing' I did not really feel like reading and just rested, somehow I would find something else that I *could* read, watch or listen to.

This is how I came to be the collector of things cat, which in the past was more directly related to 'IR', you know, how soldiers kept cats to keep them company in 'frontlines', how Twitter diplomacy sometimes really just feels like cat diplomacy, or how fundraisers and campaigns used their pets to get their message circulating, the cat memes in academic exchanges. But now, there are cats everywhere, my whole world is being filled with cats and this is a wonderful feeling—to be surrounded by the thing that holds your attention and gives you comfort. In the description of Atsushi Kaga's new exhibition 'It always comes; a solace in the cat', the Maho Kubota Gallery website contained this description which I think also captures what might be going on with us. 'The characters depicting anthropomorphized animals like rabbits, bears, and cats are still present in almost all of the works, but it feels as if they now appear as anthropomorphized ideas or messengers, rather than simply anthropomorphized characters'.* Cats as figurations of ideas or messengers, I like that—the idea that cats have messages for me when I try to stop the thing that is causing exhaustion, if I get out of the way and rest. You can see Kaga's paintings from the exhibition, 'It always comes; a solace in the cat' (I just like typing this out, isn't this a wonderful title?).†

I really like his painting, 'If you can't fly, no need to do so' because of the title and the cat butt. But the bunny is too smiley for how I feel. I'm definitely more, 'Nature may come back while we eat gherkins during the quarantine'. Even the black cat is frowning. This makes me smile.

hugs.

chine

Dear chine,

This last painting you mentioned definitely depicts the black cat as I've imagined it (or her?) and makes me smile too. I don't know why this 'not really giving a shit' kind of look brings me joy, but it does. I guess we're not the only ones, after all Grumpy Cat was one of the most popular memes for quite a while almost ten years ago.

We're definitely drawn to the same paintings by Kaga. When I visited the online gallery, I did not at first pay attention to the titles, but the black cat leaving the scene in 'If you can't fly, no need to do so' caught my attention.

---

* www.mahokubota.com/en/artists/1381/.

† It always comes; a solace in the cat by Atsushi Kaga, September 10 (Friday)–October 9 (Saturday), 2021, installation view, photo: Keizo Kioku, https://www.mahokubota.com/en/exhibitions/3287/.

I think it captures some of the essence of the black cat and how we think about her appearance as a character in this book. Something you said today in our ugly feminist collective's Zoom meeting about the black cat not being impressed at all by all the things we're supposed to be impressed by. For me the bunny in the painting is definitely impressed by the usual things; maybe the storks (?) are too. The turtles I'm not so sure about; maybe they're taking their cue from the cat and are about to leave the scene. But I'm pretty sure the bunny will soon lure or direct them back. I feel the bunny is a 'he', a gatekeeper. Of course, I'm projecting because of what we have been talking about for a long time about IR and academia. But then again, that's how art works, you can see different things in the same piece at different times. . . .

I also really like this idea of cats as figurations of ideas or messengers. I often feel like the real-life cat that I live with has only one message for me: 'I'm hungry, feed me'. Or 'please clean my litter box'. But maybe I'm not always paying enough attention to what he might want and am paying even less attention to all these figurative cats. So, I'm curious where this journey will take us all. What is your cat telling you these days?

I love, love, love this title of the exhibition: 'It always comes; a solace in the cat'! It reminds me to accept and welcome the exhaustion, instead of fighting it. Which I was doing for a long time. It's not that I'm thinking that 'after I make it through this, I'll be a better and stronger person' or some other heroic growth narrative. It's more about finding a more liveable life. I don't think there's any going back to the 'old normal', not for me personally but also on a more collective level. I think the black cat in the painting above also knows this. No matter how long we wait and eat gherkins. The bunny may think otherwise?

I'll keep this short today, but one more thing I want to pick up from your letter is this 'oh wait, there is this other big aggression against your work, and like, of course there is'. Yes, yes! Finally, I had the means (time & funding) to concentrate on what I want to do academically, but then I was simply too exhausted, but I thought that once I rest for a while, then I can be at peace and just focus on my work. But *of course*, there's all this anti-intellectualism, anti-feminism, populism etc. that join together in trying to silence us. How dare I forget that. And how dare I think that institutions (universities and funders) would somehow be proactive and useful in protecting us from the attacks.

I think I want to think more about the 'seductions of usefulness' and 'falling through the cracks' and about 'people who do/did not make it' in the upcoming weeks and letters.

Many hugs,

Zzzzzzz

Chapter 9

perverse love letter

Dear ally,

There is so much violence and shittiness around me that I have a hard time learning and sharing in conferences where we each equally get twelve minutes, stand or sit so properly in front of a room full of so equally proper and enlightened audience, so silent and so steely in how we understand equality and rigour.

[Because not all silences are the same—some are in anticipation, some are in boredom, some are in disbelief, some are in love, some are impatient, some are helpful in getting you to forget yourself and focus on the ideas, ideas, ideas; some are so loud and pregnant with resentment of its silence, though it speaks so loudly and clearly even on mute, that your ideas drown and you learn what it means to be disciplined by silence, a gaze, what is not visible but so palpably there.]

Dear ally,

There is so much violence in the staff kitchen where a 'well-intentioned' Professor Man/Woman can misinterpret the jumbled words you try to get out of your mouth as you try to get out of a conversation that you did not want in the first place. Because all you wanted was to quickly fix your coffee and get back to your office, to your Spivak, to your Trinh, but instead, out of collegiality you engage the colleague in a conversation about the hard time you had last semester with teaching. This gets immediately interpreted as a matter of rookie mistakes and experiences, as a matter of students being not smart enough or your expectations being too green and high. True, to compensate for the ineloquence and seeming withdrawn (because really, I did not want this conversation in the first place and it has nothing to do with me or you or the workplace but has everything to do with things beyond these immediate halls, this immediate place of work whereas a homeland-less academic I try to work with dignity), I overanimated my life to intersect with his. I tried to close the distance, the disconnect and maybe stood too close. He made sure a distance was maintained between us. Is it because he can't stand our proximity? our equality?

[If he were interested in listening to what I was trying to say, maybe he would have heard how I was not so much worried about how the students here are not very smart and motivated like those in elite ones across the bridge, the sea, the ocean. If he were interested in what I specifically had to say, maybe he would have realised that I was not actually overwhelmed by teaching in a new environment with new course materials. Maybe he could have learned something about me as a colleague, that I have been thinking about this very issue for a long time—longer than the split second he has given to what he thought he already knew my experiences were—and how I think that teaching and learning is shaped by a number of things like politics, different political leanings we each bring to the room but also the different understandings of politics as a discipline, the different desires students have including the desire to be disciplined, different measuring stick for validation of . . . the . . . differences all stemming from a common desire to be validated for who we think we are in daylight, in our serious mode, in our work clothes with our hair and face if not fixed up then at least glimpsed at in the bathroom mirror as we brushed our teeth, in the mode where we speak with our brushed teeth, in a mode where etiquette, hygiene, respect for another's privacy, covering up our private parts all shape how we sit, slouch, walk, look out the window, scratch an itch, eat our food, do even the most inappropriate things, in a mode that even disciplines, aestheticises how we are inappropriate.]

Dear ally,

There is so much violence in the Microsoft Word documents we receive from you in your various positions as journal editors, manuscript reviewers, mentors, collaborators, as friend, when you tell me. . . .

[Because if writing is inescapably a violence we do to our thoughts and bodies, then editing is also an inescapably violent and creative act but the editorial violence jars never purely because it never arrives as existential-in-pure-sense for brown folks, black folks, for those who think grammatically incorrect sentences, for me who spent most of my undergraduate years falling asleep in class because I was working two on-campus jobs and doing off-campus babysitting gigs in between being a student, for me who did not know beds had things called bedsheets and matching pillowcase covers until my college roommate had a stack of them and changed them every week, for me who learned her English from a Madam Lubagbas who called me into

her office to encouragingly tell me that despite not being a Filipina, I wrote a good essay, for me who write and speak English with greater ease in all contexts formal because it was the only formal education I received badly, always as a secondary citizen of this linguistic world, and speak and write Korean only in the best and most inventive ways that a self-taught person can who picked up the language as a birth-burden listening to adults, reading and writing without being corrected, for me who taught English for most of my twenties in Korea by pretending I knew less Korean than I did because only by being less Korean could my English language be fully valued, which is also the first time I ever had any money in my life and then did not know what to do with it and wanted to buy culture and class so bought many classical CDs badly until I discovered Yo-Yo Ma who I listened to religiously since high school before acquiring culture and class because his Dvorak cello concertos sang even to my uncultured ears.]

Dear ally,

There is so much violence and shittiness in the job and grant rejection letters we receive from apologetic and conscientious head of schools, search committees and administrative staff.

[Yes, this being a competitive fellowship, there being so many qualified PhDs, and yes, surely not everyone can be funded and hired, and maybe I was underprepared, not on top of my game, too green, miscalculated, had a bit of an attitude problem through the process, was too timid, hid behind a persona and a voice I thought I had to put on to be safe; misread the instructions, and god damn it, just exhausted from trying to juggle, to make it, to persevere, to be productive-despite, to value-myself-despite, to ward off cynicism, to ward off the inner demon in me that explains how I self-sabotage but also how I am able to go on. But it still really does not feel right and the necessary evaluative casting over the entire body of work you have worked so hard to create in just one talk, one document, one version of yourself that you have to crumple your feelings and be no other way but be a good sport about feels so wrong; it is the necessity and the evaluative nature of the process that injures because this idea of necessity is a funny thing. And your smugness even in your humility to admit, 'I won't have made it in the current job market', oh the smugness of drawing a line because you feel safe, the generosity that comes (only after) your wealth a little too late, a little too salty. And you still want to talk about my attitude problem.]

I do not know what to do with this violence and shittiness. I do not know how I am supposed to learn, to share, to discuss ideas and be purely intellectual, to focus and stick to the good work I am capable of doing, and make my way in this world. I do not know how I am going to make things work. I have two requests that I think might be helpful as I try to figure out how to continue.

Firstly, it would help a lot if you stopped obsessing over smart people—'She's so smart.', 'That was such a great presentation.', 'She can write her socks off.' I know it is not your intention but smartness fetish reproduces people like you and disciplines people like me, the 'belated' entrants to university/modernity/high theory who are appreciated for our new insights because of our positionality but then given extra work to then make it intelligible and intelligent to you. You are smart—do the extra work yourself and bring that into how you speak and listen. Secondly, please speak and go to bat for me—I know you do when you feel like you should or can, and I am asking you to do this more structurally and systematically—more rigorously, in conference rooms, in classrooms, in your office, in your now, now, now, which really means even when you do not feel you can or should. I guess again I am asking you to listen more than speak. I guess I am asking you to use your smartness to create less emotional work for me. Let me continue terrorising academia with my bad skills and unformed mind.

I probably wrote more than I should have. Hope you don't take this the wrong way. I don't want to sound unappreciative and you have been so generous but please do not tell me to work harder if I want to do my kind of 'innovative' writing by doing that—and blog, tweet, FB about it to reach the larger audience—but also be doing the traditional stuff in top journals. I understand changing the debates and pushing boundaries are hard work. I understand freedom is hard work. But you just don't get it. 'Innovative/creative' writing is not an option for people like me, something I do on the side for fun, to let out my creative steam. This is my mother tongue, this is the only way I can speak academese that was not created to communicate with people like me, and every time I read your academese never mind try to write in it, it is killing me. The thing about critical, feminist, postcolonial, decolonial, etc. folks is that we all think we are not mainstream. We are the good ones, the allies, the injured party, those who work to change the discipline. But the mainstream is in us, in various ways. Let us own up, let us start from an honest place.

So, I guess these are impossible requests because really I am asking you to not even think them—and yes, this is thought policing—so maybe we are at war. We are allies and also enemies. But if so, I am my worst enemy, and maybe there is really no point to this letter. I should just work on myself—the violence I feel listening to how people self-present, read, draw conclusions, ask questions is self-inflicting. I am my own oppressor.

Chapter 10

writing exhaustion—the unbearable weight of white feminism

Conversations that one forces upon a room always deplete the people who felt the need to raise an issue that exposes the limit of sociality. There is no joy in this—ever—though some of us keep finding ourselves creating the mess that no one appreciates, even ourselves-now. There is no right decision, no righting the wrong. The forced-upon conversation is impossible and the work we create for ourselves is truly unnecessary-now. Futile.

But this futility stems from the now, in the calculus of what-will-be stemming from what-is-now, that what-is-now IS, that it exists and must be taken on the 'existing' terms. This insistence on what-exists, what IS, any good critical theorist knows, can only be an effect of power. For those who exist in various intersecting positions of 'unlocation' (Tate [quoting Mirza 1997] in Tate 2017, 57) and ways of leading a life despite systems and worlds that are designed to ensure you cannot exist-in-your-terms, or exist only through depletion, accruing value in ways that never will sustain life, creation, . . . one has to experiment, one does a lot of listening, a lot of watching . . . a lot of looking around at-least-five-times before crossing the line. And yet, even these cautious belated crossings, we are told are too brash, too unclear, too radical.

This moment radicalizes and depletes at the same time.

Shirley Anne Tate (2017, 55) narrates an illustrative example of this moment:

Your new head of department is a White feminist and sees feminism as your point of commonality. She asks you to a meeting when she takes up her position to tell you that you must reconcile with another White feminist who egregiously racially harassed you three years previously. You must reconcile because you have to work closely with her due to her departmental role but most importantly

73

because she is 'the friend and colleague' of the head of department. You are told that whatever arrangements had been put into place to separate you in terms of office space from your racist harasser no longer hold and that she can be put anywhere in the building, so you should get used to that as the new approach because, after all, the person you see as your racist harasser 'just sent you some long emails'.

The occasion for this racist harassment that made her friend-less and colleague-less is significant (Tate 2017, 60):

> The programme leader was a White feminist. She wanted a White woman who was her friend to get the job that had been advertised. I disagreed and supported a more qualified and experienced Asian man over her friend, citing our responsibilities under equal opportunities legislation. She questioned my feminist credentials and asked me, 'what are you today, are you Black or a feminist?' She made it plain that the White woman would be hired because the course on which I also taught had already borne 'the brunt of employing Black people'. That brunt, of course, was me. The Asian man did not get the job, but he won his case at an industrial tribunal on grounds of racial discrimination. I was a witness on his behalf and, unlike the racist perpetrator, was not represented by university counsel. There was an internal investigation. I was spoken to by the head of department as part of the fact-find and this was audio-recorded so that no claims could be made afterwards that anything untoward had been said. I was summoned, questioned and verbally reprimanded by the vice chancellor for my disloyalty to the university. The White feminist, who walked around teary-eyed for months after the tribunal, was not reprimanded but rather pitied because of my betrayal and her public humiliation, though she kept her job until she retired. I, on the other hand, was put into a room with no windows, by myself, for two years so I 'would not experience victimization' and was 'sent to Coventry' in the department. I left the university to end my two-year stint in isolation, which makes me think that if I had stayed I could very well still be in that room.

Tate reminds her readers, 'White power is absolute and acts without qualms to favour those racialized as White, whatever their gender. . . . None of us are exempt, irrespective of institutional status, and this is an important political message and a lesson that we must remember. We must remember it because even if we feel that we are included within White sociality and White networks, exceptionality procedures mean that our inclusion is partial. This is so because Whiteness and anti-Black women racism dictate our very outsideness, our position on the margins of organizational social life' (2017, 56).

I am invested in breaking this recurring meeting point, 'what we are asked to experience' (Tate 2017, 60). The moment, the experience is all too familiar; we have the same conversations—words might change but grammar remains the same. They feel fresh, honest, progressive only for those who newly enter this space, this space where moments recur. They feel fresh, honest and progressive also only for those who keep on forgetting. But some of us cannot forget, we do not forget.

So, the fact of the matter is
We already had these conversations in public and private before
that a decision was problematic,
the author has been long overlooked,
undervalued,
the same kind of students fall through the cracks,
that the institution is failing a student is not an overstatement,
'it is so obvious to me', venya patel, a student, in a conversation on decolonising university*
I cannot tell you how, why, in a way that what I say and know can convince
in part because it seems impossible to have conversations about what is wrong
because it gets all too personal, we have to be protective, we have to be closed, we
were not there, we have moved on (so why revisit, let's do better in the future),
there is no consensus. . . .

So, we insist.
This is why we have to have more specific, specifying conversations. To discuss specific cases, specific people as people beyond the general terms of reviewing processes, in terms of principles, and how seeing the project of global feminist publishing as one of providing language-specific copyediting assistance, special mentoring review process, getting authors to become familiar with and translate their work into North American/ British/Western European style-writing and building of argumentation.
This assumption that they have to conform, that international research is 'our space' (who is this we?) is deeply problematic.

white feminists are not neutral, experienced arbiters
of what global conversations and thinking in the Rest of the World should be, where
feminist IR should be, and is, heading. Using different located 'Global South'
difference-marked feminists to shape directions with White feminists at the helm is racism.
Going global, and seeing this as geographic
has a way of keeping the world's people segregated and separated in neocolonial terms.
When a member brings a decision to attention that despite our reflexive procedures in place that she knows—it is her area of expertise, what she knows in her bones—through her skin, . . . that we want to debate this,
figure out if she is right and we were wrong . . .

---

* https://youtu.be/yRi_QnGhlk8

that this is our response:

racism

Nanoracism, achille mbembe (2019) writes, is the structured racism
imperceptible to human, the reconstruction of the human through plasticity,
necropolitics to lubricate neoliberalism.

And here we must add

                            patriarchy. hegemony. power.

So, when we say it is structural,
We mean structural.
Feeling the full injury of the structure.
That moment the small, passing comment is made.
Request for (over)explanations arrive in our inboxes.
When what you did not mean, meant.

                            our conversation should never have happened
The conversation that her email asked for . . .
        The conversation that her email asked for mediated by Her email that there
is no racism here.
        The 'open' conversation as a result.
        The flurry of side emails and chats we had to process this conversation
that should not be happening.
        A side effect of the conversations that should have never happened is that
some of us—however momentarily—turn into mouthpieces for whiteness.
        'I have been there,' says chaos.
        we all probably regretfully or even-still-unknowingly have been there.
        I know when friends bristle in discomfort, when powerful men start
getting impatient because a woman of colour has spoken out of turn, taking too
long, making long-winded arguments, is just rambling because flustered.
        At the tail end of a long meeting, when the session has already run out of
time, when the coffee is getting cold, when wine is calling our name.

                    Hey you, global south feminist, speak for all global women!
Global south spokesperson, how is it that we have created this role in academia?
        Global South as a case of 'special' care.
        Listening, I notice Global South is a catchall phrase in 'editing a feminist
journal in a non-feminist world' as this takes a hard global turn. It is immigrant,
developing countries, Africa, South Asia, non-Western, non-Anglophone, where
English-is-not-a-first-language.
        Surely, surely, addressing the effects of colonialism on research, teaching,
working means first getting rid of this Rest of the World (RoW) as an approach to
then address epistemic oppression?

How is it that the questions we ask, find ourselves responding to, is one of, 'global south readers will find the paper too sophisticated to understand' . . . so we have space for sophisticated papers written by white critical feminists about other parts of the world/their research area, but not by 'global south' scholar, someone with ties and investment in the region that is intimately a product of outliving colonialism and current racist global structure?

'This is what happens when you treat "global south" as a dumbed down space to start with', says Kali.

The Global South as a way for white feminists (in the Global North, I guess) to avoid change that requires deep reflection on the composition of their own social world, the coherent stories of the self as a (good) feminist. How can you be good when the world is so terrible? Getting rid of the good girl/feminist narrative—

down girl

This is not the right time, this is not the right way, this is not the right time.

'But I am of the opinion, if you have institutional power use it or otherwise it will rot (you)', says chine.

I think a conversation that began with, how can we make this right, rather than—explain to us again what we did wrong, what is wrong, would have led to less depleting, adversarial relation

that builds more meaningfully upon the work that feminists of colour have already done,

told us

warned us about

done the work to make visible (some by leaving this space)

Rest in power by Ugly Feminist Collective

marge had not quite put these women together until Malinda Smith's Twitter thread (2018).

                                        I wonder,
chine thought,
          What it is like to be supervised by a feminist scholar who has had these conversations in multiple locations?
          What kind of thinker, editor, writer, teacher, lover, doer, stroller, talker, listener would I be?

What would the world be like when we are able to listen to people across colour lines, free of anxieties in both ends about being mis-understood, not-understanding, mis-speaking, mis-hearing? Let's think with Jacqui Alexander (2006, 154) here:

> I would listen to endless repetitions about the forward thinking that prompted my hire. I lived all the discomfort of this tight space as I did the foundational labour for GSFT [Gender Studies and Feminist Theory] and the identity work for the School. I came to realize, however, that the same tight space carried the greatest potential for dissent, paradoxically assuming at the same time the greatest risk of being policed. Rumoured as being 'behind the students,' I felt no longer able to appear to be complicit in speechlessness, one of the major requirements of preservation. Nor could I choose complicity in conceding the collective will to struggle. Preservation was a demand to concede that will and renege on the promise I had made to myself about self-possession, not self-absorption, or self-aggrandizement, but self-possession. Taking ownership of myself.

Lingering Lily

Equal parts postcolonialism and feminism
Dash of Daoism
Sprinkle of fairytales
Big pinch hokey pokey

Serve in a teacup, sip often.

Roar—an interlude

My daughter was about two. She was getting very good at walking with that just-about-to-fall forward momentum.

I opened the door to the apartment after a day of working; I saw my friend (and sitter) asleep on the couch. I immediately looked for my daughter, who was three steps away from the light socket, metal butter knife in-hand. She held it out to press into one of the openings.

I wouldn't make it across the room in time. I did the only thing I could—I roared. As long and loud as I could.

It worked—my poor toddler dropped the knife, her whole body shaking with fear. I ran over to her, scooped her up, and apologized for having to scare her so badly. She patted me on the shoulder and said 'Monster Mama' (A book we often read together.)

Fourteen years later . . .

Still my daughter and myself, though now in a ground-floor apartment elsewhere in the Pacific Ocean. She is getting undressed one night, shades pulled down as much as possible. I hear odd noises outside by the bushes close to the window— peeking outside from the darkened living room, I saw a man masturbating as he tried to look into my daughter's room. I'd seen him walk by/loiter by the public walkway before—but not like this.

I grabbed a bat by the door, ran outside, and roared as I came around the corner. He had already jumped on a scooter (parked right by the window) and was frantically gassing the engine. I roared again and swung—just hitting the scooter. I hit the bat on the ground and stared at him as he drove off (he didn't look back).

When I came back inside, I explained to my daughter what happened. I ended it with 'I'd rather be known as the crazy mom and have you be safe. Hopefully he stays away'.

I apologized to my neighbours the next day. One confessed he had hidden behind his couch, saying 'I didn't know what that noise was—it was terrifying'.

Collage by Ugly Feminist Collective

Chapter 11

composting anger: why I/we refuse your 'diversity' and the 'womanofcolour' tag

'Flowers are budding on branches', that's what you say,
'Every cup overflows', that's what you say,
'Wounds are healing themselves', that's what you say,
These bare-faced lies,
this insult to the intelligence,
I refuse to acknowledge, I refuse to accept

For centuries you have all stolen our peace of mind
But your power over us will not work anymore
Why do you pretend you can cure pain?
Even if some claim that you've healed them,
I refuse to acknowledge, I refuse to accept.*

Urdu poet Habib Jalib has set the tone for refusal. In that mode, here is an effort at refusing to acknowledge, refusing to accept the tokenism of 'diversity' and the depoliticised label of 'womanofcolour'. Refusal is a political act, a feminist strategy that aligns with the idea of composting anger. Anger itself is seen as a negative and gendered emotion, especially when embraced by women (male anger is considered even natural and legitimate). I challenge this dominant view of anger, invoking Indian goddess Kali, whose anger is not only mythologically legitimized, but strategically deployed to counter the violence of the mainstream and normative resistance against it.

The first time that bell hooks (Lion's Roar 2017) was going to meet the famous Vietnamese Buddhist teacher and peace activist, Thích Nhất Hạnh, she had had a particularly bad day of racist and sexist insults. So she went to

---

* 'Dastoor' by Habib Jalib, Rekhta (translated by Swati Parashar), https://www.rekhta.org/nazms/dastuur-diip-jis-kaa-mahallaat-hii-men-jale-habib-jalib-nazms?lang=hi.

him and said, 'I am so angry!' And he asked her to hold on to her anger and use it as compost for her garden. She says, 'if we think of anger as compost, we think of it as energy that can be recycled in the direction of our good. It is an empowering force. If we don't think about it that way, it becomes a debilitating and destructive force'. This vignette is my attempt at composting anger in a constructive way, the first opportunity of which was provided at the ISA convention in New Orleans and the 'performative' experience of protesting the Sapphire Series Panels with Benedict Cumberbatch masks.

After a decade of (my) feminist academic life disciplined by IR, it is time to reflect on how and when I acquired the 'feminist of colour', 'woman of colour' tag along the way.

Several of my feminist friends and colleagues have conveniently internalized everyday racialized exchanges that continue to (re)produce the category of the 'other', while claiming a critical and progressive worldview. I started my academic journey on the grounds of evenness and equality that I thought was inherent within the feminist community. I found myself othered again and again to the point at which I believe that this othering must be embraced as a position of strength and negotiation, for the composted anger to feel truly liberating. It is that self-liberating experience that I seek in writing about the moments of intense anger and homelessness that the feminist IR community (re)produces for many outside its comfort zones.

White Feminist (WF): You must be part of our team when we meet the Saudi delegation. We want to show them how diverse we are.

Nuance queen: (note to self: I AM diversity? I am DIVERSITY? Hey, I know brown people/South Asians slave it in Saudi Arabia): It is a bad idea, if we are thinking about future collaboration (on violence against women!). I don't think they have travelled all the way to meet someone like me.

WF: We must show them how our universities take 'diversity' seriously.

Nuance queen: (note to self: exactly how? What about those racist insults, insinuation, exclusions, silences and erasures that I have absorbed through my skin, composting them in the dark corner of my being?). Sure, but I am NOT the kind of diversity they would be interested in. Never mind.

The meeting takes place; I am clearly an inconvenient presence for the visiting delegation. They have not travelled all the way from Saudi Arabia to the very white part of the world, to meet brown people who are like enslaved domestic workers in their part of the world. At the reception in the foyer, I am again the eyesore for the visitors. They are trying so hard to be polite, while I chuckle away enjoying the 'halal' vegetarian spread. I note how they are also brown but maybe a shade lighter? It is a chilly evening and I am wrapped in a shawl. I suddenly spot a colleague who I have been meaning to make contact with for a long time. I leap towards her with some relief of at last finding someone I could talk to. But before I could say something, she exclaims: Salaam Walaikum, how has the visit been so far?

Nuance queen: Walaikum Salaam, the visit has been excellent given I have only travelled from the fourth floor of this building!

She: Oh, I am so sorry. I didn't realise.

Note to self: That's precisely the point. you did not realise you had brown, shawl-covered 'others' working in your building. Fascinating, that 'colour' is so invisible. Wait, colour is so invisible? You mean you cannot see colour? Whiteness makes you colour blind? Or does your colour blindness (re)produce whiteness? The familiar chicken-egg dilemma. Which comes first, your colour blindness or your normative whiteness? What kinds of colours don't you see? Sometimes I think I can be visibilised when you need to show that token of doing diversity and well. It helps most often that I am the brown colleague you can be proud of or show off when it suits you. Brown is visible. But black? You don't see black at all.

This was confirmed by the black student who would wait for his meeting with his thesis advisor (white feminist professor). She had given him an appointment but was talking on the phone, while he was asked to wait outside. He was patiently waiting for an hour before I invited him into my office. I can never forget my conversation with him.

Student: I see my advisors in the corridor and they ask me my name each time, and ask me what I am doing around? They don't even remember I am their supervisee, not just a loitering student.

Nuance queen: They don't recognise you?

Student: I am a black guy, and you know I become invisible for them. It gets worse in the supervision meetings. I am not good enough for their standards. Going to the professor's room for these meetings is worse than being in the war zone in Sudan! He weeps inconsolably.

Note to self: The worst indictment of our profession. Erasures that are deliberate, from otherwise those who uphold ethical, non-racist, feminist, progressive positions as public facade. Erasures because. . . .

Have I made myself hypervisible because I fear erasure? Have I embraced positionalities, because I anticipate being silenced? And my own complicity in the silences and erasures that my privilege endorses and embodies? As I said at the Benedict panel at ISA, I, or others like me, cannot represent the global south voices in entirety. We cannot be seen as speaking for women everywhere, for those voices are more diverse and nuanced. Neither can we be seen as lending authenticity to the voices of global south women; disingenuous . . . disingenuous. We cannot be our own authentic selves too. Mohanty warned us . . . (you can fill in the blanks) and Spivak insisted . . . (you can fill in the blanks).

the (un)bearable 'whiteness' of knowledge production

When American author Katherine Mayo published her book *Mother India* in 1927, little would she have imagined that the book's dark and ominous portrayal of a colonized India would continue to find resonance in the understanding and representation of the postcolonial world in the twenty-first century. After touring India for months in which she was helped enormously by her British friends and hosts, Mayo wrote a scathing account of Indian masculinity, the widespread disease and ignorance, the archaic and regressive religious traditions and culture and above all the desperate conditions of Hindu women who could never find emancipation in the Hindu society. The core of the narrative was not only the justification of British rule over a 'backward' people who needed to be brought into modernity, but also how the colonial modernity was inevitable to 'rescue' women from the constraints of Hindu tradition and patriarchy (Mayo 1927). The religious conflicts in India existed simply because 'neither Hindu nor Muhammadan could think in terms of the whole people' (Mayo 1927, 354). She did acknowledge that her intention was not to imply that the 'unflattering things here affirmed of India are without counterpart in character and tendency, if not in degree, in certain sections of our western life' (Mayo 1927, 409). But according to her, 'India has carried the principles of egocentricity and of a materialism called spirituality to a further and wider conclusion than has the West' (Mayo 1927, 409).

The two aspects that Mayo alluded to, of lack of gender rights and equality and the inevitable nature of religious faultiness among people incapable of looking beyond their immediate interests is reflected in 'empowerment' discourses, determined by Western states with the active collusion of feminists. Indian historian Mrinalini Sinha, in her analysis of Mayo's account of India, highlighted the close association between Mayo with the US business community, notably through the Rockefeller Foundation, in the US government, the British government's Foreign Office, and the government of India. Sinha identified certain individuals such as Cornelia Sorabji, the wife of the governor of Bengal, Lady Jackson and the wife of the Viceroy, Lady Irwin, who facilitated Mayo's rather partisan assessment of the Indian society (Sinha 2006, 179). The pattern is discernible as one sees the scramble to establish the efficacy of Western concepts in bringing gender equality and justice to women in conflict areas in the global south. In that they are aided by state agencies, neo-liberal global institutions and even corporate interests who fund 'feminist' research and practical initiatives to improve the lot of the women, 'out there'.

white masks are colour blind

The Benedict masks made it impossible to see anything other than masculine whiteness. Whiteness is a mask that hides privilege, resources, access in knowledge production.

So much anger to compost. So many white feminists working so 'hard' to bring the rest of the world at par with the civilised whiteness of their lives. Yes, whiteness is civilised and civilising. The rest of us have a lot of catching up to do . . . infantilised, told off every now and then, reminded that whiteness is the only way to save ourselves and rescue others like us.

Kali to the rescue

Compost stinks; accumulated anger has to be eaten by worms to disintegrate . . . and then something good comes out of it. Or you can dance through your anger like Kali and embrace the chaos and messiness of your life.

I am always inspired by the Indian goddess Kali, our very own Monster Mama, who embodies death, destruction and time. In my admiration for her is the desire to 'become' and 'perform' Kali as the one who embodies anger in a legitimate way, while retaining her benign compassion. Definitely a feminist icon, she is dark and not aesthetically pleasing, in the main pantheon of male gods and fair goddesses serving them. She knows what it is to be racialised; she messes up binaries consistently and slays ego, mitigating the difference between the self and other. As Chhinnamasta, Kali cannibalises herself in her anger, but she also has unique ways of composting anger. She must dance to let off the energy, to speak while silent and being silenced, to write herself back into the mainstream where she is invisibilised and erased, to renew her commitment to fighting injustices, and slaying ignorance, to embrace uncertainties, ambiguities and to develop an appetite for all that is unpalatable. Kali's fearsome anger composts itself in various stages to enable a kind of fearlessness that is self-empowering, self-critiquing and . . .

refusal matters

- Because diversity is useful for white feminists to inhabit a moral universe, by pledging allegiance to it in white-only panels, or making sure at least one person of colour is included WITHOUT A VOICE (HOW MANY OF YOU NOTICED THAT IN THE BENEDICT PANEL?). UNEXPECTED: SOMEONE SINGING OR MASKED PEOPLE IN ACADEMIC PANELS

. . . BUT EXPECTED, CERTAINLY A PERSON NOT INTRODUCED OR IGNORED AND SILENCED.

- Because tokenism exists, around people and around the global south as case studies.
- Because like colonial labour on which colonies prospered, intellectual colonialism thrives on the labour of some people and some parts. White feminists are complicit. But we know there is a north in the south and south in the north.
- Because you can still argue in the ISA panel in 2018 that colonialism was good for the women of India and elsewhere.
- BECAUSE THE BROWN MAN IN CHARGE GETS MORE BROWN MEN AND CALLS IT DIVERSITY.
- BECAUSE WHITE WOMEN COLLUDE WITH WHITE MEN AND CALL IT A WAY OF DOING DIVERSITY IN THE NAME OF GENDER.
- Because feminism WAS SUPPOSED TO BE INTERSECTIONAL AND often does nothing beyond lip service to that term (Crenshaw 1989).
- Because anti-colonial resistance is yet to become anti-colonial critique in many contexts.
- Because elite feminists in postcolonial context refuse to hear indigenous minority women and LGBTQ+ people.
- Because privilege is not being interrogated anywhere near enough.
- BECAUSE despite all my privilege and location, PEOPLE somewhat LIKE ME CONTINUE TO DO THE LABOUR FOR OUR WHITE FEMINIST FRIENDS.
- BECAUSE IF I RAISE QUESTIONS, CALL OUT YOUR ETHICS AND epistemological positions I AM REMOVED FROM THE TEXT, erased AND sometimes as a favour REDUCED TO A FOOTNOTE.

I REFUSE THE FEMINIST/woman OF COLOUR TAG BECAUSE IT MAKES YOU LAZY AND IT MAKES ME PERFORM the LABOUR TO EDUCATE YOU. I refuse to be reduced to a colour! Colours don't need feminism, we do. After years of engaging on this issue, I realise that this tag has no political purchase. It simply stays as a piece of clothing on my body because of which there is no engagement with my real self. This label does not hide my nakedness nor yours.

KALI WILL HAVE TO DO THE ANGRY DANCE OF REFUSAL, TO BE HEARD, TO CREATE HER OWN SPACE, TO DISRUPT, TO DECONSTRUCT, TO DESTROY, TO SUBVERT, to unsettle and to make us uncomfortable. Kali will dance into and out of our worlds. She will speak through her angry dance. My Kali will live through my anger, and my anger through Kali, the dark one.

I am composting my anger and the compost grows by day.

Question: How do you relate to your Kali? What is your Kali telling you?

Nothing Personal

I should not expect people to hear me right when I am shouting,
when I am shouty.
I should not expect people to get on board just because I am telling them a
counter-fiction of the fiction they tell themselves.
I should not expect people to embrace discomfort as a mode of operation in
feeling out the field.
I should not take their inertia, and mine, so personally.
It's all just life, just how things are,
nothing personal.

I don't want to work . . . losing the 'self'

Have you ever bawled till you find no tears? Have you ever wept so much that you can swim in your own salty tears? Have you felt that aching emptiness, that life is worth nothing? Been there, done that, now what? A sick, mean, nasty world we inhabit . . . more often than not we are puppets and the strings pass on from one to the other. Have you ever felt that overpowering darkness from which there seems to be no escape, till you normalise it and tell yourself, this is how it could be forever . . . what is forever anyways? Life is not forever; how can anything else be? Someone will read this book, after we are all gone . . . . is that the forever, the posterity we crave? 'We' will not exist; the book will . . . it will have longevity, it will make sense or not, even if 'we' are not around. . . .

I have inhabited this darkness for most of this year. I have now normalised it, because there is no escape. . . . This darkness is inside me, outside me . . . on my body, in my head, in my heart . . . is there a heart that feels? What feels? The nerve ends connected to the mind that send signals? Happiness, sadness are all neurological conditions . . . right? But there is something visceral about our feelings. I have never cried so much in my entire life . . . tears they flow, they dry up, then my eyes well up again and there is another torrent of grief that flows from my eyes . . . all the sadness in my heart is like a lump, melting through these tears. I cannot recognise myself. I cannot find myself, I am lost. Nokia came last week and we worked together, but she sensed my 'self' has eroded. . . . I am sure she saw I am a shadow of myself. I have nowhere to hide, no place to go to, I don't want people near me. . . . I don't want books, students . . . and then the emails keep coming with 'reminders' with urgent nudges to do this and that. When will they 'know' I am lost? When I am gone fully or in parts . . . I am disintegrating but I need to take 'sick leave' to justify that I cannot function, work is not the distraction, work is work and I cannot do it. . . .

Leave me alone. Can you not see I am welling up in every meeting? Have you not noticed my dishevelled unwashed frizzy hair? Have you not seen my eyes are vacant, not kohl lined, my lip colour is missing, I am fidgety, fidgety . . . I feel like I am dying . . . life is ebbing away but I attend your meetings where you invisibilise my grief. I have lost my self, yes but you don't even recognise it. Empty screens, empty chairs, empty hearts. 'O, it's so great to see you after the pandemic' . . . really? what is so great when you are NOT seeing me. You are seeing something, someone? Who? You are looking through me, beyond me to greet the next in line. I am nobody, I don't matter. I am junk that made good due to some 'luck' and some 'favours'.

You see my tears and tell me 'let me know if I can help . . . all will be well'. . . . Help with what? Empty words. All will never be well. I am broken, scarred and will never be united with my lost self again. . . . It will come back in fragments, but my whole is gone, my core is gone. . . . Kali is dancing within me . . . she dances on corpses you know . . . my core is her corpse, her cremation ground . . . she is dancing on the embers inside . . . there is rage, there is grief, there is sorrow and she is making sense of it, in the way only she can. . . . I believe in her, I trust her. She will calm down one day . . . who knows when . . . till then . . . I cannot work, I won't work. . . . I am in search of my lost self. And pity you see me, and not, you hear me and not, you recognise me and know me not. I am a shadow of myself and this 'work' is not the only thing that defines me. . . . I am more than work, deadlines of chapters, manuscripts, reviews, making decisions, unanswered emails. Let me weep, let me weep.

Just finished a conversation with a PhD student from Indonesia. She cried and I cried. I read her this piece I am writing now . . . and she said 'but I thought you are strong, successful and confident'. Yes, an exterior that I preserve but that strength is only an acknowledgment of my accumulated vulnerability, the struggles, I tell her. She said, 'crying' is stigmatised and shameful . . . and I advised her . . . cry as much as you want . . . writing will flow through those tears. She seemed to get it . . . the overwhelming whiteness of the department doesn't. I feel so burdened as the one person of colour in an overwhelming white department. Sometimes, even my best, 'progressive' 'feminist' (white) friends do not notice how they racialise and otherise me, their students and world at large. I am frustrated at meetings and then cry in my lonely hours, thinking of the dark abyss I inhabit.

I do not want to work. I want to be rescued from carrying so many burdens, personal, professional for so long. I am tired and I am crumbling. Will there ever be a time when I can be nurtured? Someone will look at me and not see my strength and confidence and my academic status, and will recognise the fear and anxiety and sadness and grief in my eyes. Will there be love, somewhere? Let my tombstone read . . .

'She lies in fragments here, waiting to be rescued and loved as a whole.'

Chapter 12

planet white boys

Dear colleagues,

There are many strong things I could say about your letter *(but I'm going to 'restrain' myself, but still let you know how cross I am at the same time)* and campaign *(campaign? This places the letter in a fight-y realm?)*, but I really just want to ask you all one simple question that you completely avoid in your petition letter, and that can be *(can be? According to whom, you?)* answered yes or no:

Do you agree that the argument and evidence provided by X&XX in their XX article that XXXXX theory is deeply and irretrievable racist, supports and justifies their call for the closure *(they don't call for its closure)* of a very productive and widely used *(slavery was very 'productive' and 'widely used' . . .)* critical approach to security studies, and the excising of the word *(do they ask for this?)* XXXX from thinking about IR?

(Of course, the answer is—the question is problematically set up!)

If your answer to that is yes, then you and I are living on different planets in regards to what constitutes sound argument, solid evidence, and the grounds on which a particular meaning *(I would say I AM on a different methodological and epistemological planet—regardless of what my answer to that question is—there is absolutely not one form of 'sound argument'. And that the conventional forms are racist and sexist. These are some of feminism's main points . . . in my view . . .)* can be attributed to a text. X&XX's piece is a travesty of good scholarship *(by which/whose standards?)*. They do not even bother to look into what XXXXX theory could do within the context of anti-racism research *(this wasn't the aim of their article)*. If you think they have made a sound and well-supported argument *(this also is not the point or 'worth' of their article—that they pose the questions in a JOURNAL is perhaps the point—this is X&XX's point)*, then I am happy to be counted amongst your opponents *(sigh . . . it's not a war of 'sides')*.

If your answer is no, then we might stand on common ground in holding firm on the necessity to maintain the highest standards *(dear me, some of us really are steeped in the elitist myth of meritocracy)* of scholarship *(has XX not read anything on the racist and sexist basis of 'standards' of scholarship . . . ?)* at all times *(which would be to work as if there is no time, we live from and in nowhere)*. We would then differ on the narrower question of whether some special allowance *(the 'special allowance' is reserved for white masculinized methodology and epistemology)* should be made for scholars who are junior (though X&XX are hardly beginners in this business), female, non-white, or whatever categories of exemption you choose to favour *(eioww . . . white saviour logic much?)*. I don't think any academics, under any circumstances, should be allowed to make flawed arguments based on spurious evidence *(you really seem to think evidence is 'objective' . . .)*, and then call for a whole school of thought to be shut down on that basis *(where has THIS call been made?)*, without that being strongly opposed.

At the risk of stretching my luck *(sigh . . .)*, I am also a bit curious as to the strategic purpose of your campaign. I get that shifting the ground *(this is the ground—we did not 'shift' to it . . .)* to bullying is an effective rallying cry for those feeling *(feelings . . . 'I'm sorry you feel you died . . .' marginalised)* and/or victimized within the field, and pulls the focus away from the hard question of academic standards *(I mean for fuck's sake! Posing bullying as 'soft' and the spurious dead while male 'standards' as the 'right/important' Hard thing!)*. What I don't get is how trying to make enemies of the likes of me and XXX *(we are not . . . back to the fight-y war stuff . . . and it being 'about' them)*, serves the aim of getting the field as a whole to address its structural racism? I think it is fair to say that both of us, and XXX more than me, are clearly within the progressive wing *(is there such a thing . . . ? And . . . really?)* of the discipline *(and what is The Discipline? Is it a 'progressive wing' of in the federation of disciplines? who runs this federation?)*, and have actively in our work supported raising awareness of racism in IR. Are you not attacking your natural allies (and ditto for those promoting the postcolonial petition)? Frankly, this seems crazy *(mad women . . . ? hysterical women . . . ? witchy women?)* to me, since it just weakens the effort to take the discipline in the direction that both you and we *(how do you know what direction we want the discipline to go . . . ? As if The Discipline was our priority . . .)* think it should go.

I hope you will do me the courtesy of answering at least the first question. Since X&XX promise, in the publicity for their forthcoming book, to turn their guns *(can't keep away from the fight-y/war analogies! nope)* onto feminist security studies *(I haven't seen this—but I/we have big problems with FSS anyway! He assumes a lot . . .)* next, you may need to answer it in public anyway before too long. Perhaps I can learn something useful from you in how you handle that *(we can be victims of the same critiques by these 'new voices/entrants'; therefore let us join forces to strengthen our shared white? positions? who is this 'we'?)*. Or perhaps your rallying around to their defence, and our public exposure of their deepfake *(I mean for fuck's sake again! Deepfake = alt-right language?? Some deep misogyny down girl logics happening here)* methodology, will have changed their plans.

I have copied this to XXX and one or two others, and I don't mind if you wish to share it with others.

Yours sincerely,

XXXX

*   **Black cat** awakes from her sunny spot in the corner and streeeeeeeeeeeetches out her back and legs. What is this commotion in the house of IR (Agathangelou & Ling 2004) that woke her up? She slowly walks up the stairs, hasn't been around there for a while, to find out. Seems like some feminists have rearranged the furniture quite a bit since she last has been upstairs. There's a comfy and inviting couch in the corner and a group of feminists are huddled around a dining table, reading a letter. She hears quiet conversation, maybe sobbing, from the bathroom and realises that someone must be hiding from those knives thrown at the bathroom door. But what is that writing on the knives? She keeps jumping up to see better. Homophobic slur. Fatphobic slur. Misogynist slurs. Ageist slurs. One of the knives has hit a beautiful vase on a side table, so she now carefully navigates her way in the hallway trying to avoid the pieces of broken glass. But where did those knives come from? They couldn't come from the kitchen as it's downstairs. She wonders whose drawers are full of sharp knives. She looks around and sees Professor Man standing by a window. He's crying white male tears and yelling out of the window 'see how they are accusing me of this horrible thing, but I'm a good man and I've always done the right thing'. Other Professor Men are gathering around him in protective circle, some Junior Men and Junior Women hover around the circle and outside Trolls are climbing up a ladder to peek in from the window. Hard to tell exactly who threw all those knives, but it's clear that this is the direction where they came from. Black Cat moves closer to the feminist table to hear snippets of the conversation. 'How to remove those knives? . . . building shields . . . reducing the harm already caused . . .' It was like knives were coming out of the walls towards me in that hallowed ground of IR's 'genesis' . . . such misogynist violence*

a snowy interlude

Banu Subramaniam (2001, 36–41) tells a story about 'Snow Brown and the Seven Detergents' in which Snow Brown travels across the seas to the 'Land of the Blue Devils' to become a scientist. On arrival, she locates the 'Department of the Pursuit of Scientific Truth', and in the 'Room of Judgement' she is instructed by the 'Patriarch' to ask, 'Mirror, mirror on the wall, who is the fairest scientist of them all'? 'You are, O Supreme White Patriarch'! said the mirror. The Patriarch laughed . . . 'You should all aspire to . . . find Scientific Truth'.

But in her pursuit of Scientific Truth, Snow Brown kept asking the 'wrong questions' and pursuing the 'wrong paths'. Yet her obedient desire to become a scientist impelled her to avail herself of the 'Seven Detergents'. which eventually 'washed' her away and she became Snow White. And still she failed. How could she have been anything but last when judged by a mirror that wanted to produce clones of the 'Supreme White Patriarch'?

praise be to Lorde

Wallop of womanism
Bucket of anti-racism
A poem
Stir with an unmasterly tool (your middle finger, for example)
Serve in this mug:

Tears in a cup by ss

grown men yelling

I hesitate writing this in a Microsoft Word document.

Have you seen a grown man yell, yell, and yell at you, and then pretend that everything is ok? He then makes you think you are misremembering, mis-accounting what happened, creating drama when it really was not that bad, because I did not yell back, I tried to defuse the tension,

Or sometimes I yelled back, but we still hugged it out,

Or I yelled back and we fought, and I showed my ugly side mirroring Him,

Or I cried, sometimes from fear, sometimes from anger, sometimes from the sense that fuck, this situation is surreal,

So, he thinks the yelling was ok, that what your yelling revealed for me about you is just fiction, a momentary mistake, not who you really are.

But even after the hug, the handshake, the niceties, you are still haunted by the grown man yelling and then denying this is who He is, denying He is actually quite irrational so often, that forcing their views onto others by strategic removal of key details by the 'authorising voice of the authorising voice' is, feigning cluelessness and lack of foresight a way of masking how so well He knows what He wants and will use force to get it,

And yet he wants to be innocent. He believes he is innocent. Where does this delusional behaviour come from?

Why are grown men yelling?

the weight of a man's shoe

Mary Ellmann's riotous book *Thinking about Women* (1968) begins with an interview. Ellmann is being interviewed by a man who asks why she is writing about women. Ellmann's reply?

> I didn't want to overreach. Right from the start I thought, ME, you must limit yourself to *half* the human race. Man: Then you were not prompted by feminism? ME: Please. Man: Oh. Feminism is out isn't it? ME: Well, yes, in the way principles all go out before they're practiced. Man: Then, you do not have a female program of your own? ME: You phrase things peculiarly. Man: I scarcely know what word will not offend you. I will try again. You don't have a program for women? ME: No. No program. Man: Ah! But perhaps you will define the attitude of the woman toward the gun, the ship and the helicopter? ME: Impossible. Man: It's been done. A man has done it for men. ME: Indeed.

This conversation sounds very contemporarily familiar (even if the wording might change somewhat today). In a wonderful section on 'differences in tone', Ellmann places her discussion in the context of intellectual matters and specifically 'the symposium'—a conference of sorts. She suggests there are 'distinctions' between men and women in the realm of 'intellectual tone' (Ellmann is working with 'social constructionism' in her work if not using the term; she is also very much writing 'comedy' [on 'gender and tone' see debuk 2015]). The first distinction is that the male body lends credence to assertions, while the female takes it away: perhaps a statement that may not be overly palatable for a twenty-first-century audience. But here's the key phrase: 'the subliminal assumption is that from *weight must come weight*: men's shoes alone seem a promise of truth' [a glorious phrase!]. The effect is heightened by the vogue of the symposium, at least it is (persistently it seems) arithmetically intensified. 'An emblem of confidence: four men and a moderator on stage, sitting behind a long table, each with his own glass and pitcher of water. (Men also drink more water on stage than women do, and the effect of these pauses, unless the water spills, is again sober and deliberate.) Even to an audience of faint impressionability [like we might think at an ISA, EISA or BISA conference] it seems inconceivable that wisdom should not issue from such an assemblage' (Ellmann 1968, 148–49).

Ellmann's 1960s observations reverberate well into the twenty-first century. Do we have the authority or the entitlement to refuse these kinds of inheritances? Yes. But resistance to curtailing sexism, misogyny, ageism and racism is very strong and materializes in many different forms. Few would simply say no to the call to curtail these violences. But many choose not to notice and not to think. To choose to be unthinking. And to be offended. I don't get this. Well, I do. 'Whose histories are most in the weighing'?

#afeministsaiditfirst and epistemologies of ignorance, wilful omissions, mansplaining IR, feminist killjoys

take one

Picture the scene. You're at the ISA in the audience on a panel for a new "turn" (insert turn: the body; the everyday; emotions; aesthetics; narrative; the intersectional; the relational . . . #yesallIRturns). There are four panellists, three men and one woman. The chair is a woman (of course, an easy tick for the representation box), the discussant is a prominent IR male scholar (doesn't really matter who, you know the guy, the one who is seen as 'the' expert no matter the topic). The room slowly fills with 'men in ties discussing penis size. . . .' No, no! That's a joke, of course, but there are quite a few wearing ties (Cohn 1987). Most you don't recognise. That's curious because this 'new' turn isn't so new; some feminists have been working with these ideas for some time now. Maybe, hopefully, finally non-feminist IR academics have started reading and taking seriously feminist scholarship. The room is full, a good sign, right? Wonder what feminists will be mentioned as the foremothers . . . (please, can we not do this . . . ? Who decides who can be described as a mother? Not me despite my best efforts . . .).

You turn to your colleague and ask her if she knows anyone on the panel. 'I know the two women, and the "important" IR guy, but not the others. Weird given we've both been doing (insert turn) for some time now. You'd think we would recognise more people. Hmmmm . . .'

One of the panellists pours water for everyone; she spills a bit. You think to yourself that maybe you should start paying closer attention to who pours water and for whom at conferences, who tidies the table at the end of sessions? You're reminded of another conference when a female colleague was asked by a male panellist to clean up the table just prior to the start of a session. She was black. He thought she was hotel staff . . . #conferencingwhileblack.

The chair starts to make motions to begin the panel. You bring out your paper and pen, ready to quickly scribble down what are hopefully some 'nuggets' of insight into #yesallIRturns. You are hoping that you will have inspiration strike for the article which you have an R&R for. You're a bit stuck on how to develop a key aspect of (insert turn) and are a bit worried you might be barking up the wrong tree or overstating the significance.

The chair introduces the panellists and reminds them to keep to their allotted twelve minutes, they will speak in order of the table (which means the three guys first and the woman last!!), and the discussant will have ten minutes to open up the discussion. The first guy presents a Marxist analysis of (insert turn). It's interesting. He stresses the need for social transformation and restructuring of the world we live in and bemoans the marginalisation of class and political economy matters in recent conversations on (insert turn). The second presentation starts on a promising note. He briefly mentions Enloe's work on (insert turn). 'But', he says, 'whilst feminist research on (insert turn) began some important conversations about (insert turn), we can't just reduce it to "women" because it's not only or all about women. We need to move beyond identity politics.'

You pass a note to your colleague, 'what a dick. . . .'

Your colleague smiles knowingly. After all, you have a running bet on how often you will hear such phrases at ISA, BISA, EISA, PSA (#yesallconferenceswankfest #allmalepanels). She passes a note back, 'rich—from the guy who only writes about men, even if it's not framed like that. So tired of this 'only' about women bullshit. As though research that is 'just' about women has nothing to tell us about the stuff that matters in IR. So what if it is only about women?' You also think about how Enloe has become 'the' feminist to cite. Cynthia is amazing and everyone should read *Bananas, Beaches & Bases* (and more!) but there is so much other feminist scholarship out there. Probably they haven't even read it. And why are you even surprised?! Isn't this business as usual, Ginger Rogers and Fred Astaire disciplinary stuff? You're itching to say something but also know how you'll be heard if you say, 'okay, but feminists have been saying this for some time now and not just Enloe. Do some work.' Maybe not quite like that, you'll say it more nicely, obliquely. But you clamp your mouth shut instead. Let out an inside scream. Berate yourself for getting exercised about it. Let it go. Inhale. Exhale.

Finally, he stops talking. The chair looks at her mobile phone anxiously. Two speakers have already taken more than a half hour. She invites the third speaker to present and reminds him of his allotted time. You shift in your seat. He starts with a story about how he was in the shower when the importance of (insert turn) finally hit him. He was thinking about the persistence of violence and how despite so much work on its utter dehumanisation, blah, blah, blah. 'Research says, you know, the best ideas happen in the shower.' He drones on. The chair passes him a warning note. Then another. He insists he's almost done. Another two minutes.

The chair looks at her phone in alarm and finally intervenes. 'We are pushed for time.' She turns to the fourth presenter, 'can you make sure that you stick to just twelve minutes and no longer?'

The fourth presenter starts her talk. She begins with an apology and explains that she intended to present some of her latest research using (insert turn) but after listening to her co-panellists present, she feels it necessary for the sake of a more critical conversation to put (insert turn) into its feminist heritage.

Your colleague looks at you and mouths—'again'. She nods and starts scribbling a note.

Having traced three decades of feminist work in (insert turn), the fourth speaker highlights the need to reconsider perspectives offered in this panel from a feminist perspective.

You unfold the note from your colleague.

Of course—the feminist has to do the triple shift. Their own research, reminding colleagues of the feminist shoulders they are already standing on but wilfully omitting, and constantly reconceptualising research that completely fails to consider feminism even when discussing [insert turn] and makes ridiculous and absurd claims to being 'new', 'innovative', 'cutting edge' . . . and let's not even talk about the emotional labour of being on this kind of panel. . . .

Do others see it? Sense it?

You feel like a hamster on a wheel.

The discussant is up next, and he always publicly vocalises his support for feminism. The discussant says that he is sympathetic to the feminist perspective articulated by the fourth panellist, and he's always thought that it was important to include women in analysis of (insert turn). His praise, however, is lavished on the first panellist for being so radical in offering a transformative vision for how to move the (insert turn) agenda forward. He also has a list of suggestions inspired by some of his recent musings on (insert turn). These thoughts, he reminds us, have been an integral part of his oeuvre. He wonders aloud if the final panellist has read his earlier work on x. It would be really helpful, he kindly suggests, in developing a particular aspect of (insert turn) and deepen the analysis of tracing the genealogy of the (insert turn). His PhD students are taking up many of the threads from this work he began long ago.

The clock is ticking and the chair cuts in that there are only fifteen minutes left and can he leave it at that. He insists on making one final point, taking up another five minutes. Finally, the chair invites the panellists to respond to his comments and feedback. Surprise, surprise, by the time it gets to the final panellist she has thirty seconds to say something. She mutters a few words. The chair opens up to questions from the audience. With only a few minutes left, there is little point but of course there is always that someone who needs to say something and have that final word. A guy in the front row puts up his hand. The chair asks him to be brief. His question, that isn't a question, more of a reflection on the presentations and how they relate to his research, takes up the final minutes of the session. The female panellist looks pissed off. Who can blame her? She barely gets a nod from her colleagues despite the fact she's been awarded a major research grant to build on over a decade of research that she has pursued on (insert turn) and not until a man said it was it taken seriously.

You look down at your notes and scribble one final thing: #afeministsaiditfirst.

take two

It happened again. Another seminar, another (white) man, claiming to have un/dis/covered another missing link in global politics (coloniality persisting in claims to the 'new'). This time it was the everyday, him saying something to the effect that the link between the everyday and the international is virtually absent from scholarship in the discipline.

The smile in response to my challenge making clear this won't change a thing. He'll still go on and say it and be lauded for birthing this new turn. Men stealing from women.

The whine in my voice grates on my nerves. Why waste my breath? Saying something won't change anything, only leave behind the bitter aftertaste of frustrated rage in my mouth.

And do we really want them to read our work anyway? Won't they simply take credit for it anyway? Scrubbing feminists and feminisms from their memories, bibliographies, acknowledgments? Pull a Foucault? Can we trust them to treat the work with the care and consideration it deserves? To take it seriously as a starting place rather than a footnote, a quick reference before moving on to the snowy masculine precincts of knowledge? Probably not.

I could say something. Call him out. His response, likely, politely ignorant. 'Sorry, I didn't know'. The injury minimised to an 'I didn't know'. Minimised to an 'I'. A minor injury. Small. Insignificant. Unintentional. It happened this one time. But to call him out always comes with the risk of being that angry feminist.

But it's never only an 'I'. It's not just this once. A scene repeated. On repeat. The hurt and anger accumulated. The lie of 'I didn't know' covering up the accumulation of injury, the perpetuation of marginalisations, exclusions, wilful omissions, wilful ignorance.

'It was not news. Emma Goldman said it, Ma Rainey and Bessie Smith and Lucille Bogan said it even better, but when the white boy said it, the world listened, and it became philosophy, not entertainment' (Hartman 2019, 293).

Good girls, little girls, bad girls: take 1^{10} 1^{10} (Weber 1994)

Reader, add your take.

nourishing negations—the pause after the
exhale (refusal) and before the inhale

Misogyny isn't a very comfortable word and not usually used much contemporarily. But there is something about the idea of challenging work (thinking, ideas, beliefs) which nurtures misogyny and its close relations (racism, ageism, sexism), and perhaps more, *refusing its inheritance*, the trials of which we so consistently witness personally, intellectually, emotionally and politically.

Refusing damaging historical, philosophical and disciplinary inheritances is something that was at the heart of the disquiet at an event planned for the EISA conference in Sicily in September 2015. What was planned was the naming of some of the panel rooms (attaching new name plates to the doors) after scholars deemed fundamentally important to the founding of the discipline: eighteen names in total. All white, all men, all dead. The absence of women in such a list proffers symbolic injury of course; as delegates trooped in and out of panel rooms, constantly being reminded, if subtly, like a 'casual reminder' (el-Malik 2015) that the 'world of international studies' still belongs to (white) men, even the dead ones. And it's not as if the spectre of 'all white/male lineups' hadn't been of serious concern in the year previous to the EISA conference in two of the other professional organisations associated with academic theorising of the international. This was detailed in a letter prepared to send to the EISA organising committee by a group of students and scholars to protest the planned 'naming event':

The February 2015 International Studies Association annual convention was subject to much criticism for the almost complete absence of non-white scholars, and the scarcity of female scholars in its Sapphire Series, which was meant to showcase contemporary International Relations.

The April 2015 Political Studies Association annual conference starred an all-male keynote speaker lineup. When this was brought to their attention, the Association decided to ensure their 2016 conference would have an all-female keynote speaker lineup.

It seems it is still far too easy to readily remember the already and always remembered, revered and honoured, as Saara Särmä's 'All-Male Panels' tumblr strikingly and creatively illustrates. And the issue is not only that there *are* women who *have* visibly mattered in the pursuance of theorizing the 'international', remembering that there are 'others' who labour in the arena of the international who are not male or white, perhaps helps us to know better (and maybe for longer) that there are *other* 'worlds of politics' than the one(s) disciplinary boundaries capture and insist are natural. Worlds where 'different' people matter and not just those who insist, by any means, on retaining the centre and locus of importance: omnipresent white men.

The letter was sent to EISA's organising committee before the conference took place. It asked for an explanation and for some form of reparation. Additionally, action to draw attention to the 'all male lineup' at the conference was planned. I did wonder what response we might receive. I imagined that the organisers would be puzzled by the levels of frustration and anger, possibly irritated and a touch defensive too. These kinds of reactions are not unusual when sexism and even misogyny are explicitly pointed out; think of the fiasco around the new UK passport design announced in late 2015. The redesign focuses on UK figures and landmarks from the past 500 years and features seven men and two women. In his defence (or really 'assertion of innocence') of the design, Mark Thomson, director general of the Passport Office, said, 'it wasn't something where we said, "let's set out to only have two women"' (that's ok then . . .). When asked about the omission of female icons such as Jane Austen and the Bronte sisters, he said, 'Whenever we do these things there is always someone who wants their favourite rock band or icon in the book' (BBC 2015). The issue was also discussed on the BBC's 'Any Questions' radio programme; one of the male panellists expressed his exasperation, retorting that history could not 'simply be re-written'.

The thing is—it really is not that hard, not difficult *at all* to demonstrate what is wrong with these views. Of *course,* it matters in terms of symbolism, equality and justice—at a *minimum*—that women should be properly represented and included. Of *course*, there ARE women who could be named and included, even on the traditional (and thus male defined) standards of conventional institutions like academic professional associations and governmental departments. And of *course*, naming has enormous power, not least those names that clearly propel into the future unwanted legacies of the past, nurturing them through the apparent innocence of a name, or indeed a 'title'. This is my 'business card':

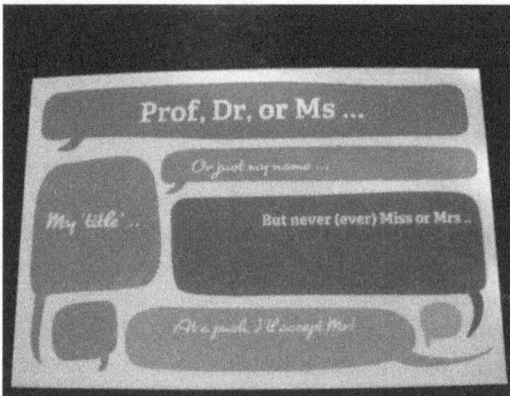

Business card by mz

Well ok, it's not really my business card; I was just getting increasingly frustrated by the constant question asked of me (and countless other women I know) in stores, online (where the first available title in the drop-down menu is most often 'Mr'), or on the phone: 'is that Miss or Mrs?' Really? In the twenty-first century?

But it's not as if decisions are not regularly made to change names, as Regina Reni demonstrated in her blog piece 'Should we rename institutions that honor dead racists?' referring to calls to rename the Woodrow Wilson School of Public and International Affairs, a Princeton institution in the United States. Given Wilson's racist credentials, Rini asks whether it is simply reasonable to wish not to study in a place that honours a man who would have you keep to your own, segregated end of the lecture hall. For students of colour, living in a society that preaches equality and practises something else suggests we should think very seriously about 'whose histories are most in the weighing'. Will we choose to continue and nurture the embarrassment of very sticky chains of racist, sexist and misogynist reference? Or will we disrupt them?

let me count the ways I hate IR
(and academia)

Listen, I was at this conference one time as a grad student and I cannot believe what happened. I presented a paper on privileges, power, and hierarchies in everyday academic contexts. My discussant was Professor Man from an Elite Institution, and he started his comments by saying how he has never been on a panel with a feminist before.

He told me that privilege can be a useful concept, but there's no need to focus only on the privileged since they are not going to give up their privileges willingly. So the more important focus would be on the underprivileged, how us feminists defend our underprivilege by sticking to our own panels and holding on to what power we have that way. FTGS is a refuge and there's strength in that. To illustrate all the power we feminists have, he said that it's like at his home where his wife and he have traditional gender roles and the kitchen is his wife's domain so when she's having a good day she might let him in there but on other days she might tell him to get out because 'this is my office'.

Oh, how I hate IR.

Another panellist, Professor Man, was *literally* applauding himself for having been to a feminist panel earlier that day and being the only man in the audience.

Later on the same evening, Very Senior Feminist Professor told me how she had approached this discussant after the panel, laying out some pretty basic stuff about feminism and feminist IR: 'there's plenty of feminist work, maybe you should read some before making judgments about a whole field . . . also plenty of men are doing feminist work these days'. Professor Man: 'they must all be gay'. True story, this really happened. In 2012.

Oh, how I hate IR. But love the feminist support.

Listen, I went to a conference on insecurity and only a few presentations actually concerned real live people. My presentation was one of those few. An older man with a long career in multinational military organization responded with a passionate speech: 'Let me tell you about reality . . . war is a permanent element of humanity and that's all we have to remember when talking about insecurity'. In the discussion that follows, other panellists took this 'fact of life' as given.

The impossibility of trying to raise issues that matter to me feels crushing in those situations where I'm immediately seen as naïve for trying to come to the issue of insecurity from another angle than the state-centric frame allows for. I keep returning to Carol Cohn's work, which allows me to explain and understand how some questions and issues are non-speakable in those situations, how the whole state-centric security discourse preempts questions that fall outside of its scope (e.g., Cohn 1987, 1993).

Oh, how I hate IR. But love feminist IR for the tools it gives me.

Listen to this one: Professor Man giving 'well-meaning advice' to a grad student about to finish her feminist PhD dissertation: 'Maybe you should look for jobs in the ministry or NGOs, it's so hard to find jobs in academia even for the *talented ones*'. Fortunately, she got a great job abroad and multiple awards for her first book. But I guess he could not see her as talented.

Oh, how I hate IR and Professor Men.

Another piece of 'well-meaning advice' from the all-male professoriate, repeated over and over again: 'gender is such a narrow approach, if you want to *make it* in academia and IR, you must do more than "just gender"'. Feminism means that you're partial, not objective, and can never appear to know about a broad range of topics; even if you've done research on multiple different topics, you remain limited, while the dude who has done his constructivist/critical realist/whatnot work on a similar number of topics, oh he's such an expert with wide range. Professor Man appeared on TV as an expert on a particular topic he was planning on maybe writing a paper on . . . someone else has written multiple articles on the topic, yet they don't think of her as an expert.

Oh, how I hate IR.

I was organizing a conference and really wanted to have some others than the usual suspects as the keynotes, but the organization was not willing to spend money on this. So, who do you think can tap into resources and to have travel money for it? Indeed, it was those usual suspects in already powerful positions and plenty of visibility in the field. Same old, same old.

Oh, how I hate IR.

Disciplining interdisciplinarity. Professor Man makes a statement that 'accidental interdisciplinarity' might be fun but not really useful, as it's not a real contribution to answering questions and addressing problems. For him disciplines exist for answering certain sets of questions and interdisciplinarity brings several disciplines together in a neat structure with a clear direction in order to accumulate knowledge about complex and difficult problems.

Oh, how I hate IR.

Visiting a well-known 'critical IR' institution abroad during my PhD studies. Over and over again at the seminars grad students asking each other 'How is this an IR question'? 'How is this IR'? Oh, that's where the gatekeeping begins, I thought. And never had to courage to present anything.

Oh, how I hate IR (and myself).

Picture this: two Grad Students—a man and a woman—at a seminar, at the coffee break of a conference, having post-seminar beers at a pub, at any sort of informal setting related to academic work. A Senior Scholar or Professor Man approaches, asks him about his work, listens carefully, maybe even offers a future funding possibility. It's like she's not even there, or like her work does not exist. Time and time again. Once Professor Man thanks her for organizing the seminar so well. 'Yes, my dissertation is proceeding nicely', she replies. Professor Man looks baffled.

Oh, how I hate IR.

Overheard in an elevator at a conference, a conversation between Senior (Professor) Men in Suits: 'I don't even know all these names on the program working on this Area'. 'Yes, so strange that this field studying the Area has grown so fast, they must not be doing very good work because we haven't heard of them'.

Oh, how I hate IR.

Living a feminist life (Ahmed 2017) is not always an active choice one makes; to me it has felt rather inevitable. There is no other way of living I could think for myself. How could I not care about inequality? How could my work not address these things I care about?

Sometimes I have wished that I could've chosen differently, that it would've been easier to live a different kind of academic life in IR. Maybe research something else, using some other approach that is not seen as overly political and thus problematic. But do we choose our topics and approaches, or do they come to us through something else than a rational choice? Rational choice would be to engage in something that was not actively disciplined out of the local IR, or marginalized.

Sara Ahmed writes about the walls that feminists come up against over and over again. Those walls are kept up, in my experience, by what Berit Ås (2004, originally published in 1978) named master suppression techniques, also known as domination techniques. These techniques can be hard to pinpoint as they are not outright hostile most of the time. Subtle silencing *makes one invisible*.

'There should be someone studying nuclear proliferation here', said Professor Man in the break room, casually, sipping his coffee. Somehow my work didn't count or register. Because the approach is all wrong. What's gender and feminism got to do with nukes anyways?

Ridicule. Another familiar domination technique. They might not ridicule your work, to your face, but others' work similar enough that you know your work does not stand a chance to register as important in their radars.

Withholding information. Men's sauna evenings, you might not even expect to be invited, but you see other more senior women to be excluded as well. Informal networking is where lot of the strategizing for various hiring processes or funding opportunities happens. Funny that it has to happen when everyone is naked.

Double binds. No matter what you do and how you act, you're doing it wrong.

Put to shame. Imply that you're to blame for your unequal position. If only you weren't too loud, demanding and difficult, you would've made it much further in your academic career, if only you behaved and were seen as one of the 'good guys'.

He's such a great guy as an argument for making things happen for someone. How is that a valid argument?

Oh, how I hate IR.

Mentoring sessions at big conferences for junior women do nothing but reproduce the US-centric masculinist game and it appears there's little room for understanding of differing circumstances and locations. 'You'll get a job, if you've published ten articles when you finish your PhD'. Career advice offered by Senior Woman Professor.

Oh, how I hate IR.

There was a point when I appeared in the media frequently. 'You've been getting a lot of visibility lately' remarked someone in the hallways. This was not a compliment.

Gatekeeping on how to be the right kind of expert, who gets to be an expert . . . not minding that, commenting on the 'trivial' and silly that other 'serious' (gender studies/feminist) scholars won't do.

Doing innovative work and being dismissed and then becoming 'famous' and the same people saying how great the earlier work was.

Oh, how I hate IR.

Collage by Ugly Feminist Collective

Chapter 13

on exhaustion and enchantment

dear Zzzzzzz,

the students in my class cancelled class today so all of the sudden I have two more daylight hours. instead of then dutifully turning to pressing things (finish next week's lecture, finish marking or even turn to my own writing), I used the first thirty to forty minutes to eat lunch and send a nice email to them about alternative timeslots they asked about, and of all the documents opened on my computer I can work on, I turned to our letter (the wrong choice, yay!). it is interesting how much I've changed this year. I would have been annoyed in the past or paranoid that this is an instance of students disrespecting me, but now I am just accepting, 'ah yes, they lost the plot today. I am glad they feel comfortable enough to make demands from their teacher so they don't have to always force themselves to fit into the schedule and ways we ask them to learn, be schooled.' I am almost proud I have helped them achieve this kind of freedom. I worry about how so many students and those around me are dealing with anxiety, or rather, how they are managing the crumbling and unkind hyper-individualised reality by becoming anxious. I do not want to contribute to that cycle, though I do not then have answers on how to get things done. hopefully with some rest and cobbling our minds together when institutionally imposed 'deadlines' for finishing up their learning come, together we will manage and we will find our way together. we would have learned somethings together. 'in-common'. I was preparing to ask them what they thought about achille mbembe's refusal of abstract universalism and building a conception of democracy using glissant's language of in-common. I was also planting a joke about how serious mbembe's global thinking is, so abstract in its very way of rejecting abstract universalism. he won't know how to talk about petty, grubby interpersonal stuff most average people have to deal with and survive with their humanity intact in the age of necropolitics.

109

or maybe he does though if he was interested in that kind of thinking, he would have become a novelist. too bad that is my brain goes even when I read theory, no escape.

if my cat, cat-x, is a messenger, she's mostly telling me, 'don't hug me too tight' and 'treat time, every time, meeeow'. I spend a lot of time looking at cat-x so she is also an idea of, just be. she is the idea where my eye rests, and when I run out of things to say to my human housemate, I ask, 'where is cat-x?' so in a way, she is also where my questions go to rest, so it is also where the mind goes to rest? maybe rather than a messenger that brings me something, cat-x takes away my muddled ideas and headache-inducing questions. I like that idea. does cat-z take stuff away or fill? what is soothing for you, when do you know you are at peace on a given day? I am definitely at peace in the morning, and when I start my morning empty I can almost touch this thing—this no-thing. I started my day today with a 7:00 a.m. meeting, I had brain fog till around 11:00 a.m. or so, till I had to shake myself up awake to prep for class which then got cancelled.

being cancelled was as energizing as having a class, such an odd thing—this thing called doing, happening, being. it is almost as if something not-happening means that actually more than one thing happens at minimum: the event that didn't happen (but played in your head as happening), and then what happened as a result of that not happening (me writing this letter) and I guess there is a third in this case, the class happening at a rescheduled time. and this is just on my end alone. no wonder work life is so productive/exhausting/endless/self-reproducing!

the book that was my inspiration for the letter exchange we got going arrrrrrived, and I took a picture for you. it is a letter exchange between two artists in korea—lee lang (indie singer and writer of many genres) and sleeq (hiphop artist) masquerading as a coauthored book, *letters with many parentheticals*. I will translate a few lines from the book in coming weeks. I think the book cover image is of their respective cats who make appearances in the book.

I had not paid all that much attention to the bunny in kaga's paintings, other than as a fluffy white thing in the middle of the picture. I like what you say about it a lot, hehe. poor bunny.

from chine

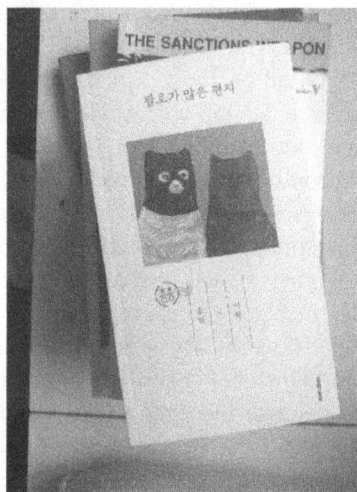

pile of books by sc

Dear chine,

I love the book cover! Looking forward to reading some translations. Reminds me of Pussy Riot. Pussy riot pussy cats? There's an excellent Turkish restaurant that I can see from my kitchen and living room windows, but before in the same spot there was a strip bar called Pussy Cat. That's apparently where my mind goes on this Friday morning. Strip bars used to be everywhere, especially after (and during) the recession in the 1990s; now there's hardly any left. I guess the internet changed that. Elina Penttinen wrote her dissertation about strip bars and much more of course.

I made some notes earlier this week. We have this morning routine, me and cat-z. I ignore him for a while when he starts to walk around and meow, then I get up and feed him and go to the bathroom and brush my teeth. I might sit on the couch for a bit watching the morning show on TV. Once I start making my coffee, I open the door to the balcony, and he goes outside. Even when it's freeeeeezing, he sits there for a few minutes. After he comes back inside, he usually goes to hide and sleep somewhere. I sit there on the couch, TV on, next to the brightlight treatment lamp, drinking my coffee and eating breakfast.

Someone said that the brightlight treatment lamp is so harsh, violent even, that they would not ever use it, but rather just slow down with the darkness. But I don't find it violent or harsh. Yes, it's very bright, and takes a moment to get used to. But without the lamp I would not ever be fully awake. I would just nap all day, like my cat. But then I would not sleep well at night.

From my notes earlier this week: 'Cat-z teaches me that routines and napping are very important. However, I can only learn one of these things, for now I'm leaning towards routines. Too much napping messes my routines up. Cat-z's routines are like clockwork, especially when it comes to being fed. But the changing light conditions, especially in the spring, do affect him too. At some point in April he starts waking me up earlier and earlier, or trying to at least. I'm pretty good at ignoring him before 8:00 a.m. even when he meows loudly right into my ear'.

I don't even care about being a productive (good neoliberal) subject. By the way, I love what you do with your students, or try to do, I think that's the only way to go, not to add to their anxieties but try to work with them in a different way. I'm so disappointed in what the university has become. There's no room for exploration and wondering and wandering about, but everything has to be so damn productive.

Being fully awake with the help of the brightlight treatment lamp is not about productivity for me; it's about surviving the dark season. There's something enjoyable, too, about the darkness, if I'm able to take things slow. I did that the year I had defended my dissertation in September, and it was quite good. Last year I was just so exhausted that around the equinox I was seriously offended by the darkening evenings and really took it personally. I remember yelling at the darkening sky one evening. For real. Fortunately, that feels like a long time ago and now I'm just like 'it is what it is'.

About ten (twelve even?) years ago I had posted on Facebook that I need to learn not to take myself so seriously. About five some years later, I had reposted the memory and made a statement that at least I have learned this lesson. Now I realized that I think I need to re-learn it again. This summer I had to take a break from vacationing to write an abstract for a conference, and I had some trouble with it, and I was wondering what the hell is going on, usually I'm pretty quick with abstracts. Took a few days, and I realized I was trying to do something far too serious, I suddenly was trying to be a serious political scientist doing serious research. What the actual what?!?

Yes, I got over myself. But there's this danger lurking, apparently. Some imaginary figure of a Real Researcher that haunts me. And it is not a useful figure, because it stops me from writing. I don't know how to shake that figure off, how to unlearn the seriousness and learn/re-learn playfulness.

Maybe the desire to be serious, to be taken seriously (Enloe writes in the *Big Push* [2017] how much easier it is afforded to some than others—nothing new there), is related to the *seductions of usefulness* that you mentioned before? Maybe I'm afraid that if I'm not serious enough, what I do won't be useful?

Last night I came across a drawing by artist Tuija Teiska on Instagram; the caption in the drawing says 'Where do all the lost cats go'? and the caption below the photo 'I ask myself every day'.* This reminded me of what you said about *falling through the cracks*. Maybe the black cat appears as such an appealing and descriptive figure for us, because we keep falling through the cracks in IR/academia. But then what happens?

We fall through the cracks because we're too much. Too feminist, 'why don't you just do gender and . . . '? Too weird, 'what is this vomit thing'? Too sensitive. Too serious (as in not ready to laugh at a sexist joke). Too this and too that, raising the wrong questions, killing the joy.

But where do the fallen/lost cats go? 'They just weren't cut out for this, you know'.

A cat always lands on its feet. But do we? Cats can be hurt too when falling from too high up. They really don't *always* land on their feet. . . .

I don't even know what I'm trying to say. Yesterday, I was riding the brand-new tram and listening on Zoom to Shirin Rai talk about the new *Oxford Handbook of Politics and Performance* (at Roland Bleiker's Visual Politics events series).† Something she said about doing interdisciplinary

---

* https://www.instagram.com/p/CULH7kRNyc3/.
† https://www.youtube.com/watch?v=ATwF4ocd7-g.

work caught my attention. It was something about using IR as a point of reference because it is so familiar, you're so much more certain of getting things right when it's the familiar literature you're working with; when working with other fields, you're so much more on thin ice. Or it feels like it. Ok, I might be paraphrasing her unfairly, or not, but this is what my brain picked up. It resonated because I do think that's why even when we (the collective 'critical' IR we) are trying to move beyond IR, we're always stuck with it.

But then I think about Astrid Joutseno's defence and what she said about being enchanted to think with, finding allies, finding kin in authors and theories . . . how different is that in contrast with the idea of sticking to the familiar so you won't make a mistake and be found out making a mistake and criticised for it.

I want to be enchanted and not afraid.

Zzzzzzz

dear Zzzzzzz,

i thought the cover felt familiar, maybe it is referencing the Pussy Riot! I will read more of the book and report back. I have had zero time to stop and think, stop and read, and definitely no time to stop enough to write beyond what I absolutely had to, which is a recipe for feeling overwhelmed these days for me. as you said about the long dark winter months, I take it personally, it feels personally offensive to be so busy, so structured by absolutes. how dare the world!

so I am sharing my scribbles, which I don't date so I have no idea when these were written in my notebook. must be quite recent, a few weeks, but this one below reads like I could have just scribbled it yesterday or even today after reading your letter. scribbling is my happy place. this morning, I was scribbling to wake myself up and realized that in Korean, a comma ',' could mean a resting point, a marking of rest (쉼표/shwimpyo). and this made me

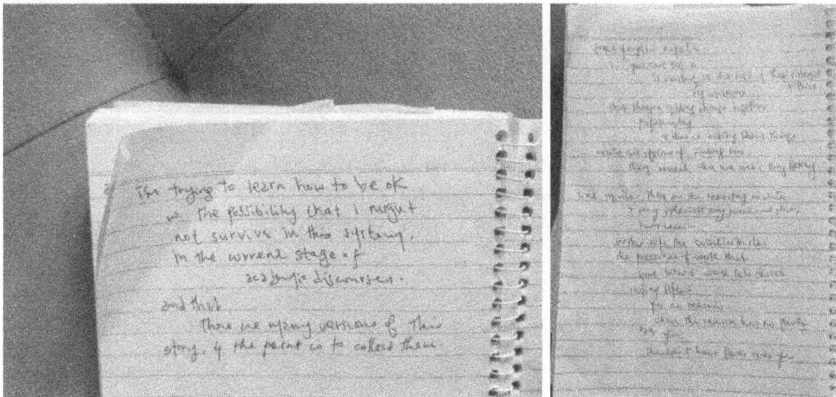

notes by sc

happy—see! I don't even want a full stop, I just want a comma, many commas, a place to rest where the breath stops, you know? just a spot to rest where there should be a rest. you wrote about routine and I thought you were also talking about rhythm, sort of a listening to the body, to a universe, which is not the same thing as doing whatever but more like an organized mess, by rest.

dear Zzzzzzz, what if we are not cats? what if we don't land on our feet, claw ourselves down to safe landing? I heard a poet, or was it a singer? I forget, she was anyway a Korean woman who was a maker of small things, and she was talking in an interview about how being a street cat in korea would be the worst thing to be born as, that the streets of urban korea are real hard places to survive—too many human residents see street cats and actually also street dogs as pests when both were brought to the cities as pets at some point, how hard it is to find food, how cold and long the winter months are, how evil humans are that they would poison the food bowls, how dangerous the streets are because of the motorbikes and cars, how crowded the concrete jungle is that even such small creatures like cats and dogs are seen as taking up too much space. I agree, cats make more sense to me as creatures to think with because they do nothing and serve no one but themselves but street cats and dogs share similar fate in the face of human abandonment. abandoned pets, is that also a problem over there or has that disappeared into the ether with the spread of internet like strip clubs?

[Imagine an image of Hello Kitty in a skull bow showing middle finger and a caption 'we are the cats that the witches you burned didn't want'.]

I think it is a shitty time to be alive, I thought I had bucked history when I found this thing called academia but no, it is just differently terrible here as the streets because it exacts so much from cats. ok, so maybe we are talking about cats, cats that even the witches abandoned because they are too angry, too emotional, etc. but also too useless, does not quite serve the purpose of where the witchcraft is now which firstly needs as its main ingredient seriousness but also in the very word suggests that making/doing/writing/thinking is a craft, a skill. I don't know if it is, I am not convinced that it is, or that that is where the emphasis should be in witchery, in magic.

ok, I'm now quite impressed I even managed to write a few new words this evening. it is always so easy to be in conversation with you, z. it is almost like scribbling ☺

can't wait to hear from you again—love getting glimpses of your apartment, what you are thinking this week, what cat-z—that grey fluff ball—has been saying to you.

hugs, chine

Chapter 14

can feminism be a comma?

dear Zzzzzzz,

thank you for sending through this meme on the messenger (about the friendship circle getting smaller each year and now consisting of only cats). I stayed home this weekend while my partner went to go hang out with his work colleagues. I really could not face meeting new people, not the least because the person whose house this gathering is happening is 'conservative', a 'covid sceptic', and a white heterosexual middle-aged man. it was going to be a gathering where I will be the lone Asian, and someone's partner at that. i'm tired of doing so much of smoothening out conversations because people are so uncomfortable with those who are different from them. either you are their pet or a wife or exotic or . . . reading your last letter, I wondered how you are being pickier, against what. I'm definitely becoming pickier about social situations where I am going to be The Different One because social gatherings and academia is so racist, sexist, heteronormative and middle class in most unimaginative ways. the neighbourhood cats are definitely my most safe and relatable friendship circle this year.

maybe we are thinking with the pets in the colonial house of IR, so not the servants, bastards, lovechildren that live in the downstairs of the house occupied by master legitimate family upstairs . . . but maybe pets need a separate conceptualization in the house of IR. I've been thinking and becoming more convinced that, for me, academic theorizing in IR makes most sense as useless writing and its political value is really in its uselessness. I think this is why my research and as a result I as an academic am more a pet than even a lovechild. I thought I was a lovechild in the colonial house but turns out, I'm a cat maybe of the servant or the lovechild, just steps away from being tossed out on the street. not sure what this means (but it is fun to think about, no?); I guess what I'm trying to say is that I really don't understand the seductions of being taken as a serious political actor, something that is taken as a given in many conversations I find myself in. I never wanted to be a serious political actor or contribute to feminism becoming a serious political actor in the world. of course I want to be taken seriously as an academic, and take feminism seriously but not in the sense that then means I want myself or want what I am part of to be taken seriously in policymaking or political movements. not so directly anyway. I don't want us to lose the value of indirectness especially if we work in the realm of changing the discourse, which is what I think theory is . . . it is work at the level of words, representation and imagination, no? I think of why people become academics in the social sciences and humanities, and I think I am not alone in my absolute lack of direction in life that led me to be here. rather than then find a purpose (or pretend one has one other than The Purpose of propping up one's social status).

I wonder if thinking with cats allows us to accept that it is ok to be without purpose, to be a resting spot in conversations. can feminist IR just be a comma, the thing that takes away a message, a spacing? and that we need commas otherwise we will be exhausted all the time, running around being so useful, so meaningful that we lose so much structure, so much that is already there? and to be good markers of rest, we need ourselves to firstly rest, to be in that at-peace state? I love the question you ask in the essay that you sent me, 'what if academia exists to serve us, not us serving it?' yes!!! if we are going to be good commas, good caretakers of imagination, of ideas and words, we need academia to be a good safe space for us as humans. at the moment, it really is not unless you live or are of use to the upstairs people of the colonial house (or to Cosmo Man as Anna and Lily put it), and we keep passing on this toxic culture to the next generation and the next and the next in the name of rigour, discipline, necessity, science, usefulness, impact. such bullshit. thank you for the collage and for the essay, I loved them both—I love how me fighting against being buried alive with my complaint by the institution creates a chain of events that shapeshifts the turd that the institutionalized people gave me into something creative, funny, joyful, persistent, thoughtful that can be shared in new forms. I am tired of whispers, rumours and the gossip corridors people have to use to deal with shit because institutions are so static and useless in dealing with what actually happens inside them, and people who can do something about the shittiness are so institutionalized that they are on autopilot, unable to make the move, make institutions move in ways that matter. I much prefer turning them into things that can be publicly shared, made public in ways that centre what we need the reality to be. next time I would also like to think a bit more about your other sara ahmed–inspired question, 'If your tombstone was a filing cabinet, what would you want to be found in the drawers when people go visit your grave'?

I thought this and then remembered, lookeeeee! turns out I actually already reserved a tombstone.* Is this what you had in mind?

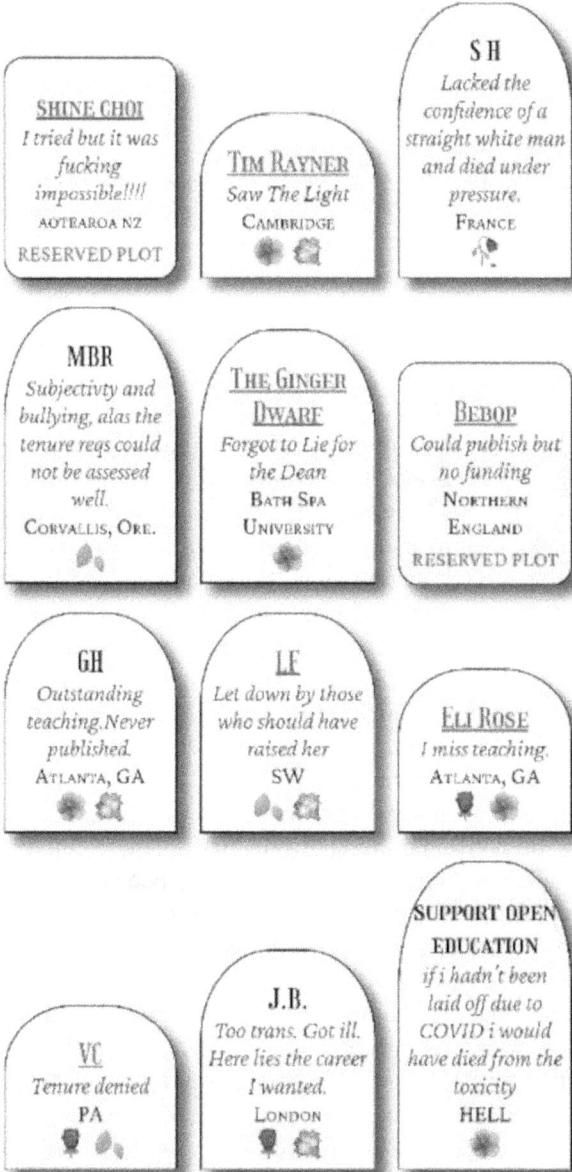

SHINE CHOI
I tried but it was fucking impossible!!!!
AOTEAROA NZ
RESERVED PLOT

TIM RAYNER
Saw The Light
CAMBRIDGE

S H
Lacked the confidence of a straight white man and died under pressure.
FRANCE

MBR
Subjectivty and bullying, alas the tenure reqs could not be assessed well.
CORVALLIS, ORE.

THE GINGER DWARF
Forgot to Lie for the Dean
BATH SPA UNIVERSITY

BEBOP
Could publish but no funding
NORTHERN ENGLAND
RESERVED PLOT

GH
Outstanding teaching. Never published.
ATLANTA, GA

LF
Let down by those who should have raised her
SW

ELI ROSE
I miss teaching.
ATLANTA, GA

VC
Tenure denied
PA

J.B.
Too trans. Got ill. Here lies the career I wanted.
LONDON

SUPPORT OPEN EDUCATION
if i hadn't been laid off due to COVID i would have died from the toxicity
HELL

academic graves by sc

* https://rip-my-academic-career.decasia.org.

I guess at the time you asked me this question, I was still in a fighting mode because I was in disbelief that the changing cast of (white) women who managed my complaint process would in private say, yes, he is x, but then decide they cannot do anything at the end of the day, and place the burden on my shoulder, well, you could have done y or z—whatever I did in response and because *I* decided that is what *I* had to do was just the wrong way to deal with Cosmo Man. but I'm no longer there now. i just want to be free and I want all of us to be a bit freer.

I started this letter thinking I was going to translate a few lines from *letters with many parentheticals*—I finished reading it this weekend but that will have to wait til my next letter. say hello to cat-z for me!

hugs, chine

Dear chine,

I was so excited when your letter arrived in my inbox yesterday afternoon. I had a piece of apple cake and read it. Now I'm having another piece and writing back. It's a vegan recipe, cardamom in the dough, very tasty.

Being pickier about people, against what. I think I'm just done with all kinds of bullshit, I'm really not interested in many people anymore. I think it relates to not wanting to smooth over anything anymore, not being willing to do the emotional work of smoothing things over and making them easier to others. It's easier for us just to refuse to engage at all? I used to joke that I hate people in general, but I really easily grant exceptions to individuals. I think those exceptions are becoming more and more rare these days. Maybe the pandemic (or depression and exhaustion, or all of them) turned me from extrovert into an introvert. Or my introvert side, the black cat, needs more space and nurturing than ever before.

You said, 'I think I am not alone in my absolute lack of direction in life that led me to be here'. You're spot on. That's how I could describe my 'career'. I feel, though, like we're surrounded by people who have had way more direction, but maybe I'm projecting my insecurities when I think others (have) know(n) what they're doing. And, like you, I also did not ever desire to be taken seriously by policy makers or desire to walk in the corridors of (state) power, but I've seen how people are drawn into it and how seductive the proximity to power can be/become. Or maybe I've judged those people wrong in the first place thinking that they share my disinterest, maybe they were aiming towards power and seriousness the whole time.

I love your thinking about the political value being in uselessness & the value of indirectness, but I also find it hard. I can feel in my body a push against these ideas, because we're constantly told that we need to show direct effects and usefulness. There's really no room for uselessness and indirectness in neoliberal academia, or whatever room there ever was is shrinking so fast that it's incredibly hard to resist, or it feels very very lonely to try to do so. That's why this book project and our conversations and these letters feel so meaningful to me, they allow me to breathe and not to be crushed by the weight of that push. Yes, this book project is the comma, the breathing space, even if even feminist IR too often fails to be that space. Thinking about and with cats is definitely opening a space I've been looking for and yearning for quite a while. The further away I can stay from the Cosmo Man, the better I feel. I think.

Maybe that's why it's been hard to write this book, if we get it finished, what then. Maybe we're all afraid this space that we have created together disappears and we're back to dealing with Cosmo Man and his friends.

Of course, sometimes I need the Cosmo Man for inspiration and rage. I think these two are often tied together—rage breeds inspiration and creativity, at least sometimes. But just at the initial stage, for doing the work, I need care, breathing space, and joy. So if I'm the cat, the pet of the servant/love-child in the house of IR, I sometimes need to sneak upstairs and see what the Cosmo Man and his allies are up to, but can't stay too long.

I'm glad you loved the essay and the collage, and it makes me happy (bittersweet happy) to be able to help you not to bury the injustice, to hold the injustice together for a moment and lift your burden. I love the virtual tombstones! When I was imagining a memorial site cabinet tombstone, I was thinking of actual artefacts that would be in the filing cabinet that people could take out and look at or enjoy, consume even, when visiting your grave. I've been thinking, for example, that if I had a memorial site people visited, it would contain a bottle of booze that people could have a drink from and whoever finished the bottle would always have to replace it. I would also maybe include some of my artwork or design an outrageous statue, or something.

It's Thursday and it's my sauna day. I usually would not leave the house after sauna, but tonight I'll go out to hear Astrid Swan play her new record live, I think it'll be a comma, too.

Hugs,

Zzzzzzz

dear Zzzzzzz,

what does a letter read eating vegan apple cake taste like? can I taste the vegan apple cake in your letter?

a hint of warm spice, yes cardamom but also cinnamon?

moistness of a vegan cake—comfort.

it has been a while since I've baked. the rare spurts of energy are used for cooking Korean food which I have no option but to make myself because I live in a small town where my people open sushi takeaways or two-dollar shops, sticking to what the locals already understand. they are just trying to make a living so they (and probably more, so that their children) can have better lives. why would they pursue something more? something riskier and 'less essential'?

my immigration status is more privileged than the sushi shop owners (I entered in a 'talent visa' issued for privileged skills category). So when I worry about the whole culture of 'essential' and 'non-essential' returning with a vengeance in the pandemic, and link it to why there are no restaurants that serve food from home, only sushi takeaways owned by people from home in this small town, this is already a luxury, something that did not have to be thought. and as luxury, crass, perverse in a crisis when so many are so busy just surviving the calculus of the pandemic politics. I guess for me this apple cake–infused letter exchange is about that—comfort, luxury, being extra.

I was also thinking about the value that poetry and other small art provide in a world where increasingly (or always) people ask what use they are to society, why they should exist, for whom they exist when sometimes so much of poetry and other small objects seem to have an audience of small and limited numbers. I wonder why large n has become the way democracies appreciate art and knowing. I am tickled by the possibility that academic political theory can be like poems, useful in their uselessness for anyone and anything directly most of the time until they do become useful in the most surprising of ways, in moments when one turns contemplative, when one needs some way to be alone but not all by oneself at the same time. this idea of useful in uselessness is from Trinh Minh-ha, a few generations before us and not even in IR (but please don't ask me to find the exact book and page number, I read her often and without taking notes, retracing my steps here . . . what use would this be?). but you are right, is this understanding no longer possible for our generation? or for someone like me, easily exhausted, more ambivalent about academia in general, less driven perhaps, have less to say and happy to just listen in (or even happier to just read and call it the day)? someone will have to explain to me why writing is privileged over listening and reading, especially now when so much published/publishable writing feels like reproduction of what is already said in tone and content, and really not new at all.

so many people (especially those who will have a hard time claiming the position of Cosmo Man given their histories, or rather given the history of Cosmo Man as a subject position) seem so sure and settled in their ways. I don't know why being settled and knowing so much are seen as good things in critical thinking *if indeed* the point of critique is to loosen up established power structures and norms, if it is meant to provide an independent view of the world that insiders and practitioners are unable to gain by themselves given the nature of their positions and work.

I love your thoughts on being a cat checking out what the Cosmo Man is up to, and in my case, it will be what the servants, bastards and the lovechildren are up to, I've forgotten the upstairs exists! maybe this is my problem, why I keep butting heads at work.

I have to read some student work now so wrapping up my writing session with just a few lines I have underlined in the first few pages of the book (I'm a very messy reader, which is mostly why I buy books rather than rely on libraries—what about you?).

안 그래도 한달 벌어 한 달 먹고사는 프리랜서 인생인데, 이제는 앞날의 캄캄함이 스페이스 그레이였다가 매트 블랙이 되어버린 기분입니다.

> already as a freelancer, I was living on what I earned month to month, I feel as if the darkness of the future has now turned from space grey to matte black. —sleeq

대재난 시대에 살고 있는 두 여성 예술가가 앞으로 어떤 편지를 주고받을지 무척 기대됩니다. 직접 참여하고 있으면서도 기다려지고 기대되는 신기한 일이네요.

> I'm looking forward to the letters the two women artists living through the age of catastrophe will be writing to each other. what a curious thing, to anticipate what I myself have a hand in making. —lee lang

when we first talked about writing letters to each other to get the book writing going again, you also mentioned autotheory, and a writer associated with it. I've written down the name but that piece of paper has escaped. can you tell me the name again? I liked the sound of it because I certainly am not interested in autoethnography but using the self or what lies around in our lives as materials-of-sorts to think with is intriguing . . . though I don't think I can do it without a series of objects to mediate and situate this turn to auto-. or maybe this autotheory is something entirely different—do tell!

chine

Dear chine,

the eternal November has truly begun here, I feel like it's getting longer and longer every year. For the last few years it's been about 100–120 days, usually about less than 100 hours of direct sunlight during that whole time. So grey and dark, although this year I'm not so afraid of it. It helps that I did not have to write any funding applications so my body is much less stressed, or not really stressed at all. Last year I learned to play video games during the dark season; it helps me to stay awake in the early evening, and this year it was actually something to look forward to, I was thinking already in the summer about the games I may want to play. Last year I played (on Nintendo Switch) Mario Odyssey and now I have started Luigi's Mansion 3. They are both easy enough and teach me what to do along the way. I never was a gamer when I was younger, but I guess it's not too late to become a casual gamer in middle age. I think this is useful uselessness also, it does not produce anything, it does not make me a better academic or thinker. It does allow me to sleep better at night, because I don't nap in the early evening. If I watch TV or read during those hours, I'll surely fall asleep and then won't sleep as well during the night. It's ridiculous how in the last few years I've gotten to that age that I'm getting more worried about sleeping well. I used to be a great sleeper and still don't suffer from insomnia or anything, but my sleep is just getting trickier. And this is apparently what I also talk about with my friends these days. My dad once said that you know that you're really getting older when every time you meet with your friends, everyone is just talking about their health issues. That's where I am at the moment. Maybe COVID-19 has also added to this illness/health talk?

You wrote: *'I am tickled by the possibility that academic political theory can be like poems, useful in their uselessness for anyone and anything directly most of the time until they do become useful in the most surprising of ways, in moments when one turns contemplative, when one needs some way to be alone but not all by oneself at the same time'.*

I love this. I think I read fiction because of this—being alone but not all by myself. Of course, at the same time learning about different worlds, different ways of seeing the world. And yes definitely, at its best academic political theory does have the same effect. Effect not being the best possible word here.

I totally agree that we should privilege listening and reading over writing and that so many things published are not creating new thinking but pretty much repeating what is already known and has been said. I have such issues with academic writing and not wanting to take part in that game and not wanting to write in that formulaic way and repeating all the things that have been said.

I definitely think one of my problems with academic writing is also the certainty, the being settled and *knowing*. It's supposed to be a conversation, but it's really more of talking past each other with a lot of certainty that I have it right and someone else has it wrong, or at least pointing out those bits where someone else has it wrong. I think that's why I was so enchanted with Astrid Joutseno's defence when she talked about being enchanted to think with others and finding great allies in theorists. I feel like that's a less certain/ knowing so surely kind of way. Less of a Cosmo Man subject position but perhaps the servants, love children, bastards and their cats can embrace this kind of allyship and enchantment?

I think that here locally the communities are so small, that I necessarily run into the Cosmo Man and see what he's up to. In broader (global?) IR it's definitely easier to forget that the Cosmo Man is out there doing his thing. In my first couple of ISAs I did occasionally go check out a panel with some Big Name Cosmo Men just to see what they look and sound like—to put faces on the curriculum I had gone through in my studies. These days I'm far less curious that way. Back then, I did walk out of a panel or a two after taking a look, don't think I ever had the interest and stamina to stay through the whole thing, such boredom, good thing they were always in those huge ballrooms so no one noticed little me taking off from the back row.

I absolutely love the translations you included. I so can relate to both. I think what saved me or pulled me through the darkness of the future that turned to matte black was this temporary financial security that I have now that I have this funding and that it allowed me to be on sick leave and take time to recover. Having access to occupational health care certainly helped too. Even though I'm not fully recovered yet, or maybe never will, the future is not such a black hole sucking up all the light but is returning/has returned to shades of grey. And I'm so very pleased that we started writing these letters; it makes me excited to see where we go, even if we're just going around in circles.

The autotheory author I mentioned is Maggie Nelson. I think she's best known for her novel *The Argonauts*. I haven't read any academic work on autotheory yet; there's this book *Autotheory as Feminist Practice in Art, Writing, and Criticism* and I noticed there's some podcast episodes as well on the publisher's website—maybe I'll listen at some point.

A friend of mine recently interviewed Maggie Nelson for a feminist magazine and the translation just came out this week. It's a lot about mothering, but I think there are things that resonate with what we've been talking about here, especially this bit:

'One thing, in both mothering and just living, that I am interested in, is hanging out in the space between attraction and aversion, and trying to experience openness and criticality together. You know, finding a way to move through the world that allows for all experiences to be novel, that preserves, maybe even augments, the space for curiosity' (Nelson in Ruot-salainen 2021).

I think that might be another way of talking about the comma, no?

You wondered 'why large n has become the way democracies appreciate art and knowing'. Is neoliberalism the answer? Or as an answer is it too easy or too complicated? Something to do with counting & the bigger the better? In the last few days there has been a heated political debate over here related to this; the government was planning on cutting a lot of the funding for small culture actors, poetry magazines and such. In the overall budget of the nation, it's peanuts, but a huge thing to a lot of freelancers who have been in that black matte future already because of the pandemic restrictions, and now they're threatened with an even darker future. How do you get darker from black matte?

I don't know how to defend the small and the seemingly insignificant, the comma, to those who have bought into the idea that everything needs to have value according to their financial/productivity/number game standards. Most will never be convinced, so why even bother. Thank whatever higher powers that I am not a lobbyist and I don't have to try. It pains me to watch some of my friends trying. It's exhausting.

But I guess just having this discussion with you is in fact defending those things, even if no one else ever reads this but us.

Have a lovely weekend!

Zzzzzzz

Omg Zzzzzzz, I have so much I want to share and write in response to your letter but I am not sure I will manage. the pressure! for now, I have to breathlessly tell you about Adrian Piper, the artist that the academic book you linked up to 'studies'. I have been reading her, her complaint letters—she had a scandalous academic professional life in philosophy as well as this amazing artistic life. the scandal being that the college cut her off from payroll a few months before she hit retirement so she does not get the pension because she's been fighting the institution for many years, sued it and lost, and one year, she moved out of her office/job/life in the United States secretly without telling anyone (not the least her employer because she was running away because of them—their harassment) and moved to Berlin where she is now self-exiled! I started looking her story up earlier this year because that college is where I did my undergraduate studies (and where CC works!), and I was a philosophy student in the department that shit on her. when I was a student, she was like a ghost figure in the small department, other professors would be like, 'we don't know what's happening to her,' 'she does not want to teach', 'she's not teaching this semester I think, she's not around.' she's this big fancy artist, you know? so I wanted to take her class (on Kant, she taught moral philosophy) but she was 'never around'. I have read all her complaint letters, her diversity report (scathing), they are all publicly available through her website (and I read her memoir, which took superhuman effort on my part to acquire . . . so yes, I was a bit obsessed for a few months). anyway, I know these professors she mentions and now wondering, wow, did they just keep students away from her to dry her out? that dick, he could have told me to go talk to her instead of telling me I need to learn how to overcome my inability to get over the fact that Kierkegaard had no regard for me as a human/reader. she as an African American woman studying Kant was uniquely positioned to teach me, make sense of the impossibility instead of brush it under the carpet. anyway, knowing her story as she told it made things click about my education.

and autotheory. I will have to read (when I'm feeling academic) but at the moment I'm reading autocritism (I think?) by autofiction writer about another autofiction novel at the moment . . . this is an interesting world, but then I think—isn't that what so many black, brown, yellow Third World feminists have been doing all this time? thinking not just Trinh Minh-ha but also Audre Lorde, June Jordan, . . . and these people have intellectual descendants, you know? what are this whole new auto-genres all about? I was also remembering a passage I read from *Revolutionary Feminisms*—it was an interview, I can't remember which contribution but one feminist said that she turned to her life because she could not afford to do any other kind of research to answer her questions. all she had was her life, where her family is from. I thought that is beautiful. yes, the turn to auto- also happens because we do not have resources (or energy) to go to archives, learn a whole new language for years, live there for months and months, or try to access the key military whatever man . . . the personal is the international because yes, it is, but also, you have to work with what you've got and you got little. in which case, the autofiction/criticism I read is in that vein—she's adjuncting, she writes through her pregnancy, she makes little money on her books—and she does her study of Hervé Guibert's novel (who also wrote autofiction). she writes about how she does not have time to work on this study, and so it is also a study about exhaustion and not doing what she's supposed to do and yet doing it dragging and kicking. this reminds me of marysia's book exquisite corpse (Zalewski 2013) and what she's said about it.

I am very gossipy and ranty today, can you tell? I got another silly idea in my head when I read your letter. Ok, so Cosmo Man can be a cat too, he can be a Cosmo Cat! so if the Cosmo Man is a cat, what would he see? And I thought, oh that dude who wrote the latest Trending Book on Academia is a Cosmo Cat, no wonder it is so annoying to read though his understanding of neoliberal university bullshit is spot on. he still wants to be a top cat.

I was surprised to read that you also remembered that incident we discussed the other day—it was barely 'an incident', almost just a thumbprint kind of light-touch encounter . . . all digitally . . . and yet it left an imprint, this nothing of a complaint and 'complaint evidence' that made me realise

I really don't get it (because others on there seemed to in their sympathetic replies). this made me a bit sad, that so many complaints that I would immediately get are not shared in such public forum because the public however informal is not a safe place to air negative experiences of the kind I'd immediately get, the complaints that Piper made. what I notice about how I used Twitter—when I write complaints, just scenes from my everyday really—is that people DM me concerned, checking in. they don't post replies directly to my post when in some ways, I think I started posting my complaints because I don't want these experiences to be private, I don't want negative experiences to be brushed under the carpet in IR all the while nothing complaint incidents get public airing all the time leaving thumbprints in the network. sharing negative experiences that most academics in IR would get and sympathise, that is ready-made, that is like . . . what we are doing here? what is IR? I keep on losing the plot.

I was flipping through the book again and these passages jumped out at me about health:

완벽히 건강한 사람이 있을까요? 그리고 그 사람이 인간 중에 최고일까요? 저는 그렇게 생각하지 않습니다. (p152)

> do you think there is such a thing as a perfectly healthy person? and do you think that person is the best of the humans? I do not think so.

이렇게 스스로 돌보지 않게 된 데는 아무래도 코로나19의 영향이 크겠지요. 갑자기 쓸모가 없어져버린 마당에 뭐하러 스스로 가꾸겠어요. 긍정적으로 생각해보려 해도 불이 붙지 않은 장작에 바람만 불어제치는 느낌인 걸요. (p. 114)

> covid19 probably explains how I came to stop taking care of myself. why would I take care of myself when I have become suddenly useless? I'm trying to think more positively but it feels like trying to get a fire going by blowing at firewood that has not been lit.

there is another passage about games, but will have to find it for you next time.

hugs,
chine

Dear chine,

Omg, omg, indeed, I can feel the same breathlessness even tho we were supposed to have this letter writing as a breathing space, a comma . . . but I guess it's more of an excitement about having this conversation and our minds racing to so many different directions at once. So it's different from that exhaustion that has us needing the breathing space in the first place. After ten months in therapy and learning to listen to myself and what I need, I can't always differentiate what makes me tired in a good way and what makes me exhausted, so that's why I can be wary of excitement and breathlessness.

Autotheory/autocriticism etc. made me think about the politics of naming things. Is this one of those cases where a thing becomes named a thing only when privileged white people start doing it? There's this whole discussion also about autofiction, where suddenly it became this amazing literary genre when the Norwegian author Karl Ove Knausgård wrote his six-part series describing his everyday life in a very detailed way. I never got past page 485 of the second book, decided to read the rest when I've retired; I think that's probably at least 2,500 pages or more to go. Prob won't even then. When women write about their everyday it's small and inconsequential. Women's things. And no woman would get published to this extent, don't know if they/we would even have the audacity to write all these thousands of pages. I know a man who is writing a trilogy and both the first and second parts have been about 1,000 pages, and while I really enjoyed both of them, there's something very gendered about the whole thing. All the women authors around me write much shorter books.

I was on a crowded tram the other day and some middle-aged white man was sitting in the middle of two seats his legs spread wide open and not paying any attention to anyone else maybe needing a seat. And I started wondering what it would be like to have grown up thinking that the whole world is for you, you can take as much space as you want anywhere, physically and mentally. And of course, I'm pretty sure people like that think that world is the same/feels the same for everyone else too. That, I guess, is the essence of the Cosmo Man/Cosmo Cat. There's this local Professor Man, or he was a professor in humanities for ten or so years, but his professorship was not a permanent one, so he recently became unemployed, and his critiques of the university system are spot on and I think he's trying to start a movement rethinking the university, but . . . he's such a Cosmo Cat, wants to be the messiah, that I cannot even think about working with him on this cause eventho I agree with most of what he says.

I love the cat picture and your analysis of it! Yes, I think you got the characters spot on, but who's the one walking away with a brush in her mouth? Kali? I think it must be Kali, she's off to paint a whole another picture. . . .

Yes, it's soooooooooo interesting whose complaints get public sympathy and whose get private sympathy (if even that), I think people are so afraid of somehow being tainted by some complaints (yours being a good example) that they either stay away altogether or just express their support in private. Of course, private support matters too, to an extent, but it does not change anything. Public at least has the potential to change things, or to reveal the extent of the support to others passing by. I don't really know what's going on with that. I'm so over being afraid of rocking the boat.

Back to autotheory, you said that the turn to auto- happens because we don't have the resources to go beyond ourselves and as you point out that has been the case for many always. It's similar to what some of my activist friends have been pointing out lately that if they had the choice not to be activists they would not be (because it's so damn exhausting), but when you're born as indigenous person or have arrived as a refugee, and are always racialized, you really don't have a choice, if you want to speak about your experiences it is perceived as activism . . . it becomes something fancy, admirable, great, when those who do have the choice choose to do it, autofiction, autotheory etc.

I had something else I meant to write to you about, but I did not write it down anywhere when the thought crossed my mind, so now I've forgotten. Maybe it'll come back to me. Have to read (about) Adrian Piper at some point, hadn't heard of her before.

Hugs,

Zzzzzzz

Chapter 15

exhausted (again) of the normal

Exhausted . . .

I'm exhausted by my university who doesn't care a whit about me, or anyone for that matter. An extra pound of flesh demanded every year. Sustenance is not forthcoming. Not now, not tomorrow, not even when I retire. If they take one more pound of flesh, I'll officially be anorexic. Too little left to give, barely enough to survive.

I'm exhausted by my body telling me how exhausted it is. Eyes twitching all day long. A patch of shingles inflaming my side. Big yawns in the afternoon. I want to put my head down on my desk and sleep. An email pings, my head jerks up. My body keeps telling me to stop. I keep hushing it up. I lullaby it into complacency.

I'm exhausted by things that are good for me. Kale. Fresh air. Savasana. Striking for equal pay, pensions, liveable wages.

I'm exhausted by the news. First it was Covid. Daily tallies of the dead. Obsessively watching the rise and fall of infection rates in my city, country, around the world. Worn down by an unfulfilled rage at the brazen racialised and gendered biopolitics of the Boris Johnson government (and most other governments). Knowing they simply don't care and berating myself for hoping otherwise. Most governments don't care but do a better job at hiding it. The daily death toll still high and always climbing but we seemingly no longer care with war upon us. And so now it's war. Exhausted knowing that war is completely pointless. The war will have to come to an end, the two sides will have to come to some kind of agreement, so why must people die when we know this must/will happen?

I'm exhausted by the return and resurgence of realist thinking in IR, in the world. . . . I know it has never gone away, but its easy return to the centre of things, to the centre stage of making sense of the world, is terrifying.

I'm exhausted by how quickly feminist and postcolonial thinking/doing is forgotten, set aside to make room for the big boys to play and have their say. Forty-plus years of scholarship sidelined. The time still not right or ripe for feminist and postcolonial thinking.

I'm exhausted by masculinity, and all sorts of versions of it. Narcissistic versions. Misogynist versions. Mansplaining versions. Comedic versions. All that bloody and deadly fragility . . .

I'm exhausted by femininity. Dressed up and arranged around a table, all bows and kitten heels.

I'm exhausted by virtual platforms. Square boxes. Stay in your box. One speaker at a time. Camera on. Camera off. Stuck in waiting rooms. Shut your fucking microphone off before I scream. Missing the fug of bodies in the ISA lobby, starving for a glimpse of a friendly face.

I'm exhausted by a conference panel that I need to prepare for, make myself presentable for, say something smart at. When is there time to be stupid with exhaustion?

I'm exhausted by a to-do list that never seems to be at a loss for things to do.

I'm exhausted by a stack of books that I want to read, need to read to nourish my greedy soul. But who has the time with such a fucking voracious to-do list?

I'm exhausted by daylight saving time. Spring has stolen an hour of my precious time.

dear Zzzzzzz,

I have so much to say, to ask what you think, but this past week has been so exhausting and I have another full week of work to face when I know what I need is to empty out a few days to get my rhythm back. I keep on thinking, 'this is normal, you've kept the work schedule normal despite the pressures to just plough through so why are you struggling?' then I thought, because normal is the problem, I refuse the normal academia, rethinking the university within the bounds of Cosmo Cat's masterscript. no, we are not all in this together; I don't know what this 'we' is that people keep on talking about in these rooms. no no no. I love what sara ahmed says in her latest book (On Complaint!) (which I wish she wrote first, before she wrote the books so many people seem to love but fear being tainted), once we blurt out the first no, a lot more noes follow. but this refusal thing takes so much energy as your activist friends say.

I've been so bothered all week by many of the normal exchanges in normal situations in normal feminist academia with people going about their work in normal ways as if the world is normal. the topics change, the networks are different but I keep on hearing myself saying (to myself, after the fact, after the exchange because a passing comment stays with you, you know? one of those sticky exchanges that stay with you which is what I find exhausting more than anything. which is why I want to just stay home—irony here is that I *am* home in all this):

Yes, I could have gotten things all wrong here but allow me this—I might be wrong in ways that you seem unable to see. All I ask is also to consider this, that what you do not see matters and please do not ask me to explain this, not now, not to you. Just give me this, that I am wrong in ways that you might be unable to understand because . . . history. I don't think we have the language yet; I don't think we are trying to get the language right hard enough.

all this to say, I am exhausted. I feel unwell but I don't think those who feel well and healthy are the best of the humans either to be working, doing the critical work.

and when we are unwell and cannot get well again and being well and healthy (again) is not an option, do we stop being humans? Isn't being unwell and dying not part of the living too? I had an end-of-semester get-together with a few students, and one of them asked me if I was happy doing what I do. this was after they shyly discussed with me that they wanted to continue their studies because they enjoyed university studies for the first time this semester, that this class made them think that maybe there is something in this thing that they mostly found alienating and oppressive in previous semesters. so you see, I had to be honest here because I did not want them to think I am well, that there is a 'we' in university, and that things will fare better in life if you stay in school versus find somewhere else to spend one's time and energy. so, all I could say was that I just try to do my job with integrity and try to be helpful, but no, I am not sure I am happy or that I find the job rewarding. on the whole, I find it impossible. I tried not to be fatalistic, to say that just because I find it this way that they will too so find something else to do. because that is not helpful. these students know so much though about 'suddenly becoming useless', about being made to 'blow at firewood that has not been lit'. I hope the teachers they meet in the future and their future studies continue building on this knowledge they bring to the university. I wish people in the university would stop gaslighting the students. so unethical!

not wishing you wellness,

chine

Chapter 16

academic friendships and angers (not?) worth holding onto

Dear chine,

you're definitely on point saying normal is the problem. Didn't Cynthia Enloe teach us to always direct our feminist curiosity to 'normal', 'traditional' etc? I think we, the feminist IR we, have not learned that lesson well enough. We don't collectively pay enough attention to the normal and refuse its pressures. And I can sort of understand why—in this hyperindividualized competition that academia has begun it makes sense to just plough on and on and on, trying to 'make it', but at what cost? At what cost to those who 'make it' and even more so at what cost to those (of us) left behind? I don't think I'll ever 'make it'; I'm too old and too tired and not willing to sacrifice my time, health and well-being to produce enough, to have enough merits to get a permanent job that would require me to work too much. . . .

But as you said that refusal is also damn hard work. I know I've probably said this before, but I did a huge amount of emotional work after getting my doctorate and when I was one foot out of the academia already for a few years, I grieved for what could've been, the research I could've done if only I had gotten that funding, and the academic friendships I could've had nurtured if I had that funding which includes travel money for research visits. I was dreaming of visiting Lily and thinking about laughter and humour with her and laughing with her. Then she died. Finally, I was ready to let go of academia for good and then I did (at the last possible round of applying) manage to get the funding. I was so exhausted, but did not let myself feel it, ploughed on and had this whole amazing trip planned for March 2020, which I had to cut short because of the pandemic. We were all meant to go to Hawai'i and I was looking forward seeing Sharain Naylor, and when it all got cancelled I was still thinking that maybe there's a way to go to Hawai'i at some point. And now she's dead. Just like that. And I don't even know how to process that information. Except by sending random thoughts in emails to you and Michelle.

I found this image by @zeppelinmoon on Instagram, it's a black cat hissing and the texts says 'would you like me if I hiss at you and won't come out to play' and I think it captures some of what we've been discussing about the servants and love children and that maybe the black cat is theirs or lives with them. Cosmo Man/Cosmo Cat definitely won't have the patience for those who hiss at him and refuse to play, but will the others who live downstairs of the House of IR have the patience to accept the black cat on the black cat's terms? Will anyone?

Sharain knew and understood black cats and wanted to adopt one, because the shelters have the hardest time finding homes for black cats (same goes for black dogs). People are prejudiced against them, but I don't even know why. Some say that these days when people want their pets to be Instagrammable, black cats are frowned upon because they are very hard to photograph well. So is it all just superficial performativity? People's willingness to care for pets or care for those who make it in academia?

I don't have experience in giving a home to semi-feral cats, but I know it takes a lot of patience and time to earn their trust and it is easier for many just to deem the semi-feral cats too difficult. Not thinking that it's us humans that have failed them, not that they are too difficult to deal with. And I think we, the IR we (and some more than others), failed Sharain. She was definitely not 'too difficult', IR could've learned so much from her, but . . .

This next image is by a Finnish meme artist 'instant coffee meme girl' and when I saw it, I thought of our conversations and the Cosmo Cat. Perfect, no? Have you watched the *Mad Men*? It's been a while since I watched the whole series, but I think these guys are the epitome of Cosmo Men.

You know, I should move on to other things, because I'm (as always) behind in two writing tasks, but . . . I wish we could meet in person again and continue these conversations. Last week, I went to a seminar in another city (stayed overnight! In a hotel!) and there were so many beginnings of thoughts I have just about embodiment and being in the same space with people, who are on the same page with you, who are excited and inspired and inspiring. And how way too often seminar rooms and situations are very restricting rather than open spaces for thinking to flow freely. Our seminar day started with an arts-based presentation and the presenters were in character as 'squirrels who have an agenda'. I realized that because I was listening to squirrels and I had no desire to judge them on the 'normal' (here we go again with the normal) standards of 'seriousness' or 'respectability' or any other academic criteria that I have internalized so very well that I often have to check myself in academic spaces so I can refuse to give in to the all these criteria when

Meme (pikakahvimemegirl Alma Tuuva)

listening to others. That's what makes listening so difficult, there are so many internalized things intervening and preventing us from hearing. I think. Internalized misogyny, ableism, etc., etc. And as said before refusal is hard work.

Of course, I've been on the other side of this too; remember the time when I presented my artwork at ISA and had the actual physical collages there and made the audience get up from their chairs and take a closer look. I can still feel some of the embodied discomfort in the room, when some serious academics did not know what to do with this whole thing, how to judge the collages because they were not conventional academic arguments presented in a 'normal' way. At an innovative panel, I managed to go too far by presenting just artwork, not giving lengthy academic justification for them.

I think our 'Benedict/Frankenstein' panels have also managed to create a different kind of space within the ISA (and the collaging panel too, of course); there has been crying and laughter and 'all the emotions' in those panels, which is rare thing in academic spaces. I said after last week's seminar day that I wish more academic spaces were as open for feeling and thinking as that seminar was. I had forgotten, but now that I think of it, most of the things we have put together have also been those kind of spaces. But then again, some panels we've been in, organized by some others, not so much. . . . I still get angry thinking about that one last panel in New Orleans. But maybe it's not an anger worth holding either.

I don't know, I'm just constantly disappointed in academia and most academics. This is nothing new, really, but I don't know how to let go. I mean how to exist in academia but let go of that feeling. Or is letting go of academia the only option? For me. But then again, there are all of you people I want to be in relation with and I don't know how if I were to leave academia altogether. I know some friendships would remain, but most probably not.

Hugs,

Zzzzzzz

dear Zzzzzzz,

I had the catmen image in my head all week since reading your letter. I think instead of us donning costumes, we should just distribute cat ears to our fellow Cosmo Man panellists and seminar attendees. I think it would help us deal with the internalized norms you talked about, sort of like visual reminders that we are in that part of the house the archetypal Cosmo Man reigns. and really, we are not even saying they should stop being Cosmo Men, but maybe try this alter ego, cosmo cat, and let's see how that goes, just a bit of fun really, to just lighten up the room a bit. I wish Zoom had a function where I can draw ears for people on my screen.

I love this phrase from your letter '*at an innovative panel, I managed to go too far*'! oh I know this feeling, when you know you've overstepped the parameters of innovation, art and creativity . . . by doing what made artistic sense for you. funny how listening to the artistic or experimental side of us often leads to doing *less* or *not* doing as expected. that in turn leads to being perceived as having gone *too* far and being *too* much in sites of academic work. I once just got a room of critically trained academics to tear from a piece of plain notebook paper and write things down on borders which I was then going to recompose to see what we learn about borders and boundaries by paying attention to not just our definitions/words but also how people tear the piece of paper. I intentionally just stayed myself (not performing the outsider artist persona, which is not me anyway) but also didn't explain the task, the conceptual logic, before the activity as my academic-self reminded me might be a good idea . . . and the Cosmo Men were the most dismissive, literally ignored the task. I learned from this experience (at a workshop on creativity!) that academics use words and theory to discipline and erase discomfort, the unsettling experiences that threaten the self-imposed image of ourselves and value of academic conversations, all the while professing that they value new perspectives, experimentation and creativity. i've since chucked this and other similar experiences where I've been dismissed as learning experiences and grown to deeply distrust critical work and 'creative' acts/methods with clear academic explanations and purpose.

not an anger worth holding either yes, I know what you mean. I'm happy to report that these disciplining experiences no longer make me angry even in the moment they happen, and I'd like to think I know how to be in the moment better now thanks to how frequently these interactions happen when I'm just going about my business and doing the work as I feel compelled to do. these exchanges are exhausting and also distracting though so I try not to be out and about too much in the world of words with what I'm working through these days. I get really angry though and hold onto anger that is more institutionally based, more just from the everyday stuff that has immediate impact on people, like how students are treated, how entitled and arrogant people are in how they do their job (coasters are the worst offenders for me, men who do nothing but whatever serves their ego and pontificate to no end in meetings), how I, friends or colleagues have no option but to deal 'rationally' with little tyrants intruding into our lives who wield the little power they have over other people to create such unnecessary drama and chain of events . . . this everyday stuff makes me so angry—*I see red*. I don't know, I think seeing the world in red is important. I see it linked to the negation that ahmed talks about in her book, the no, no, no! the exclamation might never be felt, does nothing to change people's behaviour, but in that it gained an expression somehow is in itself a shifting, a disorientation?

you also wrote '*the academic friendships I could've had nurtured if I had that funding*'. i too have been thinking about friendships in academia, what that is and whether indeed it is useful to think of relations we enter in academic feminist spaces in the language of friendship, especially when they require funding to nurture. to me, that sounds like work and there is a transactional dimension to the relationship. this is not to say it is not authentic, but more that it is driven by an objective and that can include political objective . . . even when the political objective here operates almost entirely in academic language and space. almost being key here. BUT when one leaves academia and one's political objective shifts, then it seems almost natural that the transaction-based relations also stop being meaningful and worth maintaining? I find this very unsettling because so much of my social connections are linked to academia, and part of what I'm trying to learn is to be ok with a 'not making it' is the shifting of the social. it is an experiment in small gestures at the moment but I'm loving the idea of unsettling as a way to reconstitute the social. I think I've already told you I've been quite obsessed with adrian piper, and she's been helpful for me in thinking about what reconstituting the social could be about, which I think returns us back to what it means to stand alone,

When I am alone in the solitude of my study or studio, I'm completely out of the closet: I move back and forth easily among art, philosophy, and yoga (my third hat). It's the only time I feel completely free to be who I am. So I will go to almost any lengths to protect my privacy. If I lose that, I lose everything. —from adrian piper: *the reader*

kate zambreno, the auto-criticism/fiction author I mentioned (or maybe I didn't mention her name, she wrote that book *To Write as If Already Dead*, a study on Guibert's novel that is not a study on Guibert's novel)—she also has this passage on friendship which I went back and found to show you.

Her 1966 piece *Hang Up* was partially fabricated by her friend LeWitt, a sculptural send-up of a painting, a wood stretcher wrapped with bed sheets, a long metal wire extending out of it into the space of the viewer onto the floor in front of the frame. How Hesse felt that this was the first piece that reached the 'absurdity or extreme feeling' that she desired in art. I think about how friendship can affect the limits of one's own thinking, how my friend, who was still my friend, mostly likely was reaching for a similar level of absurdity and feeling in her own life and work. I spend some time thinking about this before I have to go wake my child up from her nap. (Zambreno 2021, 52)

I find the two passages could be saying the same thing, the importance of following the limits of thinking. and that writing is not something we should be doing all the time, that writing is already happening all the time in our lives and in friendships, if we are willing enough to live it (in the) everyday. what am I trying to say? maybe that academic writing especially on the international, the law, security, global politics for me is not an escape from our everyday lives, it is an effort to connect better, more meaningfully across locations and our different experiences, right? and you said, being there for each other. nothing more, nothing less. I find that I'm able to explore and keep pushing towards the extreme and absurdity of this idea in our friendship, in friendships nurtured by trying to write This Book and in my other writing collaborations . . . though I understand sometimes this impulse probably drives people mad. this is also why I think maybe friendship is not quite the right word.

[Imagine a comic strip where a ghost is trying to scare a stick figure human three times by yelling 'boo' but nothing happens; when the ghost yells 'you should be writing' the human jumps from being frightened.]

my frustration with academic discourse on writing comes from this space. what is all this pressure academics feel about producing and writing all the time? I get it (I feel it) and I also really don't. when I see this discourse circulating these days it makes me see red, it is so harmful. so I had to do a quick edit. how would you edit this?

chine

Dear chine,

I love your idea of distributing cat ears to the Cosmo Men. Not sure they would do it, so yes, Zoom etc. drawing function would be better. Do you remember the lawyer who had accidentally left a cat filter on when appearing remotely via Zoom in court? This happened during the first lockdown, I think. Lot of memes were born out of the incident.

I remember wearing the Benedict mask briefly on one of our book related panels and feeling all kinds of weird feelings because of it. I do wonder how the cat ears would affect the Cosmo Men if they did indeed decide to play along. Maybe some mainstreamish Cosmo Man could; they really have nothing to lose. I think it's more the critical IR types who are worried about their (our?) seriousness; they are more afraid that the status of the whole critical field (whatever and wherever that is, if it even is) will collapse with any kind of playing around. Because populist politicians and journalists are attacking our work as being frivolous and ridiculous and not worthy of taxpayers' money, some critical scholars seem to now think that we should do all that we can not to give populists weapons to attack us with. They think they can still salvage criticality, if they're just serious and rigorous enough. So they actually end up accepting some of the populist rhetoric and playing by the rules set by populists. And they need the rest of us to play along and not be too weird and too out there.

You're right about the 'you should be writing' discourse. Like a lot of the other academic 'memes' I've started to see it too as more harmful than funny. I do recognize the importance of shared laughter, but a lot of these types of things just keep reinforcing the toxic academic culture of productivity rather than for real critiquing them. We laugh because it's too true and to stop to really think about it would hurt too much?

Maybe the ghost in the cartoon should say instead: 'You should be resting'. or 'You should be doing nothing'. or 'You should be taking time off'. In the same vein the second picture could also say 'You should be'. but I really like your edit. This letter writing has definitely brought the joy of writing back for me, or maybe not always joy, but a real sense of writing as thinking and academic writing as a discussion that can take us to places and push us and create openings . . . it has definitely brought writing to the everyday for me.

Every Tuesday and Friday a few of my colleagues do a three-hour writing session (3 x 45 minutes and breaks in between) at the university. There's quite a nice room with couches and a bright light treatment lamp and some big plants. We were just there, an hour into the session, when some other people needed the room. One of them was my line manager (oh, how I hate this term!) and she was really happy about the idea of writing together but remarked that her calendar is controlled by others, so she can't take the time to write. I know that it is true that there is so much admin work and meetings and everything, BUT . . . what if she just blocked some time slots from her calendar and said 'no, this time I'm not available'? And this is a more general point, if we really should be writing and if we WANT TO write, maybe we need to put writing first, maybe we just start making time for it.

I know I don't often do that either. I've read a whole bunch of writing self-help, and of course all of it says to put writing first, make it a priority, we all know all this. Yet we don't do it. What does that say? Does it say that we really don't want to or that the type of writing we do is just not meaningful enough? Or does it say something else? I don't know. For me it's about the meaningfulness/meaninglessness. I find our exchanges so very meaningful that I always look forward to writing back to you. Or that piece I wrote for a Journal. I really had things to say, so the writing came quite easily. Of course, I still thought that it'll need a lot of work and revisions, until I got the reviewer comments, which were so nice they made me cry.

Is niceness in academia that rare that once you come across it, it makes you cry? It's happened to me on more than this one occasion.

I was talking with my therapist about this: when writing comes easily, it somehow feels like it doesn't count, it couldn't possibly be real work if it is pleasant. What is up with that? Shut up you protestant work ethic police part of my brain!

I hear what you say about academic friendships being transaction-based relations, but I sort of want to yell that I DON'T WANT THEM TO BE. What I meant by needing funding to nurture relationships was referring to the possibilities to hang out in person, which the funding would allow. But yes, the shared political objectives of these transactions surely play into the maintenance of the relations.

Someone who left academia about four years ago was just writing on FB about attending an academic party last weekend and having been repeatedly asked how he now feels about his decision, and he said he found it funny because he had not thought about his decision to leave academia for several years, he was just focusing on his current job and career. I guess (and other people in the ensuing discussion pointed this out as well) that academics ask because his presence alone reminds them of the possibility of leaving that if he could make it elsewhere, maybe there's a chance for the rest of us/them too.

If I were to leave, I don't know whether I would want to have those discussions, being reminded of what could have been. I think that's also why the friendships die—one doesn't want to be reminded that there may be other ways of being (less toxic perhaps) than being an academic and the other doesn't want to think about what they may have lost by giving up on academia. Maybe.

This is getting long. Looking forward to hearing from you again!

Zzzzzzz

dear Zzzzzzz,

you are right, trying to get the Cosmo Men to entertain the possibility they might want cat ears would take monumental effort, and would indeed be a monumental achievement if this happened. I had not made the connection about how oppressively serious critical IR folks can be, but yes, it would also be for that same reason the 'non-Western' crowd at ISA would not want to wear them (unless their Cosmo Man rewards this). ISA is such an interesting microcosm of how IR and the world functions. I don't know what that says about me who thinks that; I know for many politics and feminist researchers around the world, ISA is not a particularly relevant or accessible platform and way of 'staying connected' in what's going on in the study of global politics. I was doing some ISA-thing this weekend (again delivered straight from my computer) and there was this 'oh and xx who is running for the President . . .', and I thought it was such a jarring turn of phrase. academics running to be presidents . . . of professional associations, of belonging to an association run in the logic of presidencies, of liberal democracy . . . and also, people understanding that we are talking about ISA (after all, just taking the sentence alone, one could wonder if perhaps xx is running to become the president of her country . . . or a country club). I am so far from their reality that it was actually very funny, almost like going to a wedding to support your good, good friend and rediscovering all the rituals and norms that you forgot about. this reminds me, if I was that person who left academia and got invited to an 'academic party' . . . i am not sure if I would go either.

Thinking some more about that academic party scenario and how both of us are like, 'eeek, that's no fun'. I wonder if that is why this letter writing is so much more meaningful (and fun) for us as a way to contribute to The Book. Because it is really more a sharing of ideas, thoughts and experiences wherein yes, at the moment of writing, academic-stuff is a strong theme because well, we are both in that space, but also it is couched in just two people having a conversation wherein 'the academic' is put in its rightful place—in our every-day lives—and we are not trying to have an academic anything never mind an academic party. though The Book could be read as an academic book. personally, I would be happy for it to be just a book, if some parts of it read like an academic book chapter, great, and if most of it reads like a mish-mash of things, great! if it raises questions in people and ourselves on whether it can count as an academic monograph, great!! I would be happy with that but that's just me. anyway, I don't want to ever host an academic (dinner) party ever again in my working and breathing life. I think back to those days when I hosted them (and went to a lot of them too), and I'm like, 'what was I trying to do? who was i?' I think this is why I am having such a hard time with how in-person academic workshops and conferences are already returning, because in a way, it will eventually mean a return of academic parties and I'm trying to figure out how I can do the work without the party. . . .

I was going to write about letters this round because I realized that I've been reading a lot of books written in the form of letters (and not just that one book I mentioned). funny, I looked around the house and suddenly these books are everywhere (sort of like how we talked about wanting to write about black cats and suddenly books on cats are everywhere in our respective homes). I was going to pull out all the letter books and send you a picture but it will have to wait till next time. I am so tired that don't even have the energy to do that today never mind string together sentences about them. *but I'm excited about the idea of doing this*, so I will when I'm less exhausted. even just thinking about it—the excitement—is making me feel less exhausted, and I'm coming around to the realization that that—the excitement about the idea—is enough, that I don't have to actually then do that thing. I did not get a chance to tell you before but Lee Lang, the author/singer-songwriter who inspired me to reach out to you about exchanging letters passed out from heavy bleeding recently because she was working so much right after she had her surgery to remove a cancerous tumour. she was doing work she loved but she was also very weak. I'm also thinking about Lauren Berlant, who recently passed, and in one of the essay collections remembering their life, one author recalled how Berlant was chairing a workshop they had convened but could not attend in person because they just had chemo treatment. the essay was about how despite their illness, Berlant was there for intellectual conversations and in their Zoom presence hovering over the room; there was just as much intellectual concentration, presence and clarity in their engagement, etc. when I read that I thought, yes, yes, but also whhhaaaat? what is this obsession to be working despite it all?

part of me understands. it is because one is unwell that one needs to write, to continue thinking things through with others . . . and to a certain extent, this is the only medication, but this medication also does not heal illnesses our bodies host, it does not address death. and we are living in the age of dying. so what does working even mean beyond that we need to make a living. 'make a living', what a funny English phrase. I mean, make money though. what does working even mean beyond that we need to make money to survive? when I read the news about lee lang's cancer and then saw she was still working, I worried but I also understood that she needs the money, but I also understood that it is possible she could not help herself—she needed to work—to speak, to get her voice out there—to be her, to feel herself. I don't know, I still think there is something entirely unnecessary about this.

when I opened the letter, I thought I was going to start by telling you all about this exciting gig I went to this weekend in the town I live in (so not Zoomed-in reality!); it was organized by two amazing young women who perform under the band name The Cellars who I knew nothing about. I went not expecting much, more out of curiosity and also because it was a fund-raiser for the Women's Center that I know (only in the vaguest sense of the word!) does good work to keep women safe in the community. but I was blown away, by these young musicians' performance but also all the other women—amazing voices, so much talent, so much truth in what they see, feel and communicate. and the people in the audience—I was like, these people live here? these people who are creating a safe space for the women artists to perform their voice by listening so intently and in solidarity? it was magical, something that I rarely feel in my daytime work-life. now, that is sad. why is it so hard to bring the nighttime magic into the daytime 'formal' spaces? why can't we have magical experiences as part of the job? and why can't creating magic pay better and be easier to do as one's job?

from chine

Chapter 17

on writing and on writing this book

Dear chine,

You said in your last letter: 'even just thinking about it—the excitement—is making me feel less exhausted, and I'm coming around to the realization that that—the excitement about the idea—is enough, that I don't have to actually then do that thing'. I think this is often what happens to me, I get very excited about ideas and might talk about them with someone, and somehow that often is enough. Or I don't have the stamina to actually follow through and put the ideas in writing, because when I start to write academese or 'IR' I hit a wall, I don't know how to write in the 'right' (BORING!) way. I was inspired by what you said in our Zoom meeting about wanting to write a book that you would want to read. I think that's the key to this whole thing, when I try to write something I would not even want to read, I fail. And that's why my list of publications remains short.

The other thing is what I mentioned in my last letter that somehow writing that comes easily doesn't count as 'work' or 'real writing' although those pieces that have come most easily have received the best feedback. A recently retired professor of cultural studies here has remarked that he's often ashamed to admit that writing is easy for him. Something to think about—why do we (or do we?) often talk about and think of writing as painful and hard? Is it because we don't have enough time for it (those 'you should be writing' memes)? Or is it because the format of academic writing is so boring and constricting? Or something else? Different things for different people surely, but there's this shared collective cultural thing, discourse, as well, no?

Hugs, Zzzzzzz

dear Zzzzzzz,

your question *'why do we (or do we?) often talk about and think of writ-ing as painful and hard?'* then is related to this, right? this being in control and perhaps all the energy focused—consciously—on all-knowing, all-understanding. I've had a glass of wine so I am probably not being very clear but hell, who cares? why care about clarity of the puzzle, what we cannot quite understand critically? I wonder if that was what Berlant was struggling with—this letting go (her famous yoga pose when she gave public talks)—but ultimately it is just a bad cycle, a relapse machine. 'it' being the (mind) body. Or (?) I cannot even desire to do the hard painful stuff at the moment, all I can do is comfort, letting go, enjoying my day, resting and complaining about not getting enough rest. and being ok with my unwellness and other people's. and writing from and about this place.

yes, I want to only write *what I want to read* but also what I need to read . . . which is written as if it is one's last book . . . so really nothing to hide or prove, just a free place to write and work, you know? I've been thinking about it as emptying for a long time now but also as dying, sort of like a small death, which I think is also a moment of hope because it is kind of like a small restart button forgetting the cycle. so it cannot even be a relapse, it just is. Our Book used to be part of that but somewhere, somehow, I'm so done with it. I was actually thinking, should we think about finishing up The Book for publication as just burning it? I am remembering Surprised writer's picture of her burning some horrible work emails (I think) she got and she shared that video (photo?) with us. that feels like an apt 'method' for the book, so yes, letter as a method for 'finishing up' The Book but also just burning the letters not so much as writing—so here not just letters like the ones we are exchanging but the letters as they say in English, which I think also means 'literature'/texts for the public?

I know Surprised writer is waiting for a response to her email, something that I've been thinking about, weighed down by, but I dunno. is there a book there? all I have energy for is to talk about it but putting this or some other method into action is going to be a bit of work. where is that energy going to come from? writing for work is not good for my health, I'm learning, which is why this letter with you is so interesting! this seems very good for my health and it also feels like work . . . in the sense I'm actually working (have my thinking cap on).

odd, puzzled and a bit too relaxed by the two glasses of wine I drank while writing to you. ok, dinner awaits!

hugs,

chine

Dear chine,

Being in control, disciplined into lean writing is definitely one of those things that make writing hard and unpleasant. I'm so happy about this letter writing, because it makes me think, but it is not forced at all. I can write down thoughts that are not fully formed, and maybe will never be anything more, but just putting some thoughts out there for you to read feels meaningful.

I think you have carried a lot of weight of The Book for the last few years, so I would totally be ok with you not giving it another thought or another minute of your time. Or perhaps at the end reading through and seeing that it's at least partly something you want your name on the cover, but not really putting more work into it. I'd be ok taking on more of the work, if I just know what to do and how, but maybe together with Surprised writer and Interventionist I can get things moving. I'm in such a better place mentally now than I've been for the last several years, and I'm quite happy you all did not let me quit the book when I tried, since it led to at least this letter writing. I do want to see the book finished, but am not sure whether it is possible, or what kind of book it will be. But I'm ok for it to be full of excess and don't care if some people think it is crazy and a waste of time; I'm sure it'll find some readers who get something out of it. I know some people need to read especially the kind of weird book it may turn out to be.

I keep saving things on FB as 'letters related' but then don't remember to share them with you or write about them. But here's something I read just today, I thought you might enjoy esp this part:

> I've come to a different conclusion: Forgiveness is a racket. A uniquely feminized scam to ensure the oppressed and mistreated redirect their anger inward instead of at those who have wronged them. (When it comes to harms like discrimination or sexual violence, it's also a clever way to make a systemic issue an individual problem.)
>
> In a world that tells women we're overreacting—or gaslights us into doubting our own experiences—resentment can be a radical act. Refusing to forgive acknowledges just how deep your hurt really is: When the people around you want you to just *move on* or *let it go*, your fury honors what really happened. Sometimes that feeling is the only 'proof' we have. (Valenti 2021)

Or enjoy might be the wrong word here, but you know, maybe you will get something out of it. In the emails with Marge we talked about anger that is not worth holding onto, but is sometimes resentment actually worth holding onto, like Valenti argues here? And how do we know the difference? I don't know.

But I do think it is interesting how she described that it is possible to be empathetic and resentful at the same time. I think often when we come to the conclusion that we need to let go of the anger or resentment, for our own good, we forget that maybe it is not either/or, but can be both/and?

I have to run. I'm going to lunch with a former colleague who retired this year; she's one of my all-time favorite teachers too. There's a bit of snow on the ground and it's almost sunny today. We're going to a new Georgian restaurant; the food is very good. Nice way to end the work week.

hugs,

Zzzzzzz

dear Zzzzzzz,

I have been mostly napping this week except to get up to do the absolute musts (and why are there still so many?!? aren't people tired? don't people stop?). once again, cats in internet came to justify my resting. my one regret really is not resting more all these years. chuckling here remembering how both of us answered surprised writer's question about what we would like to be doing if we did not work as academics . . . nothing, I'd be doing nothing if I did not have to work in academia or elsewhere. if I did have to work, I don't know if I need stable independent income and autonomy over my daily schedule so a low-key, low-rung academic job suits me in theory. only, I have problems with seeing too much wherever I find myself and I agree with Valenti, why should I 'forgive' the violence that the idiocy, the bullying, the arrogance of all these academics and managerial types inflict on me, the students and the world? I resent, and I hate, and I am ok holding onto my dislike of some very specific people who I specifically know harm those who are weaker than they in the name of 'discipline', 'rigor', 'neutrality', 'reason', 'seniority'—cowards. I had a colleague 'reason' with me and say, 'well, we should critique the structure and not blame the individual' followed by some excuses for the individual (he is a man of his generation, or he means well, or he is not alone, so many think this . . . etc.). well, the individuals are making these decisions when there are so many other ways they could have acted—the infinite possibilities, what happened to those? But also, I don't understand the either/or logic of 'stay structural in one's critique'. I think I can openly reject individuals who harm *with all of myself* AND at the same time, also theorize from these everyday experiences that does not necessarily lead to a call for separate worlds (or what mbembe calls a world in apartheid logic that constructs an enemy). I try to get there in my writing anyway, and I don't think holding onto my experiences and holding onto my rage is what is holding back my writing. if anything, it is probably the other way around, how it is such a process for me to take up space in writing and in 'real life'. it takes a lot to let myself be so i can get angry at what I see and experience, and hold onto that feeling to then let go and write from and for this place. I don't know what marge was specifically thinking though, we did not quite have this conversation in our brief exchange. I just get a lot of 'be reasonable' talking-to at work so I've been trying to just stay out of things as you know, but they come finding me and I have to respond. I wish I could just work and write from a place of peace, but it is a warzone here. just glad for the respite now that we are in the summer break months of the academic calendar here. at least some relief on one (home) front anyway.

I don't know why I carried The Book for us. no one asked me to, but you are right, I feel like I did and now I've exhausted myself. my own doing, benefit to no one. glad to hear you also think it is a thing though, hope the others are getting their rest too. and you. but I will just wait for instructions from the rest of you on The Book.

resting,
chine

PART III

Chapter 18

a shaking . . .

Hyvää huomenta. Dzień dobry. Maidin mhaith. 좋은 아침. Good morning. Bon dia. Bore da. Buenos días. Egun on. Aloha kakahiaka. Ata mārie.

We hope it hasn't been too much or too hard to read so far. But we think that there has to be somewhere for these sounds, thoughts and feelings to seep out, to pour out.

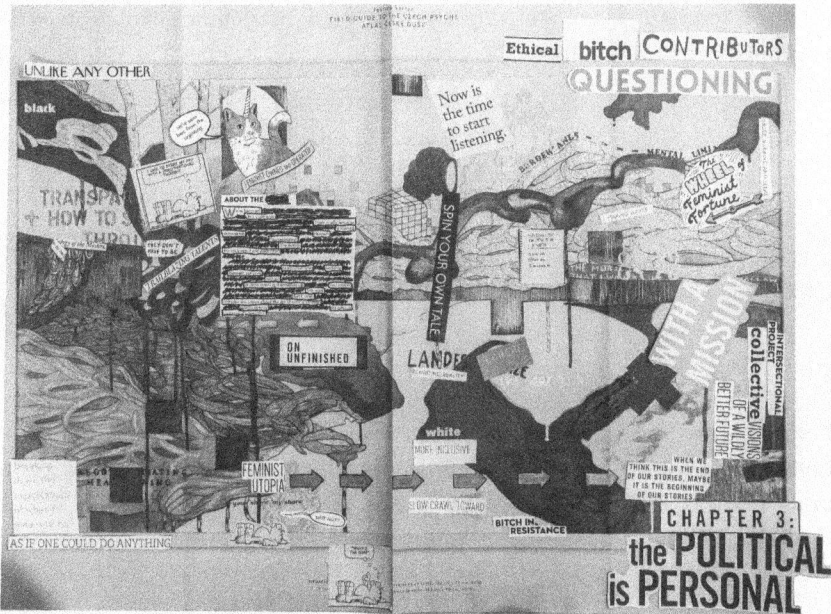

Collage by Ugly Feminist Collective

Of late our lives have been drenched with many human and nonhuman distractions which academia does not allow for and surreptitiously and/or actively discourages. We will and do allow time and space for them here because distractions matter. It matters to be distracted by bright blue skies, a doomsday clock moving closer to and then past midnight, wars breaking out, another wretched murder (of a black woman, of primary school children), the touch of a loved one, an Instagram post reminding you to take a break. We do so, too, knowing that academia is not a place that loves us (back) or a place that offers forms of living that nurture us. Loving and nurturing—relationalities we have had to cultivate through each other and through small gestures of care and support—holding space for each other, carrying the book when we have had the capacity to and asking others to shoulder the burden when we've been spent and with little left to give. Life is always happening. Demanding. Each of us have picked up (each other and the book) where and when we have been able, dipped in and out as our complicated lives have afforded us (or not) the time. Attempting, often badly, to enact little acts of love and care in the face of the gross inhumanity of the neoliberal university and a really shitty world.

None of this has been easy. For us. Or, we suspect, for you.

Despite all the words we have, all the words that tumble incessantly off our screens, out of the pages and between our virtual cybernetic connections, rage, pain, suffering and outrage at cruelties and discriminations are not meant to be t/here—well, in 'properly structured' academic writings anyway. Haunting and lurking and at the edges of this book has been a well of grief and grieving.

> For lives lost.
> For home.
> For welcoming communities.
> For better present-futures.
> For . . .

We have tried to make and hold space for these and other feelings, though allowable emotion and outrage has a heaviness in them; heavy-handedly racialized, gendering, colonizing, splitting the subject. Chaos, Black cat, Eelusive, Marge, Nuance queen, chine, Nokia, Surprised writer and Interventionist keep stumbling and tumbling, getting stuck, depressed and sick. This grief is sticky, and unapologetically so. But we also don't want to stay t/here. Pushing, pushing and pushing, it's time to shift. It's time to move our imaginations and thinking realms (though Surprised writer wonders about the idea of temporality . . .) to imagine and travel to other possible futures, on other trajectories and to other relationalities and modes of being, relating, speaking and listening. We want to feel and think more hopefully and joyfully because there is still so much work to be done—for this book and for the living that comes afterward.

To help us get unstuck, we chose to read our book with tarot cards (though our choice is [of course!] a modern witch tarot deck by Lisa Sterle). This might be a strange place to turn, or perhaps not with the idea of the frankenstinian subject as our muse. So we invite you to imagine a scene—Nokia, Interventionist and Surprised writer connect up to read a story about this book (one that has too often felt like a many-headed monster of our own making, burdensome and weighty, taking too long to figure out how to make use of its gangly limbs and walk out into the world); a story about an ugly feminist collective struggling with writing and life.

We chose a Celtic cross spread—consisting of ten cards, six in the shape of a cross and four to the right of the course; turning over three additional cards at the end of the reading an option we also embraced, to help us take stock of the 'now' and to inspire us to move in different ways. Not to leave our rage and pain behind, but to shift the centre to better make space for other imaginings and other ways of being in the world.

We invite you, dear reader, to wander into this bewitched imaginative world with us. For a little while at least. . . .

Tarot spread by mz

The first card Nokia, Interventionist and Surprised writer turn over was the *Five of Cups*. It is meant to signify the atmosphere surrounding us/the project (we and the book now cleaved together by a '/'). It's a bit of a sad card, weighed down with a sense of loneliness. There is a woman (we think she is anyway) standing at the edge of the water. Her back is turned, water lapping at her feet. The sky is grey and stormy. She appears to look mournfully downwards at the three cups toppled over at her feet—a sense of thoughtfulness, stillness and contemplation—a looking out at the water. Is it chaos trying to find some peace far away from where things are happening? Or is the figure Eelusive, working at the edge of things? Maybe it's how Marge feels in an academic discipline like IR—alone and lonely on the margins? We recognize Marge in each of us—maybe as the 'something' that drew us to one another. Or is it chine, expressing a sense of (yellow-tint) loneliness even when surrounded by people.

A bridge in the distance hangs like an invitation, but it seems too far away (it's exhausting to be Gromit—continuously building bridges and border crossing). 'It's been exhausting, it is exhausting', thinks the black cat and curls into a ball and takes a nap.

Or maybe it's not mournful sadness, loneliness or thoughtfulness at all. Maybe Nuance queen, Interventionist and Professor feminist are kicking over some (IR) cups. Or Nokia filling up the cups. Or Eelusive carefully turning over the cups to get rid of the poison in them, trying to fill them up with something else, some nourishment, something from their recent foraging excursions. And yet, the can of Spam chine added a while back can never be quite removed from the cups. Damn chine, damn Spam (damn American soldiers who introduced this expensive junk food everywhere they set foot to keep the Cold War hot). Nokia, Interventionist and Surprised writer wonder . . . is this the entangled and confusing atmosphere that has inspired the book?

Our sage suggests the *Five of Cups* holds traces of the trance of negative thinking. It also urges us to absorb successes not just (perceived) failures and the importance of shifting focus. Here we are trying to shift. All the while wearing a fabulous velvety black coat and cool boots (something Surprised writer would most definitely wear).

The next card we turn over symbolises our obstacle and is embodied in the *Knight of Pentacles*. On first look, it looks like a man on a horse—Cosmo Man on a high horse! Is *he* our obstacle? He's certainly been a thorn in our sides, but do we let him get in the way of this book? We do not think so! Though on closer inspection the knight looks quite queer and a bit sad and uncertain. Very sad. Definitely not Cosmo Man. Perhaps this look gestures to our sense of 'stuckness' and (sometimes) being at a standstill. Though it might be Chaos on the horse, unsure of how to get unstuck, hoping that the horse might make the decision for them; that it might move us despite getting stuck and working too slowly? Many other things have been stuck in place since the Covid-19 pandemic started. Maybe now is the time to ride into the sunset!

Our sage draws attention to feelings of disappointment that things are not moving forward, and instead toward unfulfilled expectations. We are drawn to the puzzle of an 'apparent' lack of progress, getting stuck in how things appear, rather than viewing the whole (thread). Time to pay attention to the details. Yup. Yup. Yup. Sometimes we get in our own way—not a failure, hardly, given the goddam obstacles. Our feelings of disappointment about the project have been because our expectations were too high and became quite serious, and our thinking happened in the scale of monuments despite our initial humble beginnings, of just wanting to stay playful, moving, laughing. But we see now, we are on a beautiful strong horse! We pick up speed. We're moving!

The Chariot represents what lies below us, the thing(s) holding us up. Our foundation(s). And what more could we ask for—a bad ass on a motorbike!! She looks amazing. Wearing a cool leather-looking jacket with moon symbols on her lapels, a wand in hand, and two regal Egyptian cats at either side. Not unthinkingly charging through though, but weaving, ducking, swerving. Wily and clever, depicting our feminist fore & present sisters and inspirers on whose shoulders we stand. In some ways too describing all of us, if differently: Chaos, Surprised writer, Interventionist, Nuance queen, Nokia, Tattooed laydee, Eelusive, chine, Marge, Professor feminist all woven together in her. Even the black cat is along for this ride, having found a companion and a counterpart. This is good. Really good. 'Keep steaming forward', it shouts at us (with our trusty animals).

One part of our cross now complete, we turn to the next.

The next card we turn over is symbolic of our past. It's *The Fool.* We rejoice. The card exudes a sense of joy and wonder. Arms open in invitation, the sun shining upon us. Full of joy and music. The Fool, like us, is so often misunderstood. It is not about being foolish in a conventional sense, but 'going gamely forward'. Being carefree, or at least having a sense that we can be unburdened; undone. This just might be the gift we first gave one another—license to be carefree because we have each other's backs. A bit of a cliff, though! But she's okay! Isn't this what we do/have to do/have been doing all along—keep(ing) at that cliff edge, dancing and laughing in the face of it? The mainstreamers are not anywhere near the cliff; they're too scared. But not us. We want to be at the precipice and we're not afraid of looking stupid with our Benedict Cumberbatch masks, making our unruly, disruptive frankenstinian way into professional spaces. Taking chances is what we embrace, even when there is a possibility of falling and failing. It's okay, we think, just wear sensible shoes (e.g., warrior sandals). Very hippy trippy and faerie like, she could fly off with her billowy sleeves. But she has a backpack on and flowers in her hair—full of lovely juxtapositions.

Though none of this is easy. But the book has always been about taking chances. Going with our gut instincts. Going lightly yet bravely has been integral to the project. There's something powerful about embracing the fool—a willingness to be foolish and experimental—in the academy. Court jesters knew what to do to save their lives. We embrace the fool!

The Fool gamely takes us to our crowning thoughts, possibilities and our future(s). We turn over *The High Priestess*. Dripping with a sense of assuredness, our high priestess is on a chair with a laptop perched on her lap, the moon purposefully pinned by her high-heeled knee-high boots. She's wearing a spectacular royal blue dress with flowing sleeves and a crown on her head. Quietly powerful. Casually in control. Very settled, but her look is a 'don't fuck with me' one. She is in command. Giving the mainstream/critical boys the side-eye.

Our sage offers wisdom: urging us to trust our instincts and transcend our fears—to touch what is limitless and make time for spirit and the spiritual. We need the spiritual for our healing, for understanding and making sense of that which seems ungraspable. Some say that the spiritual core is there inside all of us, but we assume that we have to work harder to get to it . . . actually it is about realising that the higher wisdom is within ourselves; it is another form of self-reflexivity we have been talking within feminism. Moving towards the self-realisation of the spiritual realm also means acceptance of so much that is unresolved, that will not fix itself. Remember composting anger? You can only compost if you accept that not all of it will decay in a good way. You have to choose what you compost and gradually with practice it becomes better and better . . . you begin to know instinctively what is not compostable. You start weaning them out. Spirituality helps you compost better. It helps you choose your battles, your anger that must fill up the compost. It helps you wean away the distractions. And there are too many. Nuance queen's feminist axiom is—the spiritual is the personal is the political. It is simply a greater awareness of the 'self' and its limitless potential to reform, adapt, change, rage, comfort and compost.

Nokia, Interventionist and Surprised writer move to the sixth and final card in the cross to the card signifying our present. We are gifted with the *Queen of Swords*. We like the *Queen of Swords*. We like her very much. She exudes confidence. A sword in a hand. Two feet firmly on the ground. Yet she sits on a throne high up in the clouds. A bird and butterfly carved into the throne. A far cry from the turmoil the book has been mired in for years. We've been hopping around, sometimes on one foot, at other times limping! She is steely, bringing order to the turmoil (although we will never give up on the productiveness of commotion & turmoil) through clarity and boundaries (the ones we want, not those imposed on us). We imagine ourselves and the book like her outfit: the top half like a corset, rigid and bound, but the bottom half flowy and free. Bad ass shittery wearing white boots. Oh, the energy!

Closing down boundaries between each scene. The book, so far, moving through so much complaint and grievance, it's time to shift the energy and work with creativity, fierceness, but also the need to have some steely resolve *(but don't forget, there has been creativity, fierceness and steely resolve in the complaints and grievances too, whispers chaos).* There is a sense of freedom to be found in this positionality/orientation.

Now we move on to the four cards to the right of the cross.

The first card captures *us*, our collective self. We turn over the *Six of Wands* reversed. After three rounds of shuffling at the beginning, six cards were chosen at random, reversed and placed back in the deck. It is interesting that we pulled one of these and it is the number six. It must be important.

Reversals . . . let's imaginatively 'hop' over one of those bridges for a minute—a bridge to the conventional. If we ponder the upright image of a traditional deck—the *Six of Wands* often depicts something more 'male', haughtier. And all white. The traditional tarot sense is of garnering attention through excellence. Oh my—the white masculinist 'holy grail' of so much of contemporary academia. No wonder this card appeared reversed for us! So much work to do to trample the worst, the normal of the academy. The normal measuring of citation numbers, publications, grants: 'mine is bigger than yours', the normal reviewer 2 who acts more as a bully than a colleague (no we're apparently not all in this together), the normal looking over your shoulder trying to find more important people to talk to, the normal whisper networks: 'don't ever be alone with that dude', and the other normal whisper/rumour networks: 'oh she just didn't have what it takes to make it' . . . and so many other things that pass as normal as has become evident in the previous sections of this book.

In Sterle's deck, the *Six of Wands* transgresses its figuration in the traditional tarot deck. The *Six of Wands* is embodied by a black woman. She is very cool with trendy, ripped jeans. She wears great earrings and fabulous red boots—oh yes! Very solid and firm. There's a white woman in the background holding up one of the wands. Nokia, Interventionist and Surprised writer read this in two ways: holding space for women of colour on the one hand and holding white feminism to account on the other.

Our sage offers this: don't let the opinions of others dictate how you feel about yourself. Keep your eyes on your own paper. Time to enforce an authentic sense of oneself. But we aren't sure about the authentic bit . . . what does it mean to be authentic? True?

Our hopes and fears are embodied in the *Four of Pentacles*. It very much speaks to the desire for security and safety, and perhaps a fear of exposure. What are we afraid of? She wears a big warm winter coat. A sense of Northern Novembers—maybe foretelling when the book will be finished, and with this foretelling of the place of the sense of time in the book. We read this card as symbolic of our fear of letting go of the project. She/we cling to one of the pentacles. Two others pinned underneath her/our feet. Tied down. She/we hold tightly to the thing.

The project has dragged on in all the negative senses of the word, but it has also given us something to hang on to especially in these uncertain pandemic times and proliferating 'war-times'. Nokia keeps wondering whether to stay in academia or not. Interventionist is worn out, worn down. What's going to happen to 'us'—the ugly feminist collective—when it's done? Holding onto the book. Standing on the drafts! The final draft is hanging over her/our head!

Hang on.

And where and to what have we been hanging on? What has been our hanging-on environment of late? Our environment, the cards tell us, is *The Hermit*. It feels right and it really has been our environment for the past several years. Moving slowly. Taking our time. Taking time. We have certainly done this! Slowness. Checking in. Examining feelings that have been put on ice. Wearing comfortable pyjamas. Leisure wear. No shoes. Warm, homey feeling. Laptop—opening, closing? Inside. Home. Permission for all the slowness. Maintaining trust. Peaceful. Not anxious. Healing time. Importance of getting away from the awfulness of the world/university, etc. Returning. Shutting out. Trusting our inner wise ones. Can you feel the warm embrace, dear reader?

We have one final card to turn over, the ONE signifying our 'outcome'. Yes, we turn over *The World*! Utter bliss. Kali embodied. COMPLETION! Finishing a huge life cycle. Giving birth to our project. Libidinous. Ecstatic. Happily exposed. No need for clothes or costume; a draped scarf will suffice. A wand in each hand. Kali in a silky nightie with her hair wildly down!

We draw three more cards as futures are always multiple possibilities and open trajectories: *Seven of Wands*, *Queen of Pentacles*, *The Star*. What delights! Healing time, care time. Full circles. Letting go. Rest.

Extended tarot spread by mz

Interlude: Our Tattooed laydee Sideshow

There is a small flicker of light in a darkened room. A figure sits in a chair, their back to you. They turn around, lifting their face towards the light . . . it's the Tattooed laydee.

Ah, she says, *perhaps you were expecting me earlier in this tarot spread scene.*

Right? The mystery, esoteric knowledges, and so on. That's part of it, you see. As I said earlier, often I am just an analytic.

She pauses, reflecting.

Much like 'Indigeneity' I suppose—both can be useful analytic categories. Yet they are only tangible when anchored to specific people in specific places. Otherwise people insert themselves into that analytic framework wherever they like . . . lifting us out. Appropriating or crossing boundaries.

Yes, she muses further, *tangible when anchored to specific people in specific places. And also specific times.*

She looks directly at you.

Now is one of those times.

The tattoos along this Tattooed laydee's arm seem to shift and glow slightly as she shuffles what looks like a set of tarot cards. Is this another reading?

No, she chuckles. *Well, not one for you anyway.*

You see, the 'we' in the reading in the last section is a specific one, a partial 'we' if you will. While that 'we' was and is fully meant for the people involved, there are marked differences among those who participated and those who did not. That too is part of being in this collective.

So I appear here and now, as this particular Tattooed laydee. She twirls in the chair, just once. *The analytic noted earlier has shifted, as I am now speaking from and within anchored specifics.*

She sighs. Phrasing this part is tricky. *I cannot speak for others and their practices. But as parts of the collective 'we' drew cards and entangled us all spirituality—I was also pulled in. You see, for the methods I was trained in, I do not read for people I do not know without preparation, nor do I read for people without their consent.*

She looks at you. *I do not know you well, yet.*

Reading for and as a collective can be contradictory—some may not feel it is right for them, others may be drawn to do it, knowing it is right for them, in those moments. Readings across temporalities and via different communication methods further entangle things . . . and people. Whether they wanted it or not.

This Tattooed laydee looks at her arm as one of the curls of ink around her wrist pulses. She nods, then begins to shuffle again.

Interestingly, tarot cards have a lot to do with IR; I have always seen them as a model for it. The communities I learned this skill from, the communities my families are from, use these decks and these skills in other ways besides gaining insight or clarity in times of crisis. They read cards as a way to pay their fare. As a way to feed their family (human and nonhuman). As a way to shift favour. As a way to influence those in charge. Once that I know of, as a way to avoid being assaulted.

That is not to say those card readings were false, far from it! When any of us read for ourselves or others—we are interpreters of these cards, of those forces which communicate with us in these ways. Much like IR interprets larger forces that we as nations, as communities, as families and collectives must live and work and deal with—whether we choose to or not. Cards can be useful in many ways.

This Tattooed laydee puts the deck in her lap. She opens her hands to you. *I speak from over thirty years of experience working with tarot decks as a reader. I was taught by people who, as far as I know, have learned the processes I was taught and engage with for over three centuries, roughly eleven generations. Given that the origins of what we call tarot cards are older than that, and their predecessors in reading are even older—it is likely these practices are much older than 300 years. That seems wondrous to me, yet that history is infinitesimal in the larger scale of things, as Eelusive likes to remind me.*

Still . . . these decks and what they can do are meaningful to me. Perhaps they are meaningful to you, too. That's why I am here, now. To share a few things with you, that I know are appropriate to share.

She picks up the deck again, tracing the pattern on the back of the top card. *I do want to reiterate that in this collective there are differences among how we view cards, readings, and who we read for.*

How I learned and practice and actively teach—you are entangled with those you read for.

For now, I am already entangled with these other wonderful writers here. That is without question, but I am not yet entangled with you as a reader.

And I am not ready to take on all that being entangled with others in that way entails—not right now.

If this resonates for you in whatever you are going through, know that there are ways to disentangle yourself. There are ways to put space between yourself and the person you read for so that you are not so fully enmeshed in what happens, their future choices, what they may see, do, and say about you from the reading interactions.

She pauses, then nods. *We often do this in IR when we have particularly difficult case studies or difficult subjects that are close—perhaps too close—for us.*

This research practice is not a dissimilar one, yet not exactly the same.

I touch on it because it is tangentially related and after all, this is a book that reveals IR's many forms, facets and tendrils.

This Tattooed laydee turns to fully face you, her face finally all in the light.

So I cannot read for you yet, nor will I read in front of you, entangling you and me further with what flows through this particular deck. I cannot take on that burden with everything else going on.

One of the fascinating things about being a reader? The older we get, the more knowledge and power we have working with it, yet the less we actively seem to 'do'. As women and nonbinary folks progress as readers, we are more able to actively protect ourselves working with difficult topics, with difficult people. Difficult here meaning that it is not people who are fixed as difficult, but the situations they're in, the energies they carry and exude—those can be very, very difficult to handle, to process.

We can handle that. We've learned to handle it—as another skill set.

A skill set people want to play with: laughing and dressing up on Halloween, or calling 800 numbers, hoping the person on the other end of the line has the skill set to be able to connect with them and do a reading over a distance, which is another skill.

She pauses. *Not everyone who answers or can read has that, by the way—so call or videochat carefully.*

We are caricatures, like the Tattooed laydee, operating within prescribed parameters, putting on a show. The radical work happens . . . outside of those markers.

The Tattooed laydee sits again, pulling a small table in front of her.

Truthfully, I might not have chosen a Celtic cross spread, but that was useful for the parts of us who did it. I read often with them for about fifteen years, but something in that structure was frustratingly obfuscated for me. And not in a productive way. Then, I was told I was ready to create my own layouts to use with others. So I did.

Eelusive starts to enter the scene, this Tattooed laydee spins, glares, and Eelusive recedes while mumbling about protocols and training models. Tattoed laydee turns back to you.

Eelusive isn't wrong, it is important to note protocols—but those differ and have been broken and remade and recreated. It's just not the space here for unpacking all that. What matters for us here is that I was given the OK to create this, have tested it, refined it—and can offer it.

Not as a reading here. What I want to offer you is a layout. A spread.

She chuckles.

A way to assess what the hell is going on—and what is not actually happening.

This is a layout I designed when I worked as a tarot reader as a means of income, then that tapered to reading for others I knew as a form of exchange and reciprocity.

Regardless of the exchanges, this was designed for people who had frustrating and/or urgent questions about a particular issue as people usually turn to tarot when they are a bit confused and/or unsure about what to do. I refined this for about a decade, and I am still surprised by what it can do and teach.

What I give you is a specific layout. That is to say, the position of the cards and what it represents to the questioner, the person in need of insight.

This structure offers a sharply focused meditation or response, designed for one particular topic, question, or concern. It can help guide you to see what is and what isn't. There are many different options for making choices; it gets harder when crises emerge on various scales.

Let me offer you a different one.

This Tattooed laydee reaches into her pocket, then lays out seven silver coins (it was laundry day). Two on top, then one below between them, to form an inverted triangle. She leaves a space, then places another three coins to form a triangle below that one, this one pointing up. Then one last coin between the two triangle points.

She looks at you. *Remember that order, ok? Here you have two triangles. Where the points come together has a small space between them. One final card (or other reading medium) goes there, last.*

Lay out each triangle one at a time. The first triangle is the here-and-now. You, asking. The deck and reader, responding. In the upper left of the top triangle, you have <u>What it is</u>.

Which is to say what the situation is about: What is one of those core moments that lead the questioner—I'll call them 'you' for the rest of this part—to this point?

What is one of those core drives bringing this person here, to ask about a particular situation?

If you do it for yourself—and I do suggest you do these for yourself—they can be enlightening.

They are one of a few layouts I know that can be equally clear for ourselves and for others.

Back to what it is—what brings you to this point with this layout in front of you.

Across from it, in the upper right corner is <u>What it is not</u>.

She chuckles. *Prepare for some swearing here, some denial—especially from yourself. This position signifies something you think is connected to or driving your current issue or concern. This can be something you want to be involved, or you feel sure is the cause, or perhaps it is the reason you say out loud to others but know is not true. Whatever your reasons—this position lets you know what is not your main drive and should not be the main focus.*

And in the centre, the point leading down, is <u>Advice</u>.

This offers a way to balance the two of them, lifting away the onionskin of what it is not to show more of what this situation is.

This Tattooed laydee sits back, looking at you for a moment. Then she continues.

Now we get to the bottom triangle—the yet-to-come. In the practices I learned—and the reason I designed this layout this way—what is going to be, what can be, is a tipping point. It draws from past patterns and histories to shape future possibilities.

What I referred to as the 'here-and-now' so to speak? That is balanced on top of this one.

The two move and shift. You asking about something that is clearly moving or troubling you already shifts things. Hopefully it keeps the two in more balance with each other, but I digress.

So the bottom left—<u>What it will be</u>. That is, one of the very likely outcomes. Perhaps it is one of the things perhaps you are hoping for, or perhaps . . . not. But what you get from this card here is likely to happen.

On the bottom right—<u>What it will not be</u>. This addresses future paths you are locked into: fear or eagerness or concern or stress. Whatever it is, you can let that go. Because it is likely not to be there or happen. And if it does, you can handle it, you have others and support around you.

You will be able to handle it one way or the other. Whatever is here, this should not be your main focus.

And in the centre—another point of <u>Advice</u>. Now you have two points.

The above and the below, the now and the future—or the past is future if you will.

And in the middle? There is space for one final card, a card that connects those two points.

Lay it out last, after thinking about the two triangles, and what is and is not there.

Reveal this final guide point for you after those first two triangles.

This Tattooed laydee leans back for a moment, she touches the coins, then the deck of cards.

Ah, you see I did not use cards for a very specific reason. It is too easy to get caught up in what the cards may mean, which cards may be there, or may not—instead of focusing on the positions, and the overall structure and order of what I offer.

So we'll stick with these coins.

What I find interesting about this reading is it has a lot of flexibility, it too is an analytic to assess where you are at, what you want and do not want, and how to prepare yourself for what may come or what is likely to come. As boundaries become increasingly porous between the personal and political, between spiritual work and applied IR, what I offer here is an analytic that is useful in many different frameworks.

For example, I used it at several points in my dissertation work to help me assess what I wanted to get through in a particular chapter, what I was caught up on and what I needed to let go.

This allowed me to step away from the words on the page, the words on the screen, the words in my head, and think about a particular urgent motivation and situation differently.

This Tattooed laydee's arm tattoo begins to flicker and move slightly in an area by her inner elbow. She nods, then begins to pick up the coins.

This interlude was difficult for me to navigate—but I was called here. One way of answering is with reciprocity. I am giving you a tool to assess, to read yourself or to read for others who need some guidance.

And you apply this layout with whatever you are connected to, use some of your favourite signifying objects that are of equal size and weight: dice if those have meaning for you, playing cards, coins, there are many ways to engage this. What you put in the spaces is up to you; this analysis framework is offered here as a gift.

Keep it with you as we move into the next sections and after you close this book, or shut down the computer or tablet. Or ignore it altogether—you are not obligated to accept this or carry it further. The choice is yours.

I have presented this to you because I am not ready to entangle with you, these cards, their energies and histories, my limitations within the Tattooed laydee construct . . . but what I can offer is a way for each of us to know a bit more about themselves.

For me, this is one of the most important skill sets we can pass along with these types of readings. And the most important lesson from any reading? I always ask questioners, including myself, after the cards have been shuffled, my hand on the top of the deck, but before any card is drawn: <u>What is the card you most want to see? What is the card you do not want to see at all?</u> Be honest—this is important to understand before going further.

This Tattooed laydee pockets the coins, wraps the deck in a faded cloth, and pushes back into the shadows, becoming once again an indistinct analytic—the Tattooed laydee.

What do you want to see? What do you not want to see any more of?

Chapter 19

feminist practices of
knowledge formation . . .

What are feminist practices of knowledge formation? What might they look like? How might they feel? Are there really (helpful) answers to these questions? Perhaps for thinking . . .

Perhaps it seems a 'tired' thing to say—but when feminists gather, the spectre (is she such?) of 'woman' emerges—even if tangentially and ethereally. In women's studies, in gender studies, in feminist politics, 'woman' was and continues to be a useful departure point for much writing, thinking and acting. But 'she' is always surely (just) that—an opening for moving and thinking. And 'knowing'? But 'woman' is never a destination point for feminist practices of knowledge formation. What follows or unravels from opening question(s) of 'woman' unearths hosts of questions about sex, gender, sexuality, bodies, identities (and always much more). Questions which always invite interrogation, perhaps raising anxieties for some.

But let us start again from a slightly different place. Feminist practices of knowledge formation as a project, is a project of keeping the meanings and contours of feminism and politics open as a series of question marks and commas.

Could the project also be a way of asking what feminism and what being a feminist means? asks chine, tired of people taking feminism as an identity card, a certificate, a desired postal code. professor feminist chimes in—do we need sure answers to that? Though yes—yes always to feminism! Feminism is such an organic set of things, activities, feelings, senses, ideas . . . do we need to tie it down? This group of writers, feelers, thinkers—we do know we are feminists, don't we? Even if we know we don't always 'do' feminism in the ways we might want/hope to/are expected to—how could we? It's the work, the moving forward, the pushing forward (however hard the resistances) and the commitment that makes—just makes. . . . Also yes to not privileging knowledge creation, and to remaining open to what happens when knowledge claims are expanded, interrogated, turned upside down, asked irrelevant questions, interrupted, translated, made to speak to people not at people, explored to amplify not clarity but also obscurity. . . .

Feminism works to massively reconfigure what counts as knowledge and knowing, and also importantly, works hard at 'not-forgetting' the small, banal, the seemingly trivial, the prosaic. As Adrienne Maree Brown (2017) affirms, 'How are you in this moment in history is really important and all of that small stuff matters. All of the big things we are longing for are only made up of a lot of small, personal, radical choices.' And to acknowledge feeling as knowing.

We want to work with the 'livingness' of things—viscerally working with the chaos and tumultuousness of living and being in a complex worldscape. And so, it has been very important how we have done all this—there has been much collaging, collaborating, writing, ranting, talking, falling apart, holding—together. And always working at being unfaithful and irreverent to the origins of disciplines and their governing texts. This has made us (revealed us?) as very vulnerable. Being cynical and critical can seem to be the easiest things to do in the face of—well, all 'that'. The hardest thing is to be optimistic and to fantasise; to relentlessly imagine, demand and work toward alternate and better futures. Dreaming in this sense asks something of us that being cynical and critical do not facilitate—indeed foreclose. We want to explore other ways, other trajectories. . . .

Chapter 20

trajectories . . . ?

Another day, another Zoom call, this time someone Surprised writer hadn't spoken to or seen for many years. Someone who has decided to finally leave academia after witnessing the crushingly cruel behaviour of her university in 'covid-time'. One of the most joyful, heartful people she's ever known, the conversation feels like a gift. Surprised writer has been watching the different dying stages of her bloodied violated white roses—created as a plea to art for help—and she has them in her eye line as they talk.

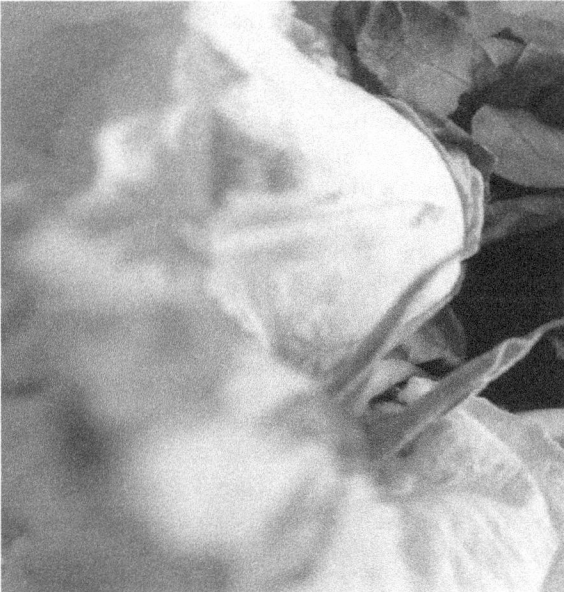

Flowers by mz

The tarot reading comes up, a little surprisingly. Tarot came by accident to Surprised writer some time ago—an old friend gifted her a (Rider Waite) deck, offering the assistance they had given her. Unnerved by the idea of tarot but curious, she started to find out how to learn about the cards. They were fascinating, though she truly hated the blokey ones! She decided she would re-gender the ones she didn't think were helpful in their cold masculinist prerogative. The gift (clearly a theme here . . .) of the possibility of thinking about and imagining diverse interpretations and varied future/s was very appealing. Though that multiplicity in life also felt impossible. Their Zoom conversation criss-crossed the corporate cowardly excesses of academia, the beauty of thinking philosophically, and reading tarot cards—which led them to the idea of trajectories. . . .

. . . .

Routes, courses, flights, paths, lines, arcs, curves, trails, traces, tracks—some of the words that the thesaurus throws up as alternatives for trajectories. Some of these seem to have more possibilities of movement and shifting than others—but still, all of them hold the possibility of movement (even lines . . .). Movement—the staggered, staggering stuff of life. Keep moving. Sometimes reduced to shuffling when the chase of colonialism, racism, misogyny, class and so much more is too heavy, too close, too populous, too intent. As we hurtle toward the middle of the twenty-first century, hot and cold wars rage, body parts (most often queered/trans/gendered feminine) criminalized and controlled by cruel states, disparities in sickness, health, wealth and the ability to just live—increasingly egregiously obscene. It is hard not to despair, to fold in and under the stinging heft of lonesomeness and hopelessness all of this engenders. Though we might remember the gifts and shifts offered through the twins of thinking philosophically and reading tarot cards to open up some different arcs and trails for you and for us: 'we do not know what we're capable of until we experience the displacement of the limits that we've been made to believe and obey' (Gago 2020, 2).

In some ways our book works with methodologies of 'the strike' as Verónica Gago articulates this. Gago tells us how striking exposes the invisibility of that which keeps worlds moving—her specific focus being on Argentina and the 'women's strike.' For us, a feminist/queer writing/thinking strike works to refuse white straight/masculinist forms of writing, thinking and being, but also to refuse to accept the invisibility of all those forms of our labour and the labour of those 'othered' which is so easily disappeared. Taking inspiration from Katherine McKittrick (2021), writing this book in this (unseemly) way is our way 'to hold on to the rebellious methodological work of sharing ideas in an unkind world' (7).

So we work here to mix everything up, epistemologically, methodologically, emotionally and psychically to help us trace the relationships between different sorts of violence which seem unconnected, yet rely on each other in layers of fraternal loyalties. We, as undisciplined frankenstinian subjects, have to keep taking these (institutionally) strange and fragmented trails to lay bare the prosaic violences and other possibilities. This trail, this path will swerve and arc, sometimes abruptly, shockingly, confusingly—here momentarily taking us to *Frankenstein in Baghdad* (Saadawi 2018). In this tale, torn and broken corpses are sutured back together—a nose from one corner of the street, ears from somewhere else—by Hadi who doesn't want the shredded dead to be treated like street rubbish. Life (re)animates and slaughter commences. Set in post-US-invasion Baghdad, this horror tale invites a retelling and rethinking of truth and violence, not least around war's absurdity. Conventional scholarly tracing through causal chains of strategy and war-laws 'leads in time to a young man with a packed lunch in his pocket blown into little more than a scarlet mist, and nothing comes of it' (Saadawi 2018). We say 'no' to thinking that leads us to bodies turned into scarlet mists and where nothing comes of it.

Conversation that feels like a gift reminds Nokia of Sámi duojár Jenni Laiti, who writes about freedom, living beautifully, and traditional Sámi art & handicrafts as gifts to one's community. Nokia wonders how we can be freer in academia, freer from the violences we impose on each other and our bodies (existing constantly at the brink of burnout is a serious violence to our bodies—and may end up killing us). Susanna Hast says that she does not believe it is possible to be free, if you don't care about others' freedom, and Jenni Laiti writes that freedom is a communal experience. Maya Angelou famously says none of us can be free until everyone is free. Freedom thus arises from a sense of belonging and being seen and not on the basis of sameness. In the process of writing (and not-writing) this book Nokia has felt a sense of belonging and being seen in ways that she finds rare in conventional academic spaces. To quote Laiti (2021): 'Freedom means living beautifully and taking care of others and your surroundings. It means I can exist as part of my community and the world as exactly the person I define myself to be'.
How do we live beautifully in academia?
Or is it an impossibility because of what neoliberal academia has become, and viscerally magnified in pandemic times?

On a small scale—like in workshops, panels, seminars, and writing this book—it is possible to work in freedom-increasing ways and practice generosity. But so often it feels in this unkind hyper-individualised environment of the academic game that people are more interested in hearing what they themselves have to say and where they say it (journals with high impact factors) than about building communities and spaces of freedom. So thinking of these things we do in academia (written texts, comments, reviews etc.) as gifts to the community seems particularly important to introduce to our everyday language about research. Not only the academic communities we want to belong to but the other communities we are part of as researchers and as humans. Here, the idea of academic 'service' could be understood differently too. Rather than approached as something that is not part of the research and a separate sphere of action within academia, what if research was seen as service too? *Interventionist asks, 'but service to whom and toward what?'*

Maria Bargh (2020) argues for a holistic approach to academic freedom which might take us some of the distance in answering this question. Bargh reinterprets the ongoing 'academic freedom' debate in Aotearoa/New Zealand (a split/cleaved socio-cultural-political reality) which tends to be simplistically performed as one about 'being a critic of conscience' conceived as being independent and oppositional to 'mātauranga Māori/kaupapa Māori approaches (where emphasis sits on community priorities driving research)' (253). By refusing the separation of academic knowledge and service to/in communities, Bargh argues for seeing academic freedom and service going hand in hand to keep power in check, and introduces the term *Take-Utu-Ea* to recast academic freedom as a mechanism of rebalancing. Take-Utu-Ea is 'a process of identifying where things have become unbalanced in people's lives and in communities, and using a mechanism to resolve disputes and rebalance' (252). Freedom as a mechanism of rebalancing rather than a mechanism of/for autonomy, service as a way to keep connections with communities and people we are accountable and connected to *and yet* are independent from which is afforded to us in academia. These insights are possible only when we insist on bringing our whole selves to academic spaces, remaining rooted and also free, staying curious about what one wants to make claims to and also what claims us despite ourselves.

A whole self like this one:

> When I was burned out, I realised afterwards that I had become extremely cynical, this meant that I did not get excited about anyone else's work nor did I feel like I had anything to say or contribute, for example in conferences and seminars. I could be immensely critical, and not in any kind of constructive way. I mainly felt that anything anyone was trying to say was meaningless, I did not see anyone's work as a gift to myself or the academic community. Rather, each

thing that I had to read or listen to felt tedious. In that mental and bodily state, it is very hard to be generous. Being burned out and depressed is an ugly living in an unkind world.

Even when I have felt better, I've realised that it may be difficult to be generous to those who are in the cynical mindset—and who in academia isn't burned out (or at least almost) especially after the last few years? But I also think trying to actively practice generosity can protect one from burning out and keep one in the realm of living beautifully. 'What if it was considered cool to express support for other people even if they're not your friends'? What if we practiced generosity all the time by telling our academic friends and those we don't yet know, but whose work we have read, how meaningful their work is and how meaningful their presence in the academic spaces is? 'What if we started making our parallel universes one week at a time [one DAY at a time even], and then expanded all of those weeks [and days] until they touched, and extended them over time, and they became just the way things are'? (Schickele 2015, 249–50)

Ugly. We call ourselves the *ugly feminist collective.* In part this is to embrace and reject all the ways in which we will have all been called or positioned as ugly—too fat, too foreign, too old, too shouty, too messy, too quiet, too bossy, too insistent, too much. Though of course we are not the 'ugly feminists'! Even though this is often a tautology for mainstreamers—ugly thinking, ugly methodology—think planet white boys. But we hope to be a lovely and generous ugly feminist collective offering this book as a gift to you—and to ourselves. That's all.

Nuance queen keeps saying that she only committed to this collective and this book when most of us managed to gather in person in Gothenburg in the summer of 2019. Chaos wants to understand this refrain but does not. That was the beginning, she thinks, we saw it as a book because it is the beginning, and the book is mostly about middling and muddling through. What does it mean to see the book as a thing? Do books that can be seen as a thing only get to exist? Nothing still has a right to exist, already exists despite our refusal to acknowledge it and express 'our indebtedness and gratitude' to it, no?

Nuance queen: I am busy, I will respond tomorrow!

A week passes by.

Another week passes by.

But who is counting these weeks matters, certainly it is not Nuance queen who is too busy just managing the work, the life situations, the emotions, the grief, the turmoil! To be living time as accountable, as a thing with clarity. So you see, dear reader, the book might always have been an effort at feeling—creating a point of nothingness so as to also experience the muddled way conversations go and do not go. Writing happens and does not happen, projects begin and re-begin each time the writerly self—is this the Real Researcher, the serious academic—returns. The sweet memory of clarity, a sense of beginning that is exhilarating, a collective in-formation is all just that—a moment captured by technology so as to make it exist, make it real . . . but the real is in the obscure, in writing darkly. Could this be a trajectory, a path? Surprised writer, what do you think?

Surprised writer: Hmmm. Let me think . . . we/I always need time to think . . . it's all too hard most of the time . . . and 'covid-time' is still shattering—and all those expectations and assumptions that swirl tightly around, wrapped up in *such* tired categories. Default mode is to shrink back—keep quiet—hide stories—always in turmoil—and exhausted—tired strangling categories.

Interventionist is tired of getting into the middle of things. She hangs up her interventionist coat. She'd rather work at the edges.

Nuance queen: Ok, I am back.

Unravelling.........the ice-cream here! :)

Ugly Feminist Collective retreat (Göteborg 2019) by sc

wine n candies ingredients for creativity.

Ugly Feminist Collective retreat (Göteborg 2019) by sc

women, monsters, friends.....thinking n writing together.

Ugly Feminist Collective retreat (Göteborg 2019) by sc

Prelude: An eel-like flash

Eelusive comes out sideways. They tumble, brush themselves off, and stand before you.

Perhaps you have been wondering where I have been. I have been here and there in the book, but this . . . is my first time talking with you.

They look down for a moment, then remember, *I should project a power body-language position. This is my serious scholarly section.* They put their hands on their hips, feel ridiculous doing so, then stop.

They go back to moving around slightly as they speak with you: hands moving, arms in motion, pacing a bit. Being in motion is soothing. Proprioception is one way they understand the world around them—and academic writing and publishing is a very weird world. They begin anyway.

My family comes from an eel community. Much like the eels that I love, and I now realize have shaped my life and work, I have gone through several cycles. This next section is me (re)turning to evolve again, to shift and change. This time though—the changes for you, and others around me.

As you read this action, know that this is a way of introducing myself. When I say to you dear reader, I am clarifying why I call you that. I hope you enjoy this ride. It is the way I think and work—ideas coming to the surface, then embedded deep within metaphor, and story—always story. Demanding that I grasp concepts, ripping and decontextualizing them out of particular places and times sometimes is not possible. But you can see them, hear them, and they will come back around again.

Eelusive jumps backwards—surprisingly graceful this time—somehow present, yet not present.

Chapter 21

imagining other futures . . .

Dear Reader,
*   This is a letter to you.*
*   Yes, you.*
*   'Dear Reader' here for two reasons:*
*   Reason #1: In the most generative way possible: you are reading this, you matter. If you are someone who has followed us along on this journey, you are dear. You are awesome (in my more informal phrasing)—I appreciate you giving us your time and attention. As I revisit this piece one last time in 2022 before we send it to the publishers, time and attention are even more precious. They are in short supply now, and in the near future time and attention will be even more precious as things escalate, implode, explode, and reform in distinct yet interconnected ways. Ancient patterns of gather->build->grow->decay->collapse/breakdown->(re)grow are cyclical and iterative. As my Nanas reminded me, nation-states come and go, our relations with the world around us can survive those when rooted and routed deeply. Knowing that right now doesn't make current cycles easy to endure—even when we have privileges to mitigate climate, state, and interpersonal impacts.*
*   Reason #2: The phrase Dear Reader has intrigued me since I was little.* The fact an author would stop to address and greet me, sometimes long after they were alive. Words that travelled across continents and decades or centuries . . . to be taken in by me, reading them in a particular place and moment. The more I read, I learned to feel when the author* meant *the words 'dear reader(s)' by what came before and*

---

*   * One curious privilege I had was that I was an avid reader and my mother worked in a thrift store. I was the first in my family to attend college. But long before that, I loved to read and write and draw—immersing myself in other worlds, other ways of sensing what was around me. Stories are powerful. My mother wanted to support me but did not enjoy books. That meant trips to the library where the librarians would help me select my picks for the week and discuss last week's selections. Books would be stacked in a wicker laundry basket, which I would push and pull down the library's front hall to wait for my ride home. I always had to return them though—even the ones I loved.*

179

*after that phrase. I hope you sense my commitment and meaning here, now, where/
when -ever you are.*

   *When my mother got a job at a large thrift store in a bigger town, that meant
I could* own *books. For her, hardcover books seemed more important. She would
bring home paper bags and boxes full of them: collections from all kinds of genres
from the 50s through to the 80s and 90s. I found the phrase 'Dear Reader' in
mysteries, horror, nonfiction—applied in many settings to whomever was reading
that particular set of words. I engage it here, for you.*

   *As I noted in the opening this is a letter to you, written by my past, present, and
future selves. The original text of this piece was in a different form—written while
in my PhD program, thinking about stories, worldmaking, kinship, and relational
networks. Now it has been read and patiently revised and edited by my coauthors,
selected parts of it are here to be revisited one last time. The original writing was
for me; I suppose a lot of academic writing is. Now, it's reworked for you. For
anyone wondering—as communities near and far, human and nonhuman, hurt and
crash—what do we do? How do we keep going? How do I help or make an impact?*

   *As someone whose life has been transformed by opening a book printed in
1963, the author long since dead, I know that impact and hope are marvellously
multitemporal.*

   *So exhale, then take in these story pieces. Keep them, or release them as you'd
like. These led me down a different path while in graduate school, into a life path
that involves teaching and making BIPOC futurisms and speculative fiction as
blueprints/guides. May they provide you with some fragments to guide you.*

The Path Without End is a short film made by Elizabeth LaPensée, retelling
aspects of Anishinaabe stories of Moon People who travelled to Earth from
the stars by canoe. In older print versions of this story, the Moon People who
travel between Earth and Space are women, a group of sisters. A human man
and his family—human and nonhuman—help him kidnap the youngest sister
(whom he finds irresistible) and help her adapt to his world and way of life.
She comes to love him but mourns her world and family—which she visits
with her child in a birch bark and cedar strip recreation of the original Sky-
Ship canoe. Humans and moon people travel/keep moving with their hybrids.

   In LaPensée's digital version of the story, they shift the emphasis from
the beauty and 'otherworldliness' of the Moon Maiden into the familiar-
yet-alien: using images of traditional materials to create the characters and
environments. Their retelling focuses on human and Moon lovers' connec-
tions to nonhuman worlds as they travel, propagate, and face the unending
chase of colonization. Furthering the place-based importance, the shapes are
all created with digital manipulations of organic matter: wood, copper, sweet-
grass, shells, etc. These hybrid human-nonhuman assemblages echo that of
native/hybrid-native families navigating multiple realms of understanding
and difference.

Screen capture from *The Path Without End* by Elizabeth LaPensée by mlb

LaPensée sees the monstrous forms that follow and hunt them as wetiko/ wétiko (excessive consumption) as exemplified by colonization. 'We have had to contend with the cannibal force of Wetiko, which consumes all—our stars, our spirits. In *The Path*, this force is forever following the lovers and at times it takes the human, at times it takes the child, and at times we over-come' (*The Path Without End*, introduction).

Powhatan and Delaware Native scholar Jack Forbes further extends this desire for control and human-devouring as colonialism: the overriding char-acteristic of a wétiko (a Cree word for cannibal or kin-devourer, which is not necessarily male or female though 'he' is used—it can infect/emerge from many sources) is 'that he consumes other human beings for profit, that is, he is a cannibal' (Forbes 2008, 5).

How to elude the ever-present 'real' monsters of colonization?

I return to you, dear reader, for a moment here.

In the intervening years since this piece was first written—I don't ask that question. I don't elude well. To elude it means to pass it along to another. I was tempted to edit that verb out, but it's an important reflection.

What I usually ask is something like:

How do I face and confront colonization where I am? What is my place in that struggle?

True perhaps to my family's reputation, I don't flee or freeze often—I get fighty. I fought, I endured.

That is important, but exhausting—feeding into cycles of not resting or recovering. [See Alisha B Wormsley and Suzanne Kite's work on Black and Indigenous rest and dreaming.] It can eat away the ability to imagine otherwise.

I have broken a few times, and seen others crash. I have lost people I love dearly. Forces of colonization—including entwined settler colonialism, patriarchy, racism, anti-trans and queer offshoots—reproduce and shift faster than we can recharge in isolated groups. They feel like the slickest robots and war/extraction machines of Western sci-fi novel covers. My thoughts in this early work were to get. . . not monstrous, but postmonstrous. Let's shift into She-Hulk instead of the Hulk in this next section.

Mutate into the postmonstrous to address colonization. That involves embracing the potential to become the monstrous, but channelling those energies by *grounding* them in renewed practices, stories and relations.

LaPensée takes these revitalized stories further—seeing mixed native and colonial identities within the Moon Person–Human hybrid children that connect with blood quantum and settler colonial definitions of belonging in Indigenous nations' current contexts. However, she keeps it placed in the speculative fiction arena and uses a nonverbal abstracted format to convey the story—eliding tensions around human hierarchies and delineated roles and allowing the story to be told in different seasonal frameworks than traditional verbal retellings permitted. Not all layers of meaning will be understood by every viewer. But the seeds are there.

In her resurgence theory text *Dancing on Our Turtle's Back*, Leanne Simpson talks about resistance and resurgence through story seeds and the importance of replanting them here and now:

> My ancestors resisted and survived what must have seemed like an apocalyptic reality of occupation and subjugation in a context where they had few choices. They resisted by simply surviving and being alive. They resisted by holding onto their stories. They resisted by taking the seeds of our culture and political systems and packing them away. . . . I am sure of their resistance, because I am here today. . . . I am the evidence. Michi Saagiig Nishnaabeg people are the evidence. Now, nearly two hundred years after surviving an attempted political and cultural genocide, it is the responsibility of my generation to plant and nurture those seeds and to make our Ancestors proud (Simpson 2011, 15).

Note for the moment the importance both Simpson and LaPensée place on story and relational practices of revitalization. While both draw on traditional Anishinaabeg and Nishinaabeg practices, LaPensée views the times Native peoples are in as post-apocalyptic.

Dear Readers—another pause if you will.
  I pluralize 'reader' here for a reflection on seeds and self.
  Seeds *as a word can evoke tangible and land-based imagery, some I am quite fond of: Farmers' Almanacs, seed catalogues and exchanges, sticky watermelon*

*seeds gleefully spit out in the heat of summer, roasted pumpkin or sesame seeds. I
expand that here to include sea grasses and seaweeds—some of those marine algae
and plant seeds are zygotes (sexual reproduction), some are asexual (reproducing
through fragmentation and division). Think of seaweed fragments or small plant
divisions released from the larger body, floating away to travel, grow and multiply.
Some divisions spread out closer to the larger plants, some are carried farther
away, following current routes, waiting to take root.*

*Returning to my pluralized opening in this section—I noted earlier that this
academic writing was initially for me. I had seen a short video clip at an amazing
fiction and SF gathering at the University of Hawai'i at Mānoa around creating
futures rooted in wonder. Indigenous Futurisms author and scholar Grace Dillon
shared the clip at the opening of a panel she co-led, LaPensée had made the clip
for her mother (Dillon) and others. The animation was modelling ways to share
their Indigenous stories widely, with deeply layered meanings that worked to keep
with their protocols around audience and season. The most precious teachings/
seeds could remain secure, but it could reach a larger audience—those seeds could
drift and travel within the video. You would need to know and have had stories
shared with you to understand the full teachings and layers of meanings between
the materials selected for certain characters, backgrounds, etc.—it was a deeply
relational approach.*

*I wasn't sure what I was responding to in the clip, but I was hooked. I showed
it to professors in my department involved with feminist technology studies—they
were unimpressed; they didn't see LaPensée's point. [Meanwhile we watched many
Western surrealist and non-narrative films in graduate classes that did not have to
'make a point.']*

*I wrote part of this as a seminar paper, then expanded it. Rereading this now I
realize my main impetus wasn't to convince my professors of the piece's worth—it
was to think on paper, allowing seed forms to take root within and around me.*

*Thus I pluralize readers here—this work has layers and seeds for me, ones
that grew into the work I do now, my articulation of relation-oriented ontologies
and methods, and nonhuman as an evocation of nourishing negation practices (as
opposed to more-than-human/other-than-human, etc.).*

*Temporalities and paths are wondrous and strange: I needed to reread and
rework this for you, so I am. Let us continue. . . .*

In *The Path Without End*, there are repeated patterns of growth and destruc-
tion that afflict the postmonstrous family of human-Moon person (alien)-and
hybrid offspring. In the short introduction to her piece, LaPensée brings up
two key points that weave into the concepts of the postmonstrous and are
illustrated by the image on page 184:

1. Organic ship matter: LaPensée notes that lack of 'proof' of earlier
Native exploration doesn't mean it did not occur, but that the materials used
for their shipbuilding have long since decayed—recycled back into a larger
system. 'We do and did have technology, but since we use(d) biodegradable

Screen capture from *The Path Without End* by Elizabeth LaPensée by mlb

materials, and thus "evidence" has faded with nature, we are told by the dominate culture that we were savage with no technology'. What do we mean by advanced technology if space exploration and development tech is only useful for ten years or less, yet remains toxic or dangerous for centuries or millennia?

Taking up this idea of all-biodegradable tech—what generative and monstrous possibilities are opened by creating fully organic/compostable posthuman components?

LaPensée elaborates on the harm done by this perceived 'lack of proof' and positing the Native as primitive in the introduction to her video: 'We often limit ourselves and discredit our ancestors by thinking they didn't possibly have the technology to travel when in fact they did have canoes and other forms of ships. To me, this is how we represent ourselves in steampunk, which is otherwise a very colonialist genre that stems from the Victorian mindset'.

Within the steampunk genre there has been Afropunk and Indigipunk movements—to (re)envision organic antique-tech worlds that include black and brown bodies and communities. This is more than just a subgenre of steampunk—it challenges suppositions about what potential futures past might be like in various parts of the world—not just London, Paris or Boston in the nineteenth century. It also challenges what technology was, is, and could be. Indigenous communities can/will/could be engaging in space/time travel, cyborgs, bodyhacking, human/nonhuman blending, and other practices often found within this genre, but view them as related and relational practices.

However, this is not carte blanche to 'learn from' or appropriate Indigenous technologies, movements, or ideas. Western institutions can't even understand a land acknowledgment is also an active form of technology, let alone more sophisticated relational and place-based encounters. As Space NDN and Navajo scholar Lou Cornum notes:

> The land acknowledgement sets us up for what kind of encounter we are going to have. I am trying to suggest we need other kinds of encounters. When being emplaced happens properly—it can be ceremony. It is what Tiffany King recognized as an intimate connection with others and coming into knowledge of that connection. . . . But is that different contact even possible in the rooms we gather in where acknowledgments are uttered? (2019)

What is interesting about recent sci fi series and films I have watched is the expansion of the idea that the ship and/or crew is haunted, cursed, or infected. If governments and agencies cannot recognize the places and materials they extract and build from, let alone actually be in-relation with those communities, what makes them think these issues will be left behind like undesirable crewmates? The infection/haunting is already inside. Returning to Cornum:

> I usually don't feel good enough about my body to allow the intimacy of ceremony, let alone in a white cube with mostly white poets, or a Hilton hotel conference room with aspiring professionals nervous about their CVs. These spaces shape what can be uttered. I believe in the material force of the speech act and that that force can misfire. Until the space of ceremony is secured for those I want to be with, I'd rather dwell in the irreconcilable. I want antagonism over inclusion, in order to prevent, as Sandy Grande has cautioned in regard to 'Indigenizing the academy', making Indigenous practices and peoples open for further extraction. It is a tricky maneuver to insist on our existence both prior and present while slipping, ghostlike, out of the enclosure of visibility.
>   We don't have to be dead to haunt the burial ground. (2019)

. . . Or the spaceship.

The spaces between Mbembe's deathworlds and Cornum's hauntings are where the second point below can emerge as seemingly new shoots from older taproots. Much like dark matter and other SF small-but-superdense energy sources, these seeds contain multitudes . . . just not for everyone.

2. Reimagining and reworlding—openings for ideas that break from colonial dis-ease patterns that limit, constrain, and extract; unleashing the freedom *to* (re)map histories and possibilities through creative storytelling. 'There is a sickness from colonization and art is our medicine' (LaPensée). Simpson also sees these stories (in song, art, and recorded words) as powerful medicines:

Our Nishnaabeg landscape flourishes with our stories of resistance and resurgence, yet through colonial eyes, the stories are interpreted as quaint anecdotes with 'rules' of engagement and consequence. Interpreted within our cultural web of non-authoritarian leadership, non-hierarchical ways of being, non-interference and non-essentialism, the stories explain the resistance of my Ancestors and the seeds of resurgence they so carefully saved and planted. (Simpson 2011, 18)

Simpson goes on to articulate that she sees these stories told in print or video/film as losing some of their emergent transformative power (34). This could be viewed as remaining within the goddess realm—fixing particular realms as Native; however, her more recent works embrace and explore multimedia resurgence stories.

LaPensée is part of a large community of Indigenous artists who see digital realms in particular in decidedly posthuman, indigenous, and monstrous contexts. In the collection *Coded Territories: Tracing Indigenous Pathways in New Media Art*, Stephen Loft has a chapter titled 'Mediacosmology', in which he takes up this idea:

A cosmological, adaptive, and decolonized cyberspace that presages its own development . . . a full circle, if you will. And, it is entirely consistent with our ways of transferring knowledge and culture. What Indigenous new media artists are doing is creating what Tuer has termed a 'hybrid subjectivity' that navigates the virtual in a fashion that overlays (thus disrupting) the colonial narrative of the World Wide Web. This is not to portray cyberspace as some pan-Indian utopia but to posit a syncretic Indigenous ontology that is material and virtual. (2014, 173)

Evoking both material, energetic, and virtual potentials, the foundational stories for the Anishinaabe contain space travel and human/nonhuman partnerships that shape their human and nonhuman communities. These communities would not view their posthuman practices as 'cyborg'—but as family and kin networks extend to the nonhuman, with these elements and species seen as older siblings, parents, and/or ancestors, embraced within the postmonstrous.

Dear reader—you made it this far and I am grateful. I want to offer more*: the urge to edit, to add more, to revise is intense. My only discipline here will be leaving this here, as-is: a postmonstrous letter from past-mes to future-yous.*

May you find the seeds that you need, that we need. Plant them across disciplines and divides within you and around you.

Let them grow fast, strong, and unruly. Like us.

Chapter 22

dreaming of other futures . . .

—imagining escaping the relentless chase of misogyny, racism—

1. A now where strangers aren't rounded up and left in cages to die slowly
2. A now where a military must have a bake sale to afford their next drone
3. A now where old people aren't expendable
4. A now where it matters to say, 'I was wrong'
5. A now where bodies, or their parts, are not the property of others
6. A now where fathers don't rule, nor do mothers
7. A now where nourishment matters everywhere
8. A now with no borders
9. A now where failure is okay—an obsolete word . . .
10. A now where we don't go back to before; maybe a now with no return? What is intolerable now? What should have been intolerable in my now that wasn't? What should be intolerable now but isn't? What are the lies that sustain us, that make it impossible to think of a now-future? Routes foreclosed. Living my little life.
11. A now with humans decentred, uncentred, off kilter
12. A now where conflict isn't resolved with the threat of death, injury, incarceration
13. A now where learning for learning's sake is (more than) enough
14. A now where the words 'productive', 'productivity' and 'output' are forthwith banned
15. A now where daydreaming is encouraged, aspired to, admired
16. A now where White Men are a thing of the past . . . anachronistic (it's a concept remember . . .)
17. A now where taking care of others is everyone's job

18. A now where there is no gender, race or class, or any hierarchical categories full stop
19. A now where abolishing is the orientation. Abolish the police, abolish the state, abolish the military, abolish the university. There are other, more capacious ways of living and being in the world. Let's find them . . .
20. A now where breathing is not optional
21. A now which isn't (bone) crushing, dream crushing
22. A now where tearing down the walls is the only option—what creative works tears at these walls? So many tears down these walls and so many tears (crying). . . .
23. A now where there is some violence we must do . . . feminism is fundamentally violent . . . feminism is always violating. It is about doing violence to hetero racialised patriarchy. Those who benefit will feel pain, there is no way around that
24. A now where there is no polite feminism
25. A now where being *nice* is not encouraged or welcome (so gendered); kindness though is highly encouraged and always welcome
26. A now where nobody should be an 'aire'/'heir'—billionaire, millionaire, heiress, but everyone should be thinking with inheritance—what we carry with us in our bodies, in our bones, on our skin, in our thoughts and feelings
27. A now where the state is not the (end) point—what is this home making, what does it mean and what does one need to shelter in place as part of a community of care?
28. What's your now . . . ?

Chapter 23

Poetics of a handbook—or some suggestions for better practices . . . (for those still in academia . . .)

Better practices?
**Sit with these words from Katherine and Yesmin for a while to envision worlds of better practices:

'. . . those of us who work

in places that weigh us down

can

carve out **surprising** and **generous** spaces
that challenge existing political visions,

allow us
to fight

against inequity and racism,

work

against racial violence,

and **collaborate**.'

(Katherine McKittrick 2021, 41)

'At the university,
the light is more opaque.
I am not engaged in daily battles with the Home Office of local authority
bureaucracy. However,
the "brick walls"
are just as solid
        if less immediately visible.
In this changing light, I have been thinking
again

about the importance of **relational** and   relationship-based work, this **labour
of love**
as a kind of activism;
small acts
of resistance which sustain the survival and growth of "space invaders"[,]
theblackandbrownbodiesofyoungpeople,studentsandacademics
whose
presence
within
disrupts and disturbs
white
space.'
(Yesmin Devici 2019, 169)

And sit with this:
 to be successful in academia (and what a word) requires embracing misogyny
and racism and ableism.
 We don't believe it is possible to decolonise the university, so our aim with this
'handbook' is not liberatory. It is not delivered in the hopes of saving academia or
saving the institution. Our aim is far (very far) less lofty, far less ideal and idealistic.
It is a small and grossly inadequate attempt to carve out moments that make
                              thinking,
                                        moving,
                                                  breathing,
          caring,
                      intervening,
                                        keeping things open and up in the air
          slightly more possible, slightly less terrible

for those in—and making use of—the university and academic spaces that we/you/
us worked to keep ourselves in.

          Take it as you will—add to it, rewrite it, tinker with it, throw it away.

Marge would like you to see if you can use the points as writing prompts. *What
fragments of memory, stories, words come to your mind in this rapid list of points?*

Marge would like you to rearrange the word fragments into a paragraph form. *What
kinds of stories, memories, moments do we need to string together the lines into a
paragraph form?*

Marge would like you to use the blank spaces in the following pages and in between
the lines.

Marge would like to see if you can give life in the pages.

Teaching

Teaching is not a curse; it is a gift. Cherish it. Look at what bell hooks (1994, 198) tells us:

> *'Professors*
> *are expected to publish*
> *but no one*
> *really*
> *expects or demands of us that*
> *we really **care***
> *about teaching in unique and different ways.*
> ***Teachers** who **love***
> *students*
> ***and are loved***
> *by them*
> *are still "suspect"*
> *in the academy.*
> *Some of the suspicion is that the **presence***
> ***of feelings, of passions,***
> *may not allow for objective consideration of each student's merit.*
> *But this very notion is based on the false assumption that education is neutral,*
> *that*
> *there is some*
> *"even" emotional ground*
> *we stand on*
> *that enables us*
> *to treat everyone equally, dispassionately.'*

- Refuse objectivity; feel the classroom and let it feel you.
- The classroom is not a space for white privilege, even if it relentlessly 'owns' this space. Recognise its diversity. There are refugees, migrants, vulnerable minorities and those with severe trauma and emotional (dis) stress in your classroom. Tread with care. Be **care-full**.
- Don't crack racist or sexist or ageist jokes (you shouldn't need reminding, but just in case you do).
- Try to leave your prejudices outside and be ready to embrace the diversity and difference in the classroom.
- Students sometimes/oftentimes have prejudices and narrow-minded world-views, which is why free exchange in the classroom is the opportunity to really help them with their thinking processes.
- If your exercise of power makes students vulnerable and fearful, you need to be on the other side of the classroom (you can literally do this, you know!).

Learning

should

never stop.

Being a productive researcher, publishing in 'top' outlets and acquiring prestigious funding does NOT automatically translate into being an effective teacher. One must work and be committed to teaching, rather than demean its importance. Universities were created to teach and disseminate ideas, not to become production houses for producing and counting publications.

Treat your students like the theorists they are. Like you, they are thinking and making claims about the world(s) they are moving through. Our job as teachers is to help them become more aware of how they are theorising about the world and how this affects their becomings and relationalities.

So approach the classroom with curiosity, openness and adaptability. Learn from and with your students. You know, students are not blank slates. You do not get to write on them. Collaboratively *learn* with each other.

You can either make the classroom a space that reproduces power, or it can be a space of subversion. Always choose the latter but also know that in subversion power is still reproduced. Accept a classroom is an either/and, and work through its ambivalence every day, in the thick mess of the everyday as human, as just a person that you are.

Supervision

- Supervision is not a power play. Hierarchies are so counterproductive. Professional boundaries can be respected with empathy, care, mutual respect and generosity.
- Do not play god. You cannot see all, you don't know all.
- Help build supportive communities that students/researchers need in this phase of their journey (whether UG, MA or PhD).

Be quick to open doors

be **slooooooooow**

to let them slam shut behind you.

Do not accept 'complaints' that 'there aren't enough women, ethnic minorities . . .'
on the programme. It hides so much: the failures at different levels,

the gaps   in talk and

action, the exclusions and hierarchies by design

that sustains heteropatriarchy, empires, colonialism

and other unnameables (how much do we really know about structures of power?).

Instead do something about it. Reach out to marginalised communities and persons in your university work. Actively do something—however small or unpressing the need to make the gesture—to help women, black and brown students, ethnic minorities and other outsiders: send them useful material; read and reread research proposals and funding applications; listen for how they are understanding the lay of the field and take the time to reflect together on possible options; . . . **shoulder some of the burden**, because when you do not, it is most likely that someone who is less privileged than you is shouldering this work.

- Have difficult conversations with yourself and your colleagues about your sexist and racist blind spots and biases. If/when you see something, say something.
- Thesis/dissertation writing, like all writing at all levels and genres, is about building community. Learning from and with each other. Help students, especially the 'least exemplary one' in your 'educated' eyes. Learn from them as much as they might learn from you.
- Model for your students—especially your PhDs—work-life balance. Take substantial breaks, use your annual and sick leaves and encourage them to do so. Don't answer emails after work or on the weekend (or at least make friends with your 'send later' email function). Treat their time with respect by doing the same with your time.
- Read their work carefully and deliver feedback generously. Don't be the supervisor who 'skims' and blags their way through supervision.
- Do answer emails from your supervisees in a timely manner! Don't be the asshole supervisor who ignores students for months at a time. This is part of your job. You are not doing students 'a favour'. Treat them with the time and respect they deserve.
- Do not treat your PhD researchers like your personal research assistants. That is not their job. It is *your job to do your field/work* and their job to do their field/work.
- Do not suggest coauthoring a journal article or book chapter with your PhD student and leave them to do the work.
- Do not sexually harass your supervisees. JUST. DON'T. (You shouldn't need telling, but just in case you do. And remember what can count under the category 'harass'.)
- DO NOT invisibilise a student of colour by not noticing them! Yes, we are all racists, but we can all unlearn and do better.
- Stop calling them your PhD *student* when they complete. They are no longer your PhD student. This maintains, rather than transforms, hierarchies. Build friendships and intellectual community with them instead.

- Do not demand conformity. To do so is to participate in the reproduction of white heteropatriarchy baked into the brick walls of the academy.
- **Listen**.

chine had a good session of listening to a PhD student: 'In the whole one-hour phone call, I mostly listened to her, and enjoyed it so much. She had disappeared for a month now? She had asked her three supervisors to stop the weekly meetings that all (but who though?) had decided was the way to get her to finally finish her phd. No more extensions, they said. This is your last chance, they said. And so we began the marathon and then she stopped it. So I just called her to see what might happen, to see if I could get through and to my surprise she picked up her phone. She sounded down. I asked her how she was doing. She mostly explained what she has been working on (I heard her saying: I have been working, I have been trying.) Something shifted in her voice, and at some point she sounded strong. Talking and thinking at the same time. All I did was listen, following what she was saying as closely as I could, as true to her words. It was music. I want to learn how to read her the way I listened today. If I can learn this, I strongly feel I can help her finish. I worry she will not get to finish her phd.'

- Knowing when you are not the right or a good supervisor.

chine stepped down from another phd supervision this week 'because listening to him was. . . . this sounds awful, torture'. It made her mind go red. she tried to learn how to listen better, to follow more closely what he was saying. she often felt the hit/heat of a violent note. . . . it was not always the words, but a sense of violence around them, something if written up in proper academic convention, it could go unnoticed. she was learning to brace herself, and this was another kind of 'mind going red'. she decided she could not do this to herself anymore, and also that if she stayed on, she would ruin his chances of finishing. she too wants him to finish; his failure would cost him so much personally. she knows that pain. getting out of the way sometimes is the best thing one can do.

Committees, panels, etc.

(all things where a group of academics decide and/or do things together . . . rather scary when put this way . . .)

- Do not have an all-white panel.

- Do not have an all-male panel.
- Do not have an all-white and all-male panel.

But, but, but . . . DON'T ALSO TOKENISE WOMEN AND PEOPLE OF COLOUR! Having a diverse range of bodies and voices in a room shouldn't be an afterthought or hard work. If you struggle with this, then perhaps you should find another line of work. If your institution only has one person of colour, you have far bigger problems.

- Do not blame job candidates for not being sufficiently 'diverse' (yes, this has happened. . . . 'it's their fault for not applying, not our fault for not doing the work, that is, having a job spec that invites applications from POCs, actively recruiting from diverse communities, interrogating whiteness in hiring processes . . .).
- Encourage 'space invaders' (Puwar 2004) to the table of so-called experts. Those whose lives are most impacted should always be at the table. If they can't because structures preclude them (e.g., exam committees, mitigating circumstances panels) then try your very hardest to make visible issues/ structures at play.
- Say nooooooooooooooo   to committee or panel work when you are unable to actually allocate time for this work in your monthly calendar. It is better to be not there than to become a token appointment who is then too busy to be in conversation with the committee/panel, or a committee/panel member who is not pulling the weight or doing the legwork.

> Always understand that legwork is as important as
> headwork when a group of academics comes together to
> make decisions and/or do things

(yes, rather scary a phenomenon, telling of how we are part components of the institutional machineries).
Recommend others for the roles who
could use the experience or platform,
even if you think they are not ready,
because more often than not, they
are/will be.

Some committees in university and other academic organisations really do not need to exist. Say no **abundantly**.

Fieldwork: whose field and whither fieldwork?

- Do not treat the 'Global South' as fieldwork sites or case studies—the 'Global South' is not the testing ground to validate your theories.
- All theories do not emanate from Western traditions or locations.
- A short touristy visit, or a plane stopover to any country does not make you an 'expert' on a country and its people. If anything, it is an opening, a moment where one respectfully listens, observes, reflects.
- Research assistants, facilitators, fixers, brokers help you navigate the field.
- So compensate them, pay them, treat them as partner travellers on the research journey who deserve respect as coproducers of knowledge.
- DON'T click pictures of random black and brown people during your privileged stays at posh hotels in the 'field' and share them on social media with the tagline 'the "butler" or "servant" you so wish you had'! (Yes, people do this!)

What to do about privilege?

Be careful—
        just 'acknowledging' is never, ever enough.
So much privilege
                —language, status, class, race—
helps get access to
        research participants,
                        to people turning themselves into participants.
In this context,
        Will you centre your privilege in your 'methodology section' and then what will you do?
        After you've said it, written it—then what?

White scholarly 'analysis' gets seen as more credible and legitimate;
                                                not so much
                                                the body
                                                of work
produced by local experts or agencies that may be intellectually more rigorous
and representative of the local conditions and voices. Even on subject matters that
require local skills and lived experiences, an intellectual assessment from a white
Western expert is treated as authoritative even if it does not speak to the empirical
evidence.

- Don't adjust your area of expertise according to the demands of the funding agencies. You may not be the right person for all opportunities, so it is important to bring others into the conversation.
- If you are a native speaker, you do not automatically qualify as the 'expert' on everything related to your area of study.

The process of data gathering and doing field work in the Global South reveals how racialized identities and hierarchies are imposed and how biases work. It is important to highlight that 'whiteness' in the field is not always about white bodies, but how researchers and the researched perceive each other and construct a knowledge space where legitimacy and authority are constantly negotiated. Just like the classroom, it is an ambivalent space; working to activate multiple, thick, messy relations is non-optional; it is everything.

How to structure working weeks and cut out bullshit and create an inner rhythm
for your own work, happiness and sustainability
Living with a double bind is unsustainable living, it is clear.
But
so many of us have been living with the double bind I describe above for
far too long.
It has outlasted the best of us.
it has survived the rigors of our analysis and critique,
our revolt and protest.
It remakes itself after the revolution.
It   is   sustainable.
It   sustains   itself.
We   are   its collateral   damage.
Stress, anxiety, depression, hypertension, domestic violence, state violence corruption,
substance abuse, poverty, animal abuse, environmental degradation . . .
these are just some of the effects of   the double bind.
And they do not cease.
This is why we need the myth of (the Pacific Island) paradise, right?
This is why we need the promise of retirement.
(Teresia Teaiwa 2021,
Sweat and Salt Water: Selected Works)

Get off email.
count how many hours you are contracted to do the job as described in the institutional document. Allocate that time to emails in ways that allows you to communicate well with collaborators, students and colleagues in the community who are working to **build, sustain and nourish**.
Emailing is not in your job description.
email is not work.

Do not be available for micro-aggressive and/or micro-managing encounters in either informal hallway encounters or formal meetings. We are here to **do the work**, not to make people feel good about themselves, or generate good feelings. While there is a fine line between professionalism and 'being cold'

gender and race serve to police this line————
Demands to be 'approachable' and 'friendly' often fall on the shoulders of brown and black folk, women and those who don't conform to the 'norm'. And again—try to stick to working your contracted hours for the institutional work you do (and also take stock regularly of the kind of work you think is not institutional work). It's really, really hard,

but to change how

the university thrives on our overwork means we must stop overworking.

Invest in your community(s) and **your own nourishment, growth and health** rather than the university. When you work too many hours one day/week/semester, **work less** the next. Claw back your time. Remember the university/academy doesn't **love or care** for/about you. Others do. Spend your **precious** time with them. Tell them all about the **radical ideas** you are **nurturing in your body**. Ask them to tell you theirs.

Make more time to read.
Read voraciously and less instrumentally.
Reading is nourishment.
The secret gift of reading—and thinking—is time.

Do not make yourself available twenty-four hours a day, seven days a week. **Empty** out your days and see what happens, what you notice, how you breathe, what you face. At the very least, **be present** when you're at work so you can **be present** when you aren't. **Liberate yourself** by removing your university email account from your phone. We don't need to literally carry work around with us. This is the one thing in your life where what you don't know will make you **infinitely** happier.   **Make friends** with the 'send later' function on your email account. This is a great way to manage expectations and pace email-driven work that demands attention from others and yourself. **Take days off**. Take your annual and sick leaves. Try really hard to not work on days you and/or the world has designated as 'weekends'. If working on these days is unavoidable on a given week or a given version of the dailies you are managing, make sure you mark these and schedule to **take these days off**—not in the abstract, but in actual calendar days.

Remember: we might plan in years or months but the years and months do not necessarily have plans to keep us here.

Plan in the now.

Stop

drinking 'the greatest thing about academia is its flexibility' juice. It's this very flexibility that the neoliberal university relies on to squeeze every drop of life out of us. Become *inflexible* in your refusal to do more (and more) work for an institution that systematically reproduces coloniality and racialised and sexualised hierarchies of harm and exclusion. Practice 'quiet quitting'—'doing your job within the confines of work hours'.

"You're still performing your duties, but you're no longer subscribing to the hustle culture mentality that work has to be your life – the reality is, it's not and your worth as a person is not defined by your labour."

That could mean ignoring work emails and calls outside of working hours, and leaving the office on time.

It could also mean declining projects that aren't part of your job description.

#quietquitting

Stop overworking. Just stop.

In all these suggestions, remember also that not all academics are doing their work with academia at the **centre of their** work **lives and vision**. They are doing political mobilisation work, trying to get a school or NGO off the ground, supporting family members to migrate, fighting local power politics, fighting the legal system, **getting food** and electricity to people so they do not have to rely on loan sharks. Or they are just trying to get through the everyday. The list goes on. **Rest** comes in small moments, when one can actually physically detach oneself from the myriad of **social connections** and responsibilities. Academia's claim to our work is just one of the many demands to work, scheme, be reachable and connected endlessly. This too is part of the double bind. It creates an unsustainable work life, and yet work-life **balance and boundaries** do not seem to quite get at the problem.

The problem is not you, it is the academy.

Better time management (*oh, be very cautious of anything 'management'— terrible word, awful idea, whispers professor feminist*) and work-life balance will only go so far.

Conferencing

For those who go to these conferences, when you hear an emerging scholar—they don't have to be young, by the way, they can be returning students or late to the academic journey—when you hear their work and you find it special, or good, or meaningful—let them know. They need it. Often they are unsure if there is a space for them within the field. Make some. Share some.
If you see or hear a paper that really is extraordinary, tell them because it can transform how they see themselves in these places.

Being a good colleague
Two ears
one mouth
In other words, listen twice as much as you talk. Don't be the asshole in every meeting who takes up all the space and air in the room.

'Don't be an asshole because assholery is contagious' (Mewburn 2013).

Do things for seemingly unimportant people.

Don't be 'upwardly toxic' (Dumitrescu 2019), a 'toxic enabler' (Dumitrescu 2021), or engage in 'toxic hypocrisy' (Dumitrescu 2020). And don't offer up admiration for this ubiquitous toxicity.

Politeness holds whiteness. Be impolite in the face of racism (and all exclusionary acts).

Be aware of the *nasty = clever* equation and resist it with **kindness** (see Mewburn 2013).

Avoid gossip. This is not the same as sharing knowledge/strategies to survive in neoliberal institutions. We mean the nasty stuff that does nothing to support or protect people.

When asked to do an administrative role, do it and do it competently. You don't need to reinvent the wheel (a tendency in neo-liberal institutions where we are expected to show 'innovation' in everything we do). Know your role, show up and don't make extra work for others. Treat the administrators with respect. Thank them for the work they do to support you and your students.

When you talk about your research, talk about its substance, not where it was published & what the ranking was. Prioritise substance over numbers.

Help each other out and check in often. Also know that you *feeling helpful* and actually *being helpful* are two different things. Be actually helpful, otherwise just let the person be.

Work daily towards be(com)ing a liberated subject.

When did you feel free yesterday?

What did this look like?

How did this disassemble the neoliberal individual subject, or the good daughter narrative(s), or the inner critic, or . . . (fill in the ellipses)?

Reviewing

'Academia's love language is feedback.' (Abdelhabi 2022)

If so, develop a **love** language that is **generous and kind** when reviewing, not a love language that cuts and cuts down. Remember there is a **living,**

       breathing,

                          feeling

human **being**

on the **receiving** end.

Reviewing is just **deep** reading, no? And saying what needs to be said from this reading experience.

                              This takes time,

so if you don't have time for deep reading at this time, say no **abundantly**, and if appropriate, recommend others who would **enjoy**, benefit from and/or learn from the experience.

And that is all, really!

Mentoring

Marge was taken aback when two early career feminist colleagues in precarious employment thanked her for being such a good mentor. Marge didn't know she was doing anything called 'mentoring'. She was just trying to help them and **be good** to them in the small ways that she could. So, for mentoring, see 'being a good colleague'.

Mentoring can take many shapes. It can be an acknowledged and more **enduring relationship** or more prosaic and fleeting encounters with colleagues that make a difference.

Ask for help, guidance, advice and opinions. Ask someone to listen to you (rage, gush, blubber), for a **shoulder** to cry on, to support you by being in the room, and for **a hug** when you need it. You don't need to do or go through anything alone.

Citation

Read Katherine McKittrick's 'Footnotes (Books and Papers Scattered about the Floor)' in *Dear Science* (2021), and don't forget to read her footnotes! Here's a teaser: 'citations as learning, as counsel, as sharing . . . a lesson in living' (26). YES!

> Then go and (re)read Sara Ahmed, *Living a Feminist Life,* pages 15–17
> and
> Clare Hemmings, *Why Stories Matter*, chapter 5

give your citation practice a good shake-up

> Don't pull a Donna Haraway (and so many others . . .)
> and paper over
>   the indigenous, black and brown feminist knowledges
informing/shaping your work
Cite creatively
>   Include all the **stuff that moves you** in your thinking-writing-feeling
practice.
>   Cite **generously** and capaciously

Collaboration

Collaboration is the academic future. Not just with individuals but with institutions. Adaptability and **mutual learning** must be the way forward.

Collaboration is hard. Try to pull your weight—pull more when you can and less when you can't. Keep the lines of communication open with your collaborators.

<u>Collaboration thrives when fed</u>. Feed it often. Almost everything we do in academia can and should be done collaboratively. Be(com)ing undisciplined **embraces** displacing the I/me.

1. **Actively practice radical acts of kindness.**
2. **Build communities that nourish you and others.**
3. **Embrace embodiment and take care of your body—all of it.**
4. **Collaborate often.**
5. **Be alone often.**
6. **Fight for liberation.**
7. **Never stop learning.**
8. **Cultivate curiosity at every turn.**
9. **Dig deep: Be down to and with earth and be brave at the same time.**
10. **Be unapologetic in be(com)ing undisciplined.**

Chapter 24

be(com)ing undisciplined . . .

This book has been an exercise in be(com)ing undisciplined. And to show it. To ragefully and gleefully burst out of dominant, deadly and unliveable ways of knowing and being in academia. To rip, to cut, to shred. Be(com)ing undisciplined is also an ongoing—living—project, one that we hope continues beyond the bounds of this book project and our ugly (unruly, wilful, wildly and monstrously excessive) feminist collective.

As we draw to a close that is not closure—it can hardly be closure in/for a book that is experimental, monstrous, undisciplined, open-ended—there is also a sense of loss, for some of us, wondering what will happen to our ugly feminist collective once this book is finished. There is also a sense of relief and curiosity about what letting go and being let go by a claim by a collective might unleash. And there are other feelings—there are always other feelings in endings and beginnings. We will continue living and live with the knowledge that writing only catches up with our lives and theory has yet to theorise the intimate details of what it takes to stay living, living our lives.

After writing 115 pages about *The Myth of Closure* psychologist Pauline Boss (2022) asks, 'And now, how do I end a book about ambiguity and no closure?' Her grandson's advice: to end it in mid-sentence, and she continues, 'True, there's no final conclusion to what I've written. Make your own sense of it. Along the way, try to find some meaning and new hope in your life. Let your tolerance of ambiguity grow, for therein lies the resilience to help us live with loss—past, present, and future'.

It feels right to leave you where we started, with an imagined/real round-table panel musing about the idea of 'becoming undisciplined' and other trails in this book. . . .

<u>Chair/Discussant</u>: Professor Woman

<u>Participants:</u>
Ugly Feminist Collective (UFC)—not all of us could be in attendance
Katherine McKittrick (KMcK)
Cynthia Enloe (CE)
Verónica Gago (VG)
The Ghost of Valerie Solanas (TGoVS)
Jack Halberstam (JH)
The Ghost of Sojourner Truth (TGofST)

. . . . picking up after an introduction by the ugly feminist collective—

KMcK: Yes, I can hear you struggling with 'being undisciplined', even as you practice it. Take heart. I think of Black undisciplined method as precise and detailed, though when you bring multiple texts together, it can be awful and it can wear you out. But wonder and curiosity, and yes, generosity, are crucial.
CE: Absolutely to that! Where would we be without all our feminist curiosities and generosities I wonder?
KMcK: The stories you unearth may have no answers though, but they do signal other ways of living—many of them deeply submerged, yet living. This is something we want, yes?
Chair/Discussant: I thought a lot of your book was interesting, but I got a little perturbed by some of the things you say, like in all the 'nows' in the section on 'dreaming of other futures.' For example where you say 'failure is okay'—or more when you say, 'where White Men are a thing of the past'. Do you really mean both of these?

TGoVS: Have you read my book?? Well, the one I seem to be most famous for (it is pretty good)—even though I was always writing, but nobody seemed to care. I mean The SCUM Manifesto! *And yes, everyone said that SCUM meant The Society for Cutting up Men! I loved the word scum—the excess, the dirty floating detritus—oh yes! What I really wanted—and I think you do too—was to get the dirty rotten system destroyed—not try to be like it—or have its leaders and sycophants give me 'rights'—haha! You've seen what's happened to rights! Did you know they cut out my uterus when they put me in the madhouse? This wouldn't happen today—or would it . . . ?? Ha!*

Chair/Discussant: [shivering a little] Does anyone else feel a draft? Maybe it's just me. Ok, sorry—Jack?

JH: C'mon—think of the joys of finding an escape from all those harsh norms and ideas that constantly monitor and regulate behaviours—'failing' might offer you that! Yeah, maybe there will seem to be some negative affect around the idea of failure—but let's poke some holes into the toxic positivity of contemporary living! Doesn't it make you curious that failure seems to end up being about blaming already disadvantaged groups of peoples? And y'know, for feminism, failure has often been a better bet than success—yes, really! What have women usually been measured by . . . ?

CE: Patriarchy!

JH: Exactly! And this connects up with the idea of 'getting rid of White Men'—do you remember when Valerie Solanas said we might 'cut up men' if 'woman' only has meaning in relation to 'man? A fabulous theoretical way of showing how white supremacy and patriarchy work. Just tinkering with the system and getting some rights here and there, which so often (always?) end up being temporary anyway—doesn't work. White Men do seem to keep on reappearing, even in the guise of white women or brown men. . . .

TGoST: oh yeah . . .

Chair/Discussant: [still shivering a little] right. . . . Ok—so I see some hands up in the audience—so you—

Audience member: I heard you talk about this project last year—I'd just started my PhD research—you were discussing the idea of the frankenstinian subject and I really wanted to ask you about this then, but there wasn't time. I guess I've got two questions—can I ask about the ways you work with the aesthetic affect of the patchwork corpse/monster to do more creative, radical work—what's it doing for you? Though also, I was reading *Frankenstein's Daughters*, which is partly about the strategies that women have used when writing science fiction, and it really made me think about method and structure, and how that all connects up with feminist and queer needs to break with white patriarchal systems—sorry, that's all a bit convoluted!

CE: They're great questions! And that's so interesting you've waited a year to ask them—maybe that tells us something about the affect of the work (and effect)—but more about what it's doing for You?

KMcK: Frankenstein's Daughters? I wonder who do we 'see' there?

TGoST: I wonder a lot—I wonder what you all think, or feel when you 'see' me—I mean that image of me which circulates so much across all your communication networks. I'm sitting seemingly quietly and calmly—knitting—so much of my pain and anguish and anger, a lot of anger, neatly concealed. It feels very white. Don't forget.

. . . . The black cat is curled up and purring, basking in the warmth. . . .
CE: Shall we continue the conversation outside in the garden? Then we can. . . .

Ugly Feminist Collective at a conference

Postscript

'This feminist collective stayed at my house in 2019 working on this book and the collages and three years later I still keep finding pieces of paper left from their collaging' (Maria Stern). The project lives on.

Bibliography: People we moved with

Abdelhabi, Eman. 2022. "Academia's Love Language Is Feedback." Tweet, July 19, 2022. https://twitter.com/emanabdelhadi/status/1549476151101366275?s=20&t=a tArXQkmoBiaeNlFHvwQAA.

Agathangelou, Anna, and L. H. M. Ling. 2004. "The House of IR: From Family Power Politics to the *Poisies* of Worldism." *International Studies Review* 6, no. 4 (December): 21–49.

Ahmed, Sara. 2017. *Living a Feminist Life*. Durham, NC: Duke University Press.

———. 2021. *Complaint!* Durham, NC: Duke University Press.

Alexander, M. Jacqui. 2006. *Pedagogies of Crossing: Meditations on Feminism, Sexual Politics, Memory, and the Sacred*. Durham, NC: Duke University Press.

Angelou, Maya. 2017. *21 of Maya Angelou's Best Quotes to Inspire*. https://www .harpersbazaar.com/culture/features/a9874244/best-maya-angelou-quotes/

Ås, Berit. 2004. "The Five Master Suppression Techniques." In *Women in White: The European Outlook*, edited by Birgitta Evengård, 78–83. Stockholm: Stockholm City Council.

Bargh, Maria. 2020. "Possible Worlds: Political Science." In *Ngā Kete Mātauranga*, edited by Jacinta Ruru & Linda Waimarie Nikora. Dunedin: University of Otago.

BBC. 2015. "Sexism Row over New UK Passport Design." https://www.bbc.com/ news/uk-34710261.

Berlant, Lauren. (2012). "On Her Book *Cruel Optimism*." Interview, June 4, 2012. http://rorotoko.com/interview/20120605_berlant_lauren_on_cruel_optimism.

Boss, Pauline. 2022. *The Myth of Closure: Ambiguous Loss in a Time of Pandemic and Change*. New York: Norton.

Brown, Adrienne Maree. 2017. *Emergent Strategy: Shaping Change, Changing Worlds*. Chico, CA: AK Press.

Butler, Cornelia, and David Platzker, eds. 2018. *Adrian Piper: A reader*. New York: Museum of Modern Art.

Christie, Heather. 2019. *The Crying Book*. Boston: Little Brown Book Group.

Cohn, Carol. 1987. "Sex and Death in the Rational World of Defense Intellectuals." *Signs: Journal of Women in Culture and Society* 12, no. 4: 687–718.

———. 1993. "Wars, Wimps, and Women: Talking Gender and Thinking War." In *Gendering War Talk*, edited by Miriam Cooke and Angela Woollacott. Princeton, NJ: Princeton University Press.

Cornum, Lou. 2019. "Burial Ground Acknowledgements." *The New Inquiry*, October 14, 2019. https://thenewinquiry.com/burial-ground-acknowledgements/.

Crenshaw, Kimberle. 1989. "Demarginalizing the Intersection of Race and Sex: A Black Feminist Critique of Antidiscrimination Doctrine, Feminist Theory and Antiracist Politics." *University of Chicago Legal Forum* 1989, no. 1, art 8. http://chicagounbound.uchicago.edu/uclf/vol1989/iss1/8.

debuk. 2015. "Crap Apps and Female Email." Blog post, December 30, 2015. https://debuk.wordpress.com/2015/12/30/crap-apps-and-female-email/.

Devici, Yesim. 2019. "In the Changing Light: Daring to be Powerful." in *To Exist Is to Resist: Black Feminism in Europe*, edited by Akwugo Emejulu and Francesca Sobande, 167–80. London: Pluto Press.

Dumitrescu, Irina. 2019. "Ten Rules for Succeeding in Academia through Upward Toxicity." *Times Higher Education*, November 21, 2019. https://www.timeshigher education.com/opinion/ten-rules-succeeding-academia-through-upward-toxicity.

———. 2020. "Struggling to Exercise Upward Toxicity? Try Toxic Hypocrisy." *Times Higher Education*, September 16, 2020. https://www.timeshighereducation .com/opinion/struggling-exercise-upward-toxicity-try-toxic-hypocrisy.

———. 2021. "Are You a Toxic Enabler?" *Times Higher Education*, September 16, 2021. https://www.timeshighereducation.com/opinion/are-you-toxic-enabler.

el-Malik, Shiera S. 2015. "Why Orientalism Still Matters: Reading 'Casual Forgetting' and 'Active Remembering' as Neoliberal Forms of Contestation in International Politics." *Review of International Studies* 41, no. 3: 503–25.

Ellmann, Mary. 1968. *Thinking about Women.* New York: Harcourt Brace Jovanovich.

Enloe, Cynthia. 2017. *Big Push. Exposing and Challenging the Persistence of Patriarchy*. Oakland, CA: University of California Press.

Forbes, Jack D. 2008. *Columbus and Other Cannibals*. New York: Seven Stories Press.

Gago, Verónica. 2020. *Feminist International: How to Change Everything*. London: Verso.

Halberstam, Jack. 2011. *Queer Art of Failure*. Durham, NC and London: Duke University Press.

Haraway, Donna. 2016. *Staying with the Trouble*. Durham, NC: Duke University Press.

Hardwick, Neil. 1999. *Hullun Lailla*. [Translated by Juhani Lindholm from a manuscript I'm still here: an unsuccessful suicide note.] Helsinki: Otava.

Hartman, Saiddiya. 2019. *Wayward Lives, Beautiful Experiments*. London: Serpent's Tail Books.

Hast, Susanna. 2022. *Ruumis/Huoneet*. Helsinki: Kustantamo S&S.

Hemmings, Clare. 2011. *Why Stories Matter: The Political Grammar of Feminist Theory*. Durham, NC: Duke University Press.

hooks, bell. 1994. *Teaching to Transgress: Education as the Practice of Freedom*. London: Routledge.

———. 2000. *FEMINISM IS FOR EVERYBODY: PASSIONATE POLITICS*. Cambridge, MA: South End Press.

Hustvedt, Siri. 2014. *The Blazing World*. London: Sceptre.

Kortekallio, Kaisa. 2020. "Writing with" *Monster Talks* podcast, episode 8, October 10, 2020. https://themonsternetwork.com/2020/10/30/monster-talks-8-writing -with/.

Laiti, Jenni. 2021. "Art Is Free When We Are Free." Kone Foundation, April 13, 2021. https://koneensaatio.fi/en/stories/art-is-free-when-we-are-free/.

Le Guin, Ursula K. 1976. *Left Hand of Darkness*. New York: Ace Books.

Ling, L. H. M. 2002. *Postcolonial International Relations: Conquest and Desire between Asia and the West*. London: Palgrave Macmillan.

———. 2012. *The Dao of World Politics: Towards a Post-Westphalian, Worldist International Relations*. New York: Routledge.

———. 2014. *Imagining World Politics: Sihar & Shenya, A Fable for Our Times*. New York: Routledge.

Lion's Roar. "bell hooks Tells the Story of the First Time She Met Thich Nhat Hanh." December 21, 2017. https://www.lionsroar.com/bell-hooks-on-meeting-thich-nhat -hanh/.

Lispector, Clarice. 2012. *A Breath of Life*. London: Penguin Books.

Mayo, Katherine. 1927. *Mother India*. New York: Blue Ribbon Books.

Mbembe, Achille. 2019. *Necropolitics*. London: Duke University Press.

McKittrick, Katherine. 2021. *Dear Science and Other Stories*. Durham, NC and London: Duke University Press.

'Mediacosmology' in *Coded Territories* eds. Stephen Loft and Kerry Swanson, 2014 (University of Calgary Press), pp. 169–186.

Mewburn, Inger. 2013. "Academic Assholes and the Circle of Niceness." Blog post, February 13, 2013. https://thesiswhisperer.com/2013/02/13/academic-assholes/.

Ngai, Sianne. 2005. *ugly feelings*. Cambridge, MA: Harvard University Press.

Pechawis, Arthur. (2014). "Indigenism: Aboriginal World View as Global Protocol." In *Coded Territories: Tracing Indigenous Pathways in New Media Art*, edited by Stephen Loft and Kerry Swanson. Calgary: University of Calgary Press.

Penttinen, Elina. 2008. *Globalization, Prostitution and Sex-trafficking: A Corporeal Politics*. New York: Routledge.

Piper, Adrian. 2018. *Escape to Berlin: A Travel Memoir*. New York: Apra Foundation.

Puwar, Nirmal. 2004. *Space Invaders: Race, Gender and Bodies Out of Place*. New York: Bloomsbury Academic Press.

Reni, Regina. 2015. "Should We Rename Institutions That Honor Dead Racists?" Blog post, no longer available.

Ruotsalainen, Nelli. 2021. "Maggie Nelson—Writing by Any Means Necessary." *Tulva* 2-3/2021. https://tulva.fi/lue/maggie-nelson-writing-by-any-means -necessary/.

Saadawi, Ahmed. 2018. *Frankenstein in Baghdad*. Translated by Jonathan Wright. London: Oneworld.

Sajid Ali. 2019. "Habib Jalib, Pakistan's Poet of Dissent Whose Lines Are Now Chanted On Both Sides of Border." *The Print*, November 28, 2019. https://theprint.in/theprint-profile/habib-jalib-pakistans-poet-of-dissent-whose-lines-are-now-chanted-on-both-sides-of-border/326475/.

Schickele, Karla. 2015. "Noisy Utopia." In *The Feminist Utopia Project—Fifty-Seven Visions of a Wildly Better Future*, edited by Alexandra Brodsky and Rachel Kauder Nalebuff. New York: Feminist Press.

Shepherd, Laura. 2015. "Size Matters: Reflecting on Perspective, Positionality and Critique After #ISA2015." Blog post, April 1, 2015, https://thedisorderofthings.com/2015/04/01/size-matters-reflecting-on-perspective-positionality-and-critique-after-isa2015.

Simpson, Leanne. 2011. *Dancing on Our Turtle's Back: Stories of Nishnaabeg Re-Creation, Resurgence, and a New Emergence*. Winnipeg: Arbeiter Ring Publishing.

Sinha, Mrinalini. 2006. *Specters of Mother India: The Global Restructuring of an Empire*. London: Duke University Press.

Smith, Malinda. 2018. Tweet thread, October 9, 2018. https://twitter.com/MalindaSmith/status/1049669274887802880.

Solanas, Valerie. 1967. *SCUM Manifesto*. Self-published. https://www.ccs.neu.edu/home/shivers/rants/scum.html and https://editions-ismael.com/wp-content/uploads/2019/05/1968-Valerie-Solanas-S.C.U.M.-Manifesto.pdf.

Stewart, Kathleen. 2007. *Ordinary Affects*. Durham, NC and London: Duke University Press.

Styron, William. 1990. *Darkness Visible: A Memoir of Madness*. New York: Random House.

Subramaniam, Banu. 2001. "Snow Brown and the Seven Detergents: A Metanarrative on Science and the Scientific Method." In *Women, Science and Technology*, edited by Mary Wyer et al., 36–41. London: Routledge.

Tate, Shirley Anne. 2017. "How Do You Feel? 'Well-Being' As a Deracinated Strategic Goal in UK Universities." In *Inside the Ivory Tower: Narratives of Women of Colour Surviving and Thriving in British Academia*, edited by Deborah Tate and Shirley Anne Gabriel. London: Trentham Books.

Teaiwa, Teresia. 2021. "Modern Life, Primitive Thoughts." In *Sweat and Salt Water: Selected Works*, compiled and edited by Katerina Teaiwa, April K. Henderson, and Terence Wesley-Smith, 237. Honolulu: University of Hawai'i Press.

Trinh, Minh-ha. 1987. "Difference: 'A Special Third World Women Issue.'" *Feminist Review* 25 (Spring): 5–22.

———. 1989. *Woman, Native, Other: Writing Postcoloniality and Feminism*. Bloomington: Indiana University Press.

———. 1992. *Framer Framed*. London: Routledge.

———. 1999. *Cinema Interval*. London: Routledge.

Valenti, Jessica. 2021. "Against Forgiveness: For Women, Resentment Can Be a Radical Act." Blog post, November 24, 2021. https://jessica.substack.com/p/against-forgiveness.

Vuong, Ocean. 2022. "When I Write, I Feel Larger Than the Limits of My Body." https://www.youtube.com/watch?v=u5NuCrAkjGw.

Weber, Cynthia. 1994. Good Girls, Little Girls, and Bad Girls: Male Paranoia in Robert Keohane's Critique of Feminist International Relations. *Millennium* 23, no. 2: 337–49.

Wołodźko, Agnieszka Anna. 2020. "Living Within Affect as Contamination: Breathing in Between Numbers." *Capacious: Journal for Emerging Affect Inquiry* 2, no. 1–2: 212–24.

Zalewski, Marysia. 2013. *Feminist International Relations. Exquisite Corpse.* Abingdon: Routledge.

Zambreno, Kate. 2021. *To Write as If Already Dead.* New York: Columbia University Press.

Index

About the Authors

shine choi works and lives in aotearoa, new zealand. Her current research interests include non-alignment, monumental politics, postcolonial korean history, aesthetics, critical/creative methods and global feminist conversations.

Saara Särmä is a feminist writer who lives in Tampere, Finland. Currently she works at Tampere University; her postdoc project *Making Meaning out of Meme-Making* is funded by the Academy of Finland (2019–2023). When not depressed and cynical, she's curious and enthusiastic about people and their ways of being in the world. Reader, taker of near daily selfies (huippumisukka on Instagram) and frequent skyline photos from her kitchen window, art lover and collector, who can watch eleven seasons of *NYPD Blue* in no time. While learning to live a post-burnout life, she is rediscovering the joy academic work can be sometimes, especially when it includes in-person meetings and wine.

Cristina Masters lives in Manchester where she teaches international politics at the oh so lofty University of Manchester. Capricorn, tiger or ox depending on the day, lover of high-quality tinned tuna in olive oil. Mostly a crap academic; works way harder at becoming a better human being. She loves eating carbs, drinking grapefruit gin, dancing salsa on2, reading all things fiction (but mostly not when written by white men). Is looking for like-minded frollegues to be unruly and make mischief with. This bunch is exemplary.

Marysia Zalewski lives in Wales and Scotland and works at Cardiff University. She thinks a lot about gender. Can drift into despair about the awful shit that happens here and elsewhere. . . . Loves writing and thinking with people (especially this lot in this book!). Though writing remains very hard!

Currently working on a project on—well, yes, gender. . . . There's always so much more to think about with gender. Would like to write a book called *Things that stay with you*. Would like to put on an exhibition. Written a good bit about 'feminist IR.' Had lots of 'real world' jobs in her former lives—though still works as a mother and daughter. Watches way too many films.

Michelle Lee Brown holds a PhD in Indigenous Politics and Futures Studies from the University of Hawai'i at Mānoa and was a recent Eastman Fellow at Dartmouth College in Native American and Indigenous Studies. Her work articulates Indigenous political praxis and futures through technologies and is part of the Abundant Intelligences A.I. initiative. Her creative works include speculative fiction, VR projects on water and relationality, and a comic based on the monstrosity of impostor syndrome. Before returning to academe, she was a tarot reader in Jackson Square, New Orleans, a barista, house cleaner, and stable hand. She is often found running by the ocean, baking, watching crows, and/or musing on whale and eel futures.

Euskalduna from Lapurdi, the Bidart/Plage D'Erretegia area, Michelle grew up on Wampanoag territories around Buzzards Bay, Cape Cod, Massachusetts. She strives to uphold her relational commitments to her woven human and nonhuman families and is grateful to be part of this unsettling deliciousness.

Swati Parashar would have liked to be a detective or a spiritual guru, but instead teaches and researches at the School of Global Studies, University of Gothenburg in Sweden. Her work is situated at the intersections of feminism and postcolonialism, but she is not a favourite of either of these 'camps', critiquing and messing around with them. She has lived and worked in many countries and is at home with her 'homelessness'. When not predicting test cricket scores, she likes to listen to Indian classical music and old Bollywood songs. Be warned that her best writings come when she is sufficiently provoked or angry.